INTERNATIONAL TERRORISM: CHALLENGE AND RESPONSE

Jerusalem Conference on International Terrorism (1979 July 2-5)

[International Terrorism:]

Challenge and Response

PROCEEDINGS OF THE JERUSALEM CONFERENCE
ON INTERNATIONAL TERRORISM

Editor:

Benjamin Netanyahu

The Jonathan Institute
Jerusalem, 1981

Transaction Books
New Brunswick (U.S.A.) and London (U.K.)

HV
6431
J47

The Jonathan Institute

The Jonathan Institute is an independent research and educational foundation established in memory of Lieutenant-Colonel Jonathan Netanyahu, who fell while leading the rescue mission to Entebbe.

Its purpose is to acquaint the public with major international issues affecting the survival and future of the democratic world. Public education on the threat of terrorism and the necessary responses to it is one of the goals of The Jonathan Institute.

The Jerusalem Conference on International Terrorism

The Jerusalem Conference on International Terrorism was convened by the Jonathan Institute to focus public attention on the real nature of international terrorism, on the threat it poses to all democratic societies, and on the measures necessary for defeating the forces of terror.

The present volume is one of a series of the Institute's publications on the issue of terrorism edited by Benjamin Netanyahu.

Editor's Note

Most of the addresses at the Jerusalem Conference were submitted in written form. For those of the participants who did not submit papers, the text is based on the transcript of their spoken remarks. The speakers alone must be held responsible for all statements included in these addresses.

CONTENTS

FOREWORD

FOREWORD

The Jerusalem Conference on International Terrorism was convened by The Jonathan Institute on July 2-5, 1979 to focus public attention on the grave threat that international terrorism poses to all democratic societies, to study the real nature of today's terrorism, and to propose measures for combatting and defeating the international terror movements.

Over the last decade terrorist activities grew tenfold and the arsenal available to terrorists has greatly improved. The current threat promises to become intolerable when terrorists gain access — as they show every sign of doing — to weapons of mass destruction, or when they gain control of whole peoples and governments and establish themselves as *de facto* terrorist states.

It was the intolerable spectacle of legitimization of terror groups and the frequent capitulation to their demands that made the Jerusalem Conference so necessary. The United Nations has proven itself to be hopelessly incapable of dealing with the problem. The Western governments themselves have too often tried to make their separate deals, fearing that a full-fledged battle against terrorists and their supporters could have negative economic or political consequences.

In the face of such paralysis, pusillanimity and impotence, the Jerusalem Conference was convened to begin the formation of an anti-terror alliance in which all the democracies of the West must join.

It was important to consider in a public forum the questions that must be answered. What are the real forces behind the alarming growth of international terrorism? Which, if any, organizations? What has been the current response of the democratic governments to the terrorist threat? What future dangers are likely to arise? Do the media of the West collaborate, however unwittingly, with the terrorists themselves? Sessions of the Conference were devoted to each of these questions.

Only by discussing in an open forum the full nature of the terrorist threat and the proper response to it can we create in free societies a united public stand against terrorism. Without this, the political use of terror will continue to spread with disastrous consequences for all free societies.

The proceedings of the Jerusalem Conference on terrorism contain such a discussion. The participants at this Conference represent a broad range of political opinion in the democratic world. Nevertheless, the consensus that emerged in the course of the deliberations concerning the causes of terrorism, its backers and promoters, and the means necessary to block and defeat it, left no room for equivocation. It constituted a message that could not be ignored and whose echoes keep reverberating around the world. As several influential commentators have noted, the Conference marked a turning point in the world's understanding of the problem of terrorism and what has to be done about it.

The Editor

Opening Session
Subject:
THE FACE OF TERRORISM
Evening, July 2, 1979*
Chairman: Professor Benzion Netanyahu

PREFACE

The speeches delivered at the Opening
Session of the Jerusalem Conference presented
the major themes of all subsequent discussions:
The moral intolerability of terrorism, its
natural connection with other forms of
tyranny, and its use by anti-democratic states.

It was noted that the present dangers
hint at the threat of still more terrible things
to come, and establish the need, as the opening
speaker put it, for ·"rallying the democracies
of the world to a struggle against terrorism
and the dangers it represents." As some nowadays satisfy themselves with the easy moral
relativism of "One man's terrorist is another
man's freedom fighter," it was important to
establish at the outset the fact that a clear
definitional framework exists, regardless of
political view. Terrorism — the deliberate and
systematic killing of civilians so as to inspire
fear — was shown persuasively to be, beyond
all nuance and quibble, a moral evil, infecting

* All sessions of the Conference were held at the
Jerusalem Hilton Hotel.

not only those who commit such crimes, but those who, out of malice, ignorance, or simple refusal to think, countenance them. The means and ends of terror groups, it was suggested, are indissolubly linked, and both point to a single direction: An abhorrence of freedom and a determination to destroy the democratic way of life.

BENZION NETANYAHU is Professor
Emeritus of Judaic Studies at Cornell Uni-
versity and author of numerous books and
studies in the field of Medieval and Modern
Jewish History. Architect and first General
Editor of the *World History of the Jewish
People*, he was also for many years Editor-
in-Chief of the *Encyclopedia Hebraica*.
Professor Netanyahu was chairman of the
Founding Executive Committee of The
Jonathan Institute.

CHAIRMAN'S OPENING REMARKS

*Mr. Prime Minister, Mr. Peres, distinguished participants in
this Conference, most honored guests and friends.*

On behalf of the Board of Directors of the Jonathan Institute, I welcome you to this Opening Session of the Jerusalem
Conference on International Terrorism and extend to you our
wholehearted wish for the success of your deliberations. I know
that this wish was shared by many around the world who are
aware of this Conference and will be following its proceedings.

May I now say a few words about the genesis of this
unique gathering and the purpose for which it was called. The
Jonathan Institute has dedicated itself to explore certain national and international problems, the treatment of which may
vitally affect the future of Israel and the entire democratic
world. Terrorism is one of these issues. It would seem almost
natural to have this issue included among the Institute's main
objects of study, simply because Jonathan fell in the battle
against terrorism, and the Institute was named after him. Yet
this was not the only reason for our special interest in this phenomenon. To the founders of the Institute it was obvious that
terrorism had become — or was becoming — one of the most
crucial issues of our time, one that presents some of the greatest threats, and was perhaps the least adequately treated.

Since the founding of the Institute over two years ago,
little was done around the world to alleviate the peril, and ter-

rorism continued its forward march with what seemed to be an inexorable force. Not only has its scope of activity broadened, its excesses become more frequent and audacious, but it has gained more support and more recognition in various parts of the world. I shall not cite examples here. Suffice it to say that in the supposed headquarters of mankind, in the United Nations, terrorism has not only gained a mere foothold. That institution now serves as a springboard and a clearing house for the terrorists' campaign.

It is evident that in their struggle with the terrorists, the attacked nations must admit to failure — that is, if their purpose was to arrest the tide of terrorism in the *world* and place the malady under control. I do not refer here to the devices which each nation has thus far employed in this contest. These too have, in most cases, been inadequate. I am referring to the measures that had to be taken *internationally* and which, if chosen wisely, might have been effective, as many believe. Here we note almost a total failure. No common line of attack upon the problem, not even a common line of defense, has been adopted. The few attempts made at forming such defense lines were vitiated by powerful opposing forces.

It would be easy to point to some of these forces — the states of the Eastern bloc and the Arab states — but this would not constitute the whole answer. The fact is that some Western states have shown a reluctance to take effective measures, or such that were generally considered effective. Immediate economic and political interests have overcome long-range, more vital considerations. But this again is not the whole answer. The virtual paralysis in which the free world finds itself, when it comes to forming an answer to terrorism, must be related to *moral*, no less than to *material* and political, causes.

Escape from Reality

It is perhaps amazing, but much of the free world refuses to recognize what it sees. What we see is quite a new breed of fighter against the established order of things, one who styles himself a revolutionary, but who differs radically and fundamentally from all revolutionaries known to us from the past.

Men like Andreas Hofer, Kossuth and Garibaldi would have shuddered at the thought that they might be classed in the same category with the terrorists of our time. It is commonplace, and almost superfluous to point out that the freedom fighters of previous generations were bound by certain rules of behavior which form cornerstones of our ethics; that they drew a sharp distinction between soldiers and small children, between repressive authorities and helpless women, between governmental agents and ordinary citizens, between a military outpost and a common dwelling place. The terrorist, however, knows no such distinctions. He has no moral restraints in the choice of his objectives, as he has none in his methods of warfare. His objective is indeed the *whole country* on which he concentrates his attack; his target is its entire population. In these limits he recognizes no innocents, no bystanders, not even strangers. He respects no code of law which was ever established for war or peace. He is above the law, indeed a law unto himself. He speaks of justice, but he cannot see that often there may be two sides to a question. "Just" is to him only what is good for himself. As Goering said: "Justice is what is good for Germany." In this respect, as in the genocidal attitude he takes toward the societies he assails, whether it is Ireland, Lebanon, or Israel, he is an offshoot of Nazi philosophy.

And yet, he speaks of "humanitarian" and national causes, he pretends to fight for "freedom" against oppression, he keeps speaking of "legitimate rights," and many wonder what he is really like — an idealist or a nihilist, a champion of rights or an extreme egotist who follows strictly his own passions and relies on nothing except brute force.

The Task Ahead

It will be the task of this Conference to define the terrorist, this so-called new revolutionary of our time, and throw light on his real aims. For here, with respect to his aims, the confusion is even greater. Indeed only such a state of confusion can explain why governments of great nations like the United States can describe terrorist atrocities as "senseless acts."

You may define these acts any way you wish, but senseless they most definitely are not. Terrorism is carried out purposefully, in a cold-blooded, calculated fashion. The declared goals of the terrorist may change from place to place. He supposedly fights to remedy wrongs — social, religious, national, racial. But for all these problems his only solution is the demolition of the whole structure of society. No partial solution, not even the total redressing of the grievance he complains of, will satisfy him — until our social system is destroyed or delivered into his hands.

Ladies and gentlemen, it is quite clear that the terrorist has declared war on the society of free men — from America to Japan, from Ireland to Italy, from Germany to Israel. There is bewilderment in the democracies about the ultimate aims of this war, and about who is behind it, or who will gain from it. Our Conference will no doubt delve into these questions and try to determine what the real case is. But, in addition, it is expected to deal with measures designed to stem the tide of terrorism which, unless checked in time, will continue to spread until it threatens to engulf us.

This, of course, is not one of those situations that can be remedied by legal or technical measures alone. As in every great conflict in history, you have here primarily a battle of ideas and a battle of wills. Those who have the deeper convictions, the stronger wills, the greater determination, these will triumph. Those who will be paralyzed by indecision, troubled by doubts, hampered by narrow interests or by cynicism, those who will think of today and not of tomorrow, they will inevitably succumb.

This Conference was called to serve as the beginning of a new process — the process of rallying the democracies of the world to a struggle against terrorism and the dangers it represents. Against the international front of terrorism we must build an international front of freedom — that of organized public opinion which will move governments to act. Despite all that has been said about the decadence of the West, its death-wish and moral degeneration, we believe that the free societies of the world still possess a tremendous will to live and enormous powers of recuperation. If these powers are identified and mobilized, and harnessed in time by men of vision and courage, they will save the day for mankind.

SHIMON PERES is the Chairman of Israel's
Labor Party and leader of the *Ma'arakh*
opposition. Among other government posts,
he served as Minister of Defense from 1974
to 1977, and earlier as Minister of Communication and Transportation. Mr. Peres is the
author of *David's Sling, From These Men,*
and other works.

THE THREAT AND THE RESPONSE

It was a Fourth of July that coincided with our Sabbath.
Israel's people were deeply concerned with the fate of the hundred passengers, hostages in a faraway country. Everything
seemed to be working against us: A distance of 4,000 kms
from our country and our army; a Ugandan government headed
by one of the most bizarre and irresponsible leaders imaginable;
a cruel band of terrorists who could become trigger-happy;
and the unknown overshadowing the known.

The families of the passengers had reached the heights of
their concern, and in a way, the nation and those families were
like one family. We had at our disposal only the courage of
young volunteers and their responsibility both for the hostages
and the safety of future travellers. The alternatives open to us
were not considered without doubt or misgivings. To submit
to the demands of the terrorists and to release prisoners pre-
viously found guilty of attempts on the lives of innocent people, and who, once freed, might return to their bloody vocation, would surely be an encouragement to repeat more and
more of the same. The morale, the fantasies and the actions of
the terrorist groups would be boosted to unprecedented
heights.

Yet to try as we did to overpower the hijackers in that
faraway place carried its own risks. The most brilliant planning
can never assure a faultless operation, given not just the human

factor involved, but also the technological sophistication required. I believe we made the right choice because, deep down, there is no contradiction between moral judgment and pure logic: Surrender begets surrender, bravery begets bravery. As you know, the results of the Entebbe operation were not too bad.

In the center of this operation stood a young man, an officer concerned with the problems of his people and his generation, fully aware that when few are against many, it is quality and not quantity that will carry the day. He was in love with poetry, in search of philosophy, an example to his fellows, a leader to his men — the unforgettable Yonatan Netanyahu. This Conference was not convened simply to honor his memory and salute his wisdom and courage, but also to draw lessons which may be cherished by posterity.

The Strategy of Terror

The second part of the 20th century has seen national and ethnic conflicts expressed in two different strategies: The strategy which stems from the existence of nuclear arms and the strategy which is based upon the outburst of repeated terror. Strangely, the more deadly the weapons, the less dangerous they are. I believe that negotiations on disarmament are an example of an effort aimed at having moral responsibility overcome the forces of technology. It is the symmetry between the results of using those arms and not using them which has brought their possessors to a strategic understanding that we hope will continue.

Terror is an expression of virulence and extremism based upon a hope that the weaker side, the victim, will eventually give in to its lack of logic and restraint. You cannot bring an end to terror around a negotiating table, because the motive of terror is to exact a surrender by terrorizing the other side. You can negotiate with groups who have embarked upon the path of terror only after their leaders are totally convinced that terror itself will bear no fruit. In the case of sophisticated arms, negotiations may precede their usage; in the case of terror, only when it ceases can negotiations proceed.

Terror, aside from affecting its victims, engenders a refusal to negotiate within its own ranks. Rifles in the hands of
many without the rule of majority and without legitimacy
create a permanent dialogue of fire. There is no room for
moderation as long as the first to shoot can lead the group. I
would not be surprised to learn that the number of victims
within the terrorist groups exceeds the number of victims outside the terrorist groups. Terrorists live under the impression
that their way of fighting is strategy and not just tactics. It
becomes a way of life for them, an illusion which must be
destroyed.

Fighting Terror

I believe that in fighting terrorism we have to follow several
basic rules:

- There should never be a surrender to terrorism.
- We must have an elaborate intelligence system apparatus,
  a well-organized early warning system and properly trained
  people. Only these can nullify the terrorist advantage of
  surprise and indiscriminate attack.
- We must fight terrorists not only in the operational field
  but also on the psychological one. The tendency of terrorist groups to bedeck themselves with such titles as
  "The Red Army" or "The Liberation Organization,"
  should not beguile us or our often bewitched media.
  Those groups do not carry any message to the working
  class nor any message of liberation to their own people.
  They base their strength upon the promise of murder
  and it is murder which eventually replaces all promises.
  Terrorist groups should be described in their true colors —
  groups which are impatient with democracy, which are
  undisciplined, corrupted in their attitude to life and
  unable to free themselves from the domination of murder
  and hatred.
- Terror has become international and must be fought
  internationally. The terrorists consider most free nations
  and peoples as their enemies; countermeasures must
  therefore be internationally coordinated. The earlier this

is done, the better will be the anti-terror operation. Since terror is carried out in the dark and clandestinely, it cannot be met squarely in the open field; its tactic of surprise must be met by a well-prepared strategy of surprise on the part of the international community.

Yet remembering Yoni, it is *courage* that counts. We do not lack courageous people. They are entitled to live in a world where courageous and responsible policies will ensure fulfillment of their potential. It is with this aim before us that we have met today to cherish a memorable individual and contribute to a better future. If we succeed, it may be as significant as the negotiations on arms limitations could be in our era. The Jonathan Institute will make it its business to contribute to this important effort: To enable a world of many opinions and different desires to conduct a dialogue without the murder and death of the innocent.

PAUL JOHNSON is a noted British writer
and historian. He was for many years editor
of *The New Statesman*, one of England's
leading weeklies. Mr. Johnson is the author
of *Elizabeth I, Pope John XXIII, A History
of Christianity*, and *Enemies of Society*, as
well as numerous articles on literary and
political subjects.

THE SEVEN DEADLY SINS OF TERRORISM

Before describing what I believe to be the correct approach
to the problem of terrorism, let me indicate what I am certain
is the wrong one. The wrong approach is to see terrorism as
one of many symptoms of a deep-seated malaise in our society,
part of a pattern of violence which includes juvenile delinquency, rising crime rates, student riots, vandalism and football
hooliganism, which is blamed on the shadow of the H-bomb,
Eastern materialism, TV and cinema violence, rising divorce
rates, inadequate welfare services and poverty, and which
usually ends in the meaningless and defeatist conclusion that
society itself is to blame and — to quote the caricature psychia-
trist, 'We are all guilty'.

Such a loose, illogical and unscientific line of thought will
get us nowhere. The truth is, international terrorism is not part
of a generalized problem. It is a specific and identifiable problem
on its own; and because it can be isolated from the context
which breeds it — it is a remediable problem. That is the first
thing we must get clear.

When I say it is remediable, do not for one moment think
I underestimate the size and danger of the terrorist phenomenon. On the contrary, I take the view that it is almost impossible to exaggerate the threat which terrorism holds for our
civilization. It is a threat which is in many respects more

serious than the risk of nuclear war, or the population explosion, or global pollution, or the exhaustion of the earth's resources. I believe these dangers to our civilization can be, have been, or are being contained. I believe the threat of terrorism is not being contained — that it is, on the contrary increasing steadily. I believe that one central reason why it is such a formidable threat is that very few people in the civilized world — governments and parliaments, TV and newspapers, and the public generally — take terrorism seriously enough.

Most people have only a very superficial knowledge of history. They tend, therefore, to underestimate the fragility of a civilization. They do not appreciate that civilizations fall as well as rise. They can be, and have been, destroyed by malign forces. There have been at least three Dark Ages in our recoverable history. One occurred in the 3rd millenium BC, and, among other things, smashed the great civilization of the Egyptian Old Kingdom, the civilization which built the Pyramids. Another occurred towards the end of the 2nd millenium BC, and destroyed Mycenaean Greece, Minoan Crete, the Hittite Empire and much else. We are more familiar with the third, which destroyed the Roman Empire in the West in the 5th century AD. It took Europe 800 years to recover, in terms of organization, technical skills and living standards, from that disaster. Now these great catastrophes had many and varying causes. But there was a common factor in all. They tended to occur when the spread of metals technology and the availability of raw materials enabled the forces of barbarism to equal or surpass the civilized powers in the quality and quantity of their weapons. For in the last resort, civilizations stand or fall not on covenants, but on swords.

Edward Gibbon, at the end of his great book on the *Decline and Fall of the Roman Empire*, asked: "The savage nations of the globe are the common enemies of civilised society, and we may well inquire with anxious curiosity whether Europe is still threatened with a repetition of those calamities which formerly oppressed the arms and institutions of Rome." Writing in the 1780s, on the threshold of the Indus-

trial Revolution, Gibbon thought he could answer his own
question with a reasonably confident negative. He rightly esti-
mated the strength of the civilized world to be increasing, and
he believed that the scientific and rational principles on which
that strength was based were becoming more firmly established
with every year that passed.

Civilization Threatened Anew

Now, nearly 200 years later, we cannot be so sure. The principles of objective science and human reason, the notion of the
rule of law, the paramountcy of politics over force, are everywhere under growing and purposeful challenge, and the forces
of savagery and violence which constitute this challenge are
becoming steadily bolder, more numerous and, above all, better
armed. I will not dwell on the huge and alarming disparity
between the armed forces of Soviet barbarism, and those of
the civilized world. More to our purpose here is that arms
available to terrorists, the skills with which they use them and,
not least, the organizational techniques with which these
weapons and skills are deployed, are all improving at a fast and
accelerating rate — a rate much faster than the countermeasures
available to civilized society.

Let me give only one example, from Northern Ireland. In
the month of April, 1979, the Provisional IRA and the left-
wing Marxist terrorist group, INLA, succeeded in killing 4
police officers and 8 soldiers. They suffered no casualties
themselves. The last terrorist to be killed by the Security
Forces was as long ago as November, 1978. This is due to two
reasons. The first is the replacement of the old amateurish IRA
structure by what the BBC defense correspondent calls "a
modern clandestine force, organised and well-equipped, with a
classic cellular structure which is strong and almost impossible
to penetrate or break." The second is that the range and quality
of weapons now used by terrorists in Ireland are becoming
very formidable indeed. On 17 March, 1979, the Provisional
IRA detonated a controlled device which contained well over
half a ton of high explosive. They are using some very sophisticated radio-controlled devices in growing quantities, a range

of heavy weapons including mortars firing 100-lb bombs, and, in the case of INLA, advanced bombs of the type which killed Airey Neave. On the night of 6-7 March, 1979 they were able to plant 49 bombs in 22 towns throughout Northern Ireland, which, again according to the BBC, 'must have meant staff work of a very high standard.'

These menacing improvements in weaponry and organization have been brought about by the international availability of terrorist support, supply and training services, and made possible, of course, by the relative freedom with which the terrorists can operate across the Northern Ireland border, within the Irish Republic. As a result, the terrorists have unquestionably strengthened their military position in relation to the Security Forces. In this theatre, at least, barbarism is winning ground from civilization. And it is winning ground precisely because it can turn to an international infrastructure. Terrorism is not a purely national phenomenon, which can be conquered at a national level. It is an international offensive — an open and declared war against civilization itself — which can only be defeated by an international alliance of the civilized powers.

When I say that terrorism is war against civilization, I may be met by the objection that terrorists are often idealists pursuing worthy ultimate aims — national or regional independence, and so forth. I do not accept this argument. I cannot agree that a terrorist can ever be an idealist, or that the objects sought can ever justify terrorism. The impact of terrorism, not merely on individual nations, but on humanity as a whole, is intrinsically evil, necessarily evil and wholly evil, and it is so for a number of demonstrable reasons. Let me outline to you what I call the Seven Deadly Sins of Terrorism.

Idealization of Violence

First, terrorism is the deliberate and cold-blooded exaltation of violence over other forms of public activity. The modern terrorist does not employ violence as a necessary evil, but as a desirable form of activity. There is a definite intellectual background to the present wave of terrorism. It springs not only from the Leninist and Trotskyist justification of violence, but from the post-war philosophy of violence derived from Nietzsche through Heidegger, and enormously popularized by Sartre, his colleagues and disciples. No one since the war has influenced young people more than Sartre, and no one has done more to legitimize violence on the Left. It was Sartre who adopted the linguistic technique, common in German philosophy, of identifying certain political situations as the equivalent of violence, thus justifying violent correctives or responses. In 1962 he said, "For me the essential problem is to reject the theory according to which the Left ought not to answer violence with violence." Note his words: Not "a" problem, but "the *essential*" problem.

Some of those influenced by Sartre have gone much further — notably Franz Fanon. His most influential work, *Les Damnés de la Terre*, which has a preface by Sartre, has probably played a bigger part in spreading terrorism in the Third World than any other tract. Violence is presented as liberation, a fundamental Sartrean theme. For a black man, writes Sartre in his preface, "to shoot down a European is to kill two birds with one stone, to destroy an oppressor and the man he oppresses at the same time." Thus the terrorist is born again, free. Fanon preached that violence is a necessary form of social and moral regeneration for the oppressed. "Violence alone, violence committed by the people, violence organised and educated by its leaders, makes it possible for the masses to understand social truths and gives the key to them." The notion of "organized and educated violence", conducted by elites, is, of course, the formula for terrorism. Fanon goes further: "At the level of individuals, violence is a cleansing force. It frees the oppressed from his inferiority complex and from his despair and inaction."

It is precisely this line of thought — that violence is positive and creative — which enables the terrorists to perform the horrifying acts for which they are responsible. Of course the same argument — almost word for word — was used by Hitler, who repeated endlessly, "Virtue lies in blood." *Hence the first deadly sin of terrorism is the moral justification of murder not merely as a means to an end, but for its own sake.*

Rejection of Morality
The second is the deliberate suppression of the moral instincts in man. Terrorist organizers have found that it is not enough to give their recruits intellectual justifications for murder: the instinctive humanity in us all has to be systematically blunted, or else it rejects such sophistry. In the Russia of the 1880s, the Narodnaya Volya terror group favored what they termed "motiveless terror" and regarded any murder as a "progressive action." Both the Arab and the Irish terror groups of the 1970s have drifted in this direction. Once indiscriminate terror is adopted, the group rapidly suffers moral disintegration — indeed, the abandonment of any system of moral criteria becomes an essential element in its training. The point is brilliantly made in Dostoievsky's great anti-terrorist novel, *The Possessed*, by the diabolical Stavrogin, who argues that the terror-group can only be united by fear and moral depravity: "Persuade four members of the circle to murder a fifth," he says, "on the excuse that he is an informer, and you will at once tie them all up in one knot by the blood you have shed. They will be your slaves." This technique is undoubtedly used in the various Arab terrorist groups. In these groups, too, women recruits are subjected to repeated rapes and are forced to take part in communal acts of sexual depravity, to anesthetize moral reflexes and to prepare them for the gross travestying of their natures which their future work entails. The theory is based on the assumption that neither man nor woman can be an effective terrorist so long as he or she retains the moral elements of a human personality. One might say, then, that the second deadly sin of terrorism is a threat not merely to civilization, but to humanity as such.

Renunciation of Politics
The third, following directly from the first two, is the rejection of politics as the normal means by which communities resolve conflicts. To terrorists, violence is not a political weapon, to be used *in extremis*; it is a substitute for the entire political process. The Arab terrorists, the IRA, the Baader-Meinhof gang in Germany, the Red Army in Japan and else-

where, have never shown any desire to engage in the political
process. The notion that violence is a technique of last resort,
to be adopted only when all other attempts to attain justice
have failed, is rejected by them. In doing so, they reject the
mainstream of Western thinking, based, like most of our political grammar, on the social-contract theories of the 17th century. Hobbes and Locke rightly treated violence as the antithesis
of politics, a form of action characteristic of the archaic realm
of the state of nature. They saw politics as an attempt to
create a tool to avoid barbarism and make civilization possible:
politics makes violence not only unnecessary but unnatural to
civilized man. Politics is an essential part of the basic machinery
of civilization, and in rejecting politics, terrorism seeks to
make civilization unworkable.

Promotion of Totalitarianism

Terrorism, however, is not neutral in the political battle. It
does not, in the long run, tend towards anarchy: it tends
towards totalitarianism. *The fourth deadly sin of terrorism is
that it actively, systematically and necessarily assists the spread
of the totalitarian state.* The countries which finance and
maintain the international infrastructure of terrorism — which
give terrorists refuge and havens, training camps and bases,
money, arms and diplomatic support, as a matter of deliberate
state policy — are, without exception, totalitarian states. The
governments of all these states rule by military and police
force. The notion, then, that terrorism is opposed to the
'repressive forces' in society is false — indeed, it is the reverse
of the truth. International terrorism, and the various terrorist
movements it services, is entirely dependent on the continuing
good will and the active support of the police-states. The terrorist is sustained by the totalitarian tank, the torture-chamber,
the lash and the secret policeman. The terrorist is the beneficiary of the Gulag Archipelago and all it stands for.

Subversion of Progress

Which brings me to the fifth deadly sin. Terrorism poses no
threat to the totalitarian state. That kind of state can always

sustain itself by judicial murder, preventative arrest, torture of prisoners and suspects, and complete censorship of terrorist activities. It does not have to abide by the rule of law or any other considerations of humanity or morals. Terrorism can only get a foothold in a state like the Shah's Iran, where the executive is under some kind of restraint, legal, democratic and moral. The Shah's regime was overthrown — and terrorists played a huge part in that overthrow — not because it was too ruthless, but because it was not ruthless enough. And the effect of such terrorist victories is not the expansion but the contraction of freedom and law. Iran is now a totalitarian state, where the rule of law no longer exists, and a state from which the terrorists can operate with safety and active assistance. *Hence, the fifth deadly sin is that terrorism distinguishes between lawful and totalitarian states in favor of the latter.* It can destroy a democracy, as it destroyed the Lebanon, but it cannot destroy a totalitarian state. All it can do is to transform a nation struggling towards progress and legality into a nightmare of oppression and violence.

Exploitation of Freedom

And that leads us to another significant generalization about terrorism. Its ultimate base is in the totalitarian world — that is where its money, training, arms and protection come from. But at the same time, it can only operate effectively in the freedom of a liberal civilization. *The sixth deadly sin of terrorism is that it exploits the apparatus of freedom in liberal societies and thereby endangers it.* In meeting the threat of terrorism, a free society must arm itself. But that very process of arming itself against the danger within threatens the freedoms and decencies and standards which make it civilized. Terrorism, then — and it is this we must get across to the intelligent young people who may be tempted to sympathize with it — is a direct and continuous threat to all the protective devices of a free society. It is a threat to the freedom of the press and the freedom of TV to report without restraints. It is a threat to the rule of law, which is necessarily damaged by emergency legislation and special powers. It is a threat to *habeas corpus.* It is a threat to the continuous process of humanizing the legal code. It is a threat to the civilizing of our prisons. It is a threat to any system designed to curb excesses by the police, the prisons authorities or any other restraining force in society.

Enervation of Democracy

Yet the seventh deadly sin of terrorism operates, paradoxically, in the reverse direction, and is yet more destructive. A free society which reacts to terrorism by invoking authoritarian methods of repressing it necessarily damages itself, as I have argued. But an even graver danger — and a much more common one today — is of free societies, in their anxiety to avoid the authoritarian extreme, *failing* to arm themselves against the terrorist threat, and so abdicating their responsibility to uphold the law. The terrorists succeed when they provoke oppression. But they succeed far better when they are met with appeasement. *The seventh and deadliest sin of terrorism is that is saps the will of a civilized society to defend itself.* We have seen it happen. We do see it happen today. We find governments negotiating with terrorists — negotiations aimed not at destroying or disarming the terrorists, for such negotiations may sometimes be necessary — but negotiations whose natural and inevitable result is to concede part of the terrorists demands. We find governments providing ransom money to terrorists — we find governments permitting private individuals to provide ransom money, even assisting the process whereby it reaches the terrorists. We find governments releasing convicted criminals in response to terrorist demands. We find governments according terrorists the status, rights and advantages and, above all, legitimacy, of negotiating partners. We find governments according terrorist convicts the official and privileged status of political prisoners, always and everywhere a blunder and a surrender of the first magnitude. We find governments surrendering to demands — an invariable and well-organized part of terrorist strategy — for official inquiries, or international inquiries, into alleged ill-treatment of terrorist suspects or convicts. We find newspapers and TV networks —

often, indeed, state TV networks — placing democratic governments, and their officials and servants, and the terrorists, on a
level of moral equality. We find governments failing, time and
again, in their duty to persuade the public — and this is the
real heart of the matter — that terrorists are not misguided
politicians: they are, first, last and all the time, *criminals* —
extraordinary criminals, indeed, in that they are exceptionally
dangerous to us all and pose a unique threat not merely to the
individuals they murder without compunction, but to the
whole fabric of society — but criminals just the same.

    In short, the seventh, and deadliest, sin of terrorism is its
attempt to induce civilization to commit suicide.

Arresting the Tide

I have indicated seven distinct ways in which terrorism threatens civilized society. But the point, above all, which I wish to
stress is that terrorism is not a static threat — it is an increasing
one. Not only is the international infrastructure of terrorism
becoming better organized and more efficient, but the terrorists' own sights have been raised. By helping to destroy the
legal government of Iran, they have secured a new base and
access to formidable sources of finance and arms. They are
now a factor in the struggle for control of the oil supplies of
the Middle East. Who can doubt, after their success in Iran,
that the terrorists will be emboldened to attempt the subversion
of the even wealthier state of Saudi Arabia? This state is already
a major contributor — perhaps the biggest — to terrorist funds;
but that is no guarantee of immunity to attack. On the contrary. We cannot rule out the possibility that terrorists may
one day secure direct access to Saudi wealth through a revolutionary government they will help to install. Other oil-states
on the Gulf are even more vulnerable targets. We must, therefore, expect and prepare for yet further improvements in the
types of weapons terrorists deploy. Indeed, without wishing to
seem alarmist, we cannot rule out the possibility that terrorists
will obtain access to nuclear devices, or even to their production process.

Terrorism, in short, is no longer a marginal problem for the civilized world, something to be contained and lived with, a mere nuisance. It is a real, important and growing threat to the peace and stability of all legitimate states — that is, all those states which live under the rule of law. It is an international threat — therein lies its power. That power can only be destroyed or emasculated when there is international recognition of its gravity, and international action, by the united forces of civilization, to bring it under control.

HUGH FRASER has been a Conservative Member of Parliament since 1945. He served as Undersecretary of the War Office and the Colonial Office from 1958 to 1962, and later as Secretary of State for Air from 1962 to 1964. In addition to his parliamentary duties, he is also a banker, company director and journalist. Mr. Fraser has written articles on the Middle East, Africa and the politics of oil.

THE TYRANNY OF TERRORISM

For the human race, neither terrorism nor tyranny are novelties. Indeed, of the hundred and fifty or so states represented at the United Nations, less than thirty can properly claim to have free and fully democratic institutions. Terrorism and the politics of violence have been growing, even if they are not on the same scale as at the end of the Roman Empire or at the collapse of that of the Incas in South America, or at the time of the religious wars in Europe or at that of the wars of wandering in South and Central Africa in the 1840s.

But project Ulster's 1,700 deaths by political violence over seven years from Northern Ireland to larger countries like Great Britain and the U.S.A. and you get the terrifying figures of 60,000 and 233,000 human beings slaughtered.

In the past, terrorism against tyranny and the doctrine of legitimate tyrannicide has been, and indeed still is, a morally-approved instrument of betterment. But what I call "modern terrorism" — that is, the random destruction of innocent civilians — falls into a different category. In the political spectrum of the politics of violence, it stands at an intermediate stage somewhere between the violence of the politically-motivated mob and the internationally-directed "guerrilla" movement. Morally, it can only be totally condemned. Practically, its effect is to destroy the law itself — the only thing which stands between humanity and a state of permanent terror.

To refer to the tyranny of terrorism is, I hope, a precise and exact description. The terrorist slaying civilians makes the tyrant's claim that he is above the law and by his random action endeavors to place the civilian outside the protection of the law. His object is essentially the object of political theater; however meaningless or brutal an act, it is to impress the public on the one hand and encourage on the other the State itself to move to tyrannical systems of oppression. Terrorism's continuance blights the whole democratic process. Terrorism, if it becomes an accepted disease, can rot the moral fabric of societies, until — as when an endemic cattle plague suddenly becomes mortiferous — there are set in motion cures as dangerous and tyrannical as terrorism's own murderous intentions. The direct or indirect destruction of the rule of law and its replacement by the tyranny either of the individual or of the state is the only rational and connecting purpose or effect in the endless current catalogue of seemingly mindless and anarchic acts of terrorist brutality.

Ripe Targets in a Faltering Age

It is my fear that for a variety of reasons the threat of terrorism to individuals and to institutions, far from diminishing or petering out in failure, as waves of terrorism have done in the past, is on the contrary likely to grow. And both by accident and by design its worst impact will be on the democratic and liberal, fully-developed and largely Western countries. These are the states that are the most communications-conscious and the most communications-prone; the most glued to their television sets; the richest for plundering; the most humane, compassionate and tolerant; the most materialist and yet the least conscious of on what a knife-edge hangs civilization and their own prosperity. They are also the least prepared, because like Babbit they believe "it can't happen here".

The peoples of these states are coming to believe that neither clear moral nor physical authority is necessary for the maintenance of freedom: that freedom needs no defence because it has fully flourished for a few scores of years. I will not go on — far better to re-read Solzhenitsyn's lecture to the West.

But to look to the future: Made febrile by the new revolution of falling rather than rising expectations, social frictions — especially amongst the educated and easily-frustrated — are likely to grow, and with them extreme right to extreme left (or simply dotty) manifestations, despairing of the speed either of democratic change or Marxist victories. In an era of what could be prolonged recession, the spectrum of the politics of violence — which necessarily includes terrorism — is likely to expand, and workers as well as bourgeois and intellectuals become involved.

Hitherto, the aiding and abetting and full exploitation of terrorist situations, either by international terrorist organizations or by hostile authoritarian powers, has been sporadic and — except in such massacres as those at Lod and Fiumicino airports — indirect and limited to money, arms, and occasionally to training. The pot has been stirred, but the kitchen has not been commandeered. But now some new and ominous trends are emerging.

Such recent phenomena as the P.L.O.'s involvement in the Shah's overthrow, East German terror training camps in South Yemen and Zambia, and the stepping up of Libyan activities seem to indicate the potential of the concerted use of terror — both as a military and a political instrument — from which Israel already suffers.

New and more precise terror weapons are coming into service; new targets, such as government and military computer centers and oil or nuclear installations, and the causing and· spreading of panic at moments of increasing international tension or even of red alert (terrorist Sixth Columns in effect), are no longer threats which are remote or easily discounted.

Until now, the use of terror as an instrument for advancing Communism has been discouraged by the Kremlin. Stalin, it is true, successfully robbed the bank in Tiflis, murdered Trotsky and imposed the worst internal reign of terror in Russian history. But ever since Kropotkin and Most quarrelled with Marx, and Trotsky with Stalin, terror has been discouraged — not on moral grounds, but as being elitist, adventurist and counter-productive; and in Russian history, as elsewhere — romantic but politically unsuccessful. For this deviation, no party was more brutally treated than the German Communist Party in the Thirties by Moscow. But with the contemporary decline of left-wing parties in the West, the simultaneous resurgence of the Right, and the emergence of a world recession, the incompetent Che Guevara may be in for reassessment, if not rehabilitation. This could have considerable implications with Brezhnev departing imminently, and tensions remaining unresolved between Moscow and Washington.

Psychologically the impact of terrorism, the quintessence of fear itself, on a national mood in a society which is optimistic, or faithful, or forward-looking, can be negligible; but reverse that mood into one of depression bordering on cosmic despair, and popular reaction and counter-reaction could be violent and difficult to control.

I do not think I exaggerate in my projections — if anything I have discounted some of what are claimed to be the facts about the current international nature of terrorism. But as someone with some experience, first as a guerrilla myself with the Resistance in the last war, then as a director of counter-terrorism in Malaya and Kenya and finally as a personal target for assassination, I remain surprised by the failure to exploit new technical terrorist techniques given current opportunities. I only hope I will continue to go on being surprised. Politicians are not only sitting but frequently popular targets. As our poet Hilaire Belloc wrote in his *Epitaph on a Politician:*

"While all of his acquaintance sneered and slanged
I wept: for I had longed to see him hanged".

It behooves each of us of course at this prestigious Conference to contribute something as to what can be done. So far, except in the realm of hijacking which is a limited field and in whose combatting Israel has played a notably heroic and leading part, not much has been achieved by international action. The United Nations Committee on Terrorism set up in 1974 drones on. The European Convention still remains ineffective —

in parts unratified, in practice nearly always disregarded. If only by our meeting we can shake the world leaders into acknowledgment of the need for action to stamp out this danger, something will have been achieved.

A Change of Attitude Needed
In the international field there are, I believe, two steps and one change of attitude which could be useful.

The first step is the recreation of efficient Western intelligence systems on an international basis. The damage done to the Central Intelligence Agency by attack, disparagement and reduction of funds has done quite incalculable damage to world security. To a lesser extent, some past political hostility to our own Secret Service has considerably damaged British world coverage.

The second step is to seek some international control of the reportage of terrorist outrages. There should be an effort made *now* to modify by international agreement and convention — or if needs be by unilateral U.S. action — the monitoring of the satellite television systems. This would be a real step, denying to terrorists the world stage which they so dearly seek, and on which their influence so much depends. What should be sought is not a "black-out" but a "brown-out", so to speak, of terrorist activity. It is a form of censorship, but incidentally world press coverage all but gave away the Mogadishu raid, and *did* give away a new anti-terrorist device, whose novelty was of great importance.

As to the change of international attitude: What is to me inexplicable is the defeatist, almost supine, attitude of the West towards totalitarian, barbarian or piratical support for or instigation of attacks on our individual security or national interests. What has inspired this dereliction? Vietnam withdrawal symptoms, guilt complexes, sacrificial pacifism, bogus Christianity, vote-catching — I neither know nor care. In a world of reality it is not just unrealistic, but highly dangerous. The totalitarian East is profoundly more unstable than the West: poorer, dependent on us for markets, for cash, even for food, certainly for new technologies. It is in debt to the tune of well over sixty billion dollars, with Moscow unable even to build the stadia in time for the next year's Olympics without the assistance of Western architects, technicians and artisans.

For every would-be Western statesman, Professor Raymond Aron's new book, *In Defence of Decadent Europe*, should be compulsory reading, and a replay of the Pope's visit to Poland compulsory televiewing. It is ridiculous that we tolerate East German terrorists in Zambia, or P.L.O. and Communist terror camps in South Yemen. I am not asking the Marines to add Aden or Lusaka to their battle honors won at Tripoli where they smoked out the Barbary pirates at the turn of the last century. I seek concerted political and economic action against infamous terrorism, and if need be — and only if need be — its being backed by minimal and suitable local force. There is no Leftist monopoly of just causes in the under-developed world. We should declare a policy of "both hands off"; or if one plays, two can; and the West could carry a heavier bill and weightier pecking powers. I could even feel quite sorry for Cuban and East German lads seven thousand miles away from homes and hospitals.

Internationally, general exhortations have failed to put any check on international terrorism. The conspirators continue to conspire. It is time the Western powers started their own positive deliberations on getting to the root — and, even more, the more defenceless limbs and tentacles — of this international problem.

If they do not — if *we* do not show that we are prepared to crack down on international manifestations of terrorism — the persons on whom the blanket of fear and of blackmail will descend will be precisely those people on whom the West so relies: the members of the Gulf oil sheikhdoms, the Saudi Royal Family itself.

If we delay, it will be neither Mexico nor Great Britain but Arafat or Habash who will be lolling and gun-toting in OPEC's fourteenth and fifteenth chairs at its plenary sessions.

British Conceptions of Terror
Determined international action against terrorism depends

primarily, of course, on individual national awareness and determination on action at home. In conclusion, therefore, I will say something about the condition of the United Kingdom.

In Northern Ireland, of course, terrorism continues: for the moment chiefly Catholic, in part working class. It shows no signs of abating. The rest of the U.K., unlike Ulster which has an open frontier with an unwilling host nation for terrorists in the shape of Eire, has a considerable physical anti-terrorist and anti-kidnapping advantage in being an island. Historically there is no tradition of indigenous terrorism since Catholic attempts at regicide in the 16th and 17th century. Recently mob violence has increased in the U.K., but our belief in the ballot box is general and healthy. Assassination and terrorism are foreign or Irish, both in popular belief and in practice. If we have a native mainstream of violence it is in occasional rebellions. Perhaps this has something to do with our famous "team spirit". But an ancestor of mine was the last rebel lord to have his head cut off as long ago as 1747. Historically we have a noble tradition of political asylum, including amongst its recipients not a few human monsters. Our literature is packed with revolutionary and even anarchist heroes.

We have a highly efficient Special Branch, anti-terrorist wing and general police force. Over 80% of those engaged in acts of terrorism on the mainland are identified or have been arrested. The force's contact with its European colleagues is good and swift.

Today's passive support for terrorism and for the P.L.O. comes largely from middle class fringe political groups and intellectuals. As far as the police is concerned, our main problems are the growth of violent crime, racial tension and extremist political demonstrations. The call for better law and order is general and popular; however, as far as terrorism is concerned, except in the immediate aftermath of some IRA outrage, we tend to think — "It can't happen here".

Unfortunately, it can: Physically and geographically, Great Britain might be an Island, but we are no more isolated from the winds of economic change, conspiracies and danger than the rest of the world. However efficient the police are, the sheer volume of incidents could be overwhelming. Our libertarian traditions, the preservation of whose liberal essentials is the prime national objective of all our main political parties, inevitably offer hostages to fortune.

Vigilance Against Tyranny

In all democratic institutions, however ancient and established, there sneaks like a serpent the syndrome of a Weimar Republic. Liberty has only one price, and that is eternal vigilance.

To combat the threat of the tyranny of terrorism, vigilance and action should be exercised *now*, before — however remote a chance it might seem — a surge of violence should cause panic and the institution of real repression. And let us not underrate this as a terrorist objective, with the current world swing of what Tolstoy called the "unconscious general swarm of mankind" towards right-wing political solutions.

It is said that when Confucius was asked what should be the first action of the new Governor of a Province he replied: "First he must reform the language". I feel now surrounded by Confuciuses, and by past, present and future Governors of Provinces.

But in the welter of words concerning violence, civil war and terrorism, the first essential is precision regarding not the intention or political excuse, but the nature of an act. For instance, Mr. Nkomo, by shooting down two unarmed civil planes is not primarily a freedom fighter or a guerrilla or a partisan, but a terrorist, a murderer and a criminal. This need not stop him becoming a Prime Minister, but rulers, politicians and communicators must give a lead in the proper use of language. To mince words on the subject of terrorism is just to make a meal of human beings for the murderer and criminal.

The second misconception of which we must disabuse ourselves is the idea that modern, organized terrorism can be bought off by social reform or political maneuvres. It is the essence and nature of organized terrorism to knowingly make impossible political demands; without that impossibility, terrorist leadership in itself is in constant danger of being out-flanked or betrayed. Terrorism against Israel and Ulster are prime examples. Against organized terrorism, civilized man can only have one mission: it is to contain and destroy.

I and others have already talked of the need to reach agreement — one hopes — with the media regarding the cove-age of outrages, the need for more police forces that are better, friendly and socially-alert (if I might say so, ten good police-men on the beat are worth their weight in computer software at Wiesbaden), the need to control not freedom of speech but marches and demonstrations which in some European countries have on occasion almost assumed the shape of armed insurrection and certainly lead to abrogation of police power and authority.

Finally, I would like to turn to the present adequacy of the law and its penalties. First there is the question of proving the crime of harboring, hiding and abetting terrorists. Above all this is a police function — and a most complex one for the forces of detection and for a socially well-oriented police force.

But beyond this theme there is the wider and more grue-some question of whether a return of the penalty of death for the planned but random killing of innocent civilians would add effectively to the force and majesty of law and justice.

In logic, as I see it, a terrorist whose aim is to destroy such a democratic State puts himself outside the protection of that State or of any social contract; similarly a foreign terrorist who so murders, whether he be in or out of uniform, acts as a war criminal outside any binding international convention on war. Both, in every sense, are outlaws as well as criminals. In support of the rule of law, guilt must be established by trial. But I see no moral reason why the State should show mercy.

To me, the question at issue is not of morality but of policy. I will not rehearse the arguments of "stone dead hath no fellow" against Sir Winston's famous dictum that "grass never grows over the gallows tree". I appreciate all the legal and police problems of death sentences. I know, too, from per-sonal experience that death by firing squad is a deterrent.

No, my reason for having changed from being an aboli-
tionist to one advocating the return of the death penalty is a
different one: essentially it is a people's argument. It is not
just that their sense of outrage against some mindless massacre
should find expression and embodiment in the law. It is more
profound: terrorism is the battle for the summoning of fear
from the deep and dark recesses of the minds of each one of
us.

It is not the fear of detention: it is the fear of destruction.
Even more, unless the supreme penalty is available, the people
will demand more and more checks and removals of freedom
and liberty, until finally fear is only checked with terror,
or the law taken into the people's hands. It will be the new
heyday for McCarthys, Titus Oateses, new spies and new in-
formers.

It will not be the law or freedom which will have won, but
terrorism which will have imposed an absolute tyranny.

My friends, each morning as I shave I see it: It is not the
shadow of assassination, it is a fear more profound — it is the
dread that within each one of us is the spirit of violence — the
curse of Cain.

I recall to you those awful lines of Beckett:
   "We have met the enemy, and he is us."

HENRY M. JACKSON is one of the leading
members of the United States Senate. He
has been a Senator from the state of Washington since 1952. He is currently Chairman
of the Senate Energy Committee and of the
Armed Services Committee. Senator Jackson
is a leader of the campaign for human rights
and freedom throughout the world, and has
sponsored much legislation in these areas,
including the Jackson-Vanik Amendment,
which has facilitated emigration from the
Soviet Union.

TERRORISM AS A WEAPON
IN INTERNATIONAL POLITICS

*Mr. Prime Minister, Mr. Peres, Professor Netanyahu, distin-
guished participants in the Jerusalem Conference on International Terrorism, ladies and gentlemen:*

As we gather here this evening our thoughts turn to Lt.
Col. Jonathan Netanyahu. We recall the quality of his personal
character, his inner devotion to the public good, his voluntary
performance of the most demanding duties that the defense of
democracy entails, and the sacrifice consummated in the
heroic rescue at Entebbe. Jonathan's heritage is an unpurchase-
able treasure of the spirit that moth and rust cannot consume
nor thieves break through and steal.

When in George Bernard Shaw's play, they tell Joan of
Arc that they are going to burn her at the stake, she foresees
the effect upon the people. "If I go through the fire," she says,
"I shall go through it to their hearts for ever and ever." So
Jonathan went through the Entebbe fire to our hearts for ever
and ever.

A Broad Campaign
I believe that international terrorism is a modern form of
warfare against liberal democracies. I believe that the ultimate
but seldom stated goal of these terrorists is to destroy the very
fabric of democracy. I believe that it is both wrong and fool-

hardy for any democratic state to consider international terrorism to be "someone else's" problem.

If you believe as I do, then you must join me in wondering why the community of liberal democracies has not banded together more effectively to oppose these international murderers — and to loudly and vigorously expose those states which cynically provide terrorists with comfort and support. One of the great coverups of this century is the effort by Western governments, who know better, to muffle the facts about Soviet-bloc support for international terrorism.

I'm not talking about individual acts of madmen. I'm talking about highly organized groups with international connections and support who systematically rely on major acts of violence as a political instrument.

I'm thinking of the Basque and Puerto Rican terrorists, the European terrorist groups, and the PLO attacks, or threats of attack, against moderate Arab states which might be motivated to support the Egyptian-Israeli peace agreement.

I have in mind the PLO attacks against moderate Palestinians — the murder of a moderate leader in Gaza is a recent, brutal example.

I am reminded of radical Palestinian terrorist attacks on airliners servicing Israel.

I'm thinking of the Palestinian operations in Lebanon, and the activities of Turkish terrorists.

Such acts of terrorism are part of a broad campaign aimed at the disintegration of democratic societies through undermining the confidence of their citizenry in their governments.

International terrorism is a special problem for democracies. To a totalitarian regime like the Soviet Union, it is mainly a nuisance. The government applies whatever force is needed to liquidate the group and its members; borders are closed to unwanted entry or exit; individual rights are held subservient to "law and order"; publicity can be denied by fiat. The biggest difference between the Soviet Union and such states as Libya, Iraq, and Iran is that these governments are not as efficient — yet.

A democratic government, on the other hand, rests on the consent of the governed. It is responsible for assuring the democratic freedoms of speech, assembly, travel, press and privacy. These conditions, obviously, facilitate terrorist operations, directed against a particular government or as the battleground for opposing terrorist groups. When the PLO and Iraqi terrorists were at war, they chose to fight it out in Europe, not in the Middle East.

Warfare by Remote Control

Terrorism is not a new phenomenon. What is new is the international nature of the terrorism.

Today's terrorists have modern technology to help them — permitting rapid international communications, travel, and the transfer of monies; they can work with others of like mind across the international borders of the world's free nations.

More important, however, these groups receive extensive support from the Soviet bloc. Most terrorists use Soviet or East European weapons; they have been trained in Warsaw Pact countries — or in such Middle East countries as South Yemen and the PLO-controlled areas of the Lebanon; they generally flee for protection and rest to Eastern Europe or to such countries as Libya. The primary supporters of international terrorism are the Soviet Union and those states which the Soviets support — the Warsaw Pact and the radical Arab camp.

Modern terrorism is a form of "warfare by remote control" waged against free nations or against non-democratic but moderate states which dare to sympathize with freedom. In this kind of war, the totalitarian regimes see little risk of retribution directed at them.

What can be done?

Recognizing the Common Threat

First, and foremost, liberal democracies must acknowledge that international terrorism is a "collective problem."

Everything else follows from this. When one free nation is under attack, the rest must understand that democracy itself is under attack, and behave accordingly. We must be allied in our defense against terrorists.

The cooperative effort of Western European countries to combat terrorism in Europe is a major step in the right direction. But we must go further. Terrorists must know that when they operate against any liberal democracy, they will receive no sanctuary and no sympathy in any free nation. By not making our position crystal clear, we allow fanatic groups to think we tolerate policies like those emanating from Iran concerning the Shah, members of his family, and certain others. I quote an Iranian announcement:

"Anyone who wants to assassinate these people in Iran or outside (could be) free anywhere to carry out the order of the court. They cannot be arrested by any foreign government as a terrorist because they will be carrying out the order of Iran's Islamic revolutionary court."

And let me emphasize two propositions whose truth should be evident to all democracies:

To insist that free nations negotiate with terrorist organizations can only strengthen the latter and weaken the former.

To crown with statehood a movement based on terrorism would devastate the moral authority that rightly lies behind the effort of free states everywhere to combat terrorism.

Resisting the Corruption of Language
Second, every free nation must work against Soviet and radical state efforts to define away terrorism.

The idea that one person's "terrorist" is another's "freedom fighter" cannot be sanctioned. Freedom fighters or revolutionaries don't blow up buses containing non-combatants; terrorist murderers do. Freedom fighters don't set out to capture and slaughter school children; terrorist murderers do. Freedom fighters don't assassinate innocent businessmen, or hijack and hold hostage innocent men, women, and children; terrorist murderers do. It is a disgrace that democracies would allow the treasured word "freedom" to be associated with the acts of terrorists.

Exposing the Sponsors
Third, we must turn the publicity instrument against the terrorists, and we must expose Soviet and other state support of terrorist groups whenever we identify it.

When PLO terrorists toss a bomb into a marketplace, or murder a holy man, or shoot rockets randomly at a village, each and every democracy in the world should stand up to condemn those radical Arab states and the Soviet Union who train, arm, finance, harbor, and encourage them.

When an act of terrorism occurs, and the odds are it will occur in one of the free countries, democracies should unite in sponsoring resolutions in the United Nations condemning the act. Where we have evidence of support for the terrorists by some other state, this support should be censured in the strongest terms. If the Soviet Union, its allies, and the radical Arab and Third World states want to vote against such resolutions — let them.

Let's educate the whole world as to who opposes and who tolerates international terrorism.

I am convinced that this will make a difference; I am convinced, for instance, that the exposure of East European support for European terrorism has contributed to the lessening of this support and to the signs of some cooperation to combat terrorism between these countries and the nations of Western Europe.

Punishing the Protectors
Fourth, liberal democracies must work together to apply sanctions against countries which provide sanctuary to international terrorists.

The Bonn Anti-Hijacking Agreement is a good start. It is ironic that the pilots and the airlines, and not our statesmen, provided the leadership which led to this agreement.

We can do more. For instance, is it moral to trade openly and freely with states who use the profits from such trade to finance the murder of innocents? Why should those who conduct remote control warfare against us rest easy that we will contribute to financing our own destruction.

Building the Machinery

Fifth, within each of our own countries, we must organize to combat terrorism in ways consistent with our democratic principles, and with the strong support of our citizens.

Israel has long done this. And the nations of Western Europe are moving in this direction. In my country, we are making some progress in organizing federal, state and local agencies to deal more realistically with terrorist threats. A number of my colleagues in the U.S. Senate are working to improve our counter-terrorism capacities.

As I see it, the best means to cope with terrorism is to structure national programs to reinforce the capabilities of local authorities. Local police and governments know their area; they know their people; they are the primary link between citizens and government.

Now this final word:

In providing for her own defense against terrorism, Israel's courage has inspired those who love freedom around the world. The Entebbe rescue was a classic lesson for all free nations that terrorism can be effectively countered with strength, skill and determination.

These are qualities in short supply in many countries where freedom comes more easily. Indeed, the great need in the world today is for men and women who stand in the tradition of Jonathan Netanyahu — strong, dedicated, courageous, dependable.

My friends, I know that we shall return home from this historic Conference more determined and better prepared to do what we can to combat the menace of terrorism and to defend the freedom of us all.

MENACHEM BEGIN has been the Prime
Minister of Israel since 1977. The head of
the Herut Party since its founding in 1948,
he served as Member of Knesset and as
Leader of the Likud Opposition coalition.
In 1978 he was awarded the Nobel Peace
Prize. Mr. Begin is the author of *White
Nights* which describes his experiences in
Russian labor camps during World War II,
and *The Revolt*, an account of his days as
leader of the underground organization
Irgun Zvai Leumi prior to the establishment
of the State of Israel.

FREEDOM FIGHTERS AND TERRORISTS

*Mr. Chairman, Professor Netanyahu, the father of our nation's
and mankind's hero, Lieutenant-Colonel Yonatan, my friends
Senator Jackson and Mr. Fraser, my friend Shimon Peres, the
leader of the loyal Opposition, and the respected writer, Mr.
Paul Johnson, ladies and gentlemen, dear friends.*

What is the difference between a fight for freedom or
liberation on the one hand and terrorism on the other? For the
answer to this question, one should apply two criteria: the aim
and the methods.

Terrorist Aims
Fights for liberation have taken place throughout the centuries
from ancient times to our own days. There are historians who
maintain that the most justified fight in the annals of mankind
was that of Spartacus. That revolt took place in ancient Rome,
and ended when Crassus crushed it by raising a sea of crosses
on which the rebels were slowly extinguished. It was justified
because it was a fight not merely for political independence,
but also for physical liberation in the literal sense of the word,
a fight for breaking the shackles of the slaves and gladiators.

There is, however, a third kind of fight — a fight for
physical survival. That was the fight we, the Jews, conducted

in the country historically known as *Eretz Israel* or the Land
of Israel since the days of the Prophet Samuel.

When we fought, our aim was to save our people from
utter destruction. What happened in Europe everybody knows.
In those days Palestine, promised as the National Home for the
Jewish People, was shut off to every and any Jew. And great
tragedies, which remind us of the present too, took place at
sea. Were it not for our fight for liberation, independence
and survival, our people would have suffered total extinction.

And now I will pause for a while in order not to commit
sacrilege. I will now ask about the organisation known in our
time as the PLO, where the "L" supposedly stands for "liberation." There is a so-called Palestinian charter and its Article 1
stipulates:

"Palestine is the homeland of the Palestinian Arab people
and an integral part of the great Arab homeland. The people
of Palestine are part of the Arab nation."

What does that mean? The State of Israel must disappear.
There are some learned people who call it "politicide," the
destruction of country. I disagree, because it would be
genocide all over again. The Jewish people cannot exist without this country of its forefathers. That has already been
proved.

But pay attention, ladies and gentlemen, to this sentence:
"They are part of the Arab nation." If this is the case we must
remember that the Arab nation has now as an expression of its
inherent, undeniable right of self-determination twenty-two
sovereign states. The proposition is that the Arab nation should
have twenty-three sovereign states, and the only Jewish country
should disappear from the earth. This is the aim.

In Article 6 it is stipulated, Jews who were living permanently in Palestine until the beginning of the Zionist invasion
will be considered Palestinians. What do the words *Zionist
invasion* mean? According to the interpretation given by the
authors of this document, they mean the Balfour Declaration
of November 1917. In those days there were in Palestine
60,000 Jews. Now there are 3 million 200 thousand Jews. In
other words, all the others will have to leave. This is a repeti-

tion of the Nuremberg Laws, because then the Jews would lose even their citizenship. You must listen to the Iraqis who recently promised they will fight on until all the Jews who came to Palestine will be sent back to the countries of their origin.

And ultimately we come to Article 22 of the Palestine National Covenant:

"Zionism is a political movement organically related to world imperialism. It is hostile to all movements of liberation and progress in the world. It is a racist and fanatical movement in its formation."

I have been a Zionist 60 years. I have studied almost every book, almost every article and almost every speech written or spoken about or on behalf of Zionism. I learned what Zionism is from Herzl, Nordau and Jabotinsky, who were men of great learning, who were renowned writers and orators. These are some of the greatest liberals in the 19th and 20th centuries, who imbued us with the idea that nothing that is human should be alien to us Zionists.

The authors of this document have the impudence to say that this movement is racist. All of us sitting here who call ourselves Zionists have learned through personal experience that Zionism is the purest, most humanitarian, liberation movement of a people wandering throughout the world for nineteen centuries. A people humiliated, oppressed, assaulted, persecuted, ultimately physically destroyed by racism. And this pure, great, idealistic movement is called "racist" and other such names.

Now you can understand the aim of this so-called PLO. Not to *save* a people, but to *destroy* a state and a nation together.

Terrorist Methods

What is the method? Well, I will call as witnesses many commanding officers of the British army in Palestine. And they can offer testimony in every court, after many, many battles between their army and the Jewish fighting underground.

Those commanding officers used to comment, "It was a fair battle." During nearly five years of combat against a mighty power, which we had to engage in to save our people from the danger of utter destruction, no British child was ever hurt, no British woman was ever injured, no citizen of Britain was ever attacked. Only armed men against armed men.

British armed men were also human beings. We never rejoiced when we had to hurt them. And on our side we used to take all the risks. And we always regretted whenever there were casualties on either side.

Yes, there was a unique case about which I will tell you at the end of my remarks, the revelation of which I myself learned about only a few weeks ago. But the method was to never hurt a civilian or a man, woman or child, whether Jew, Arab or British.

How does this compare with the so-called PLO?

The civilian population is the target of their attacks. During all the years they have never attacked a military installation. Only civilians. Therefore they have an unaccountable number of living targets, actually three million two hundred thousand living targets.

At Nahariya, just to give you an example, they took a father and girl of four. They shot the man and then they shot the girl. But the girl did not die of the bullet, so the two-legged beast smashed the head of the four-year old girl with the butt of his rifle. Then he raised his hands in surrender. He saved his life and was arrested.

At Petah Tikva, a young mother of 24 and a baby girl were blown up; at Ma'alot, boys and girls 14 years old were ordered to lie down on the floor and machine-gunned. Israel is the only country in the world in which all our schools are being guarded arms in hand by the parents, by the teachers and by special guards. Why? Because they come to our schools to kill our children.

I could give you endless examples. The method is genocide. Kill the Jew because he was born a Jew. This is racism in its basest expression. Kill an Israeli because he was born an Israeli. Again the same racism.

So now we have the answer. Their aim is not to save or liberate a people; 22 sovereign countries is sufficient expression of the self-determination for a nation. It is not necessary for fractions of nations to have separate states. Otherwise what would happen to the map of the world? To any country? And the terrorist method is absolutely genocidal, for the target is always the civilian population.

The New Left
Now, I would like to tell my friends from Europe, and ask them to tell their respective governments, that you have your *own* problem. In our time it is called the New Left. And usually, because of a well-known propaganda success, a man who says that he is on the left is absolutely convinced that he represents human progress. The New Left is one of the darkest reactions in human history. They fight democracy; they are enemies of democracy. I, myself, a former underground fighter, state here and now, that wherever you can decide issues by the ballot you must under no circumstances use the bullet. From either direction, either right or left. Therefore the New Left, that reactionary dark movement, fights democracy in Italy and in France, in Germany, Japan and other countries, but mainly in the European countries, where Jewish blood flowed from the Rhine to the Danube, and from the Bug to the Volga.

Destroying Terrorism
The European countries cannot expect to overcome terrorism in their own midst if they give comfort and support to the so-called PLO, the basest armed organisation since the days of the Nazis. You cannot expect to overcome your own terrorism if you permit offices of the PLO in your capitals, if you accept them into the United Nations, if you give their representatives the right to sit around the table of the Security Council.

Now ladies and gentlemen, there are some who say for many years to come we shall have to live with terrorism, that is is impossible to overcome. Respectfully, I disagree. During the 19th century there was a phenomenon of armed anarchism throughout Europe. Ultimately it was smashed and it disappeared. And that anarchism indeed launched a famous or infamous slogan, "There are no innocents," repeated now by the terrorists of our time. There are no innocents. Everybody should be a victim.

Yet, we can hit them and we can overcome. And it may pass. Let me give you an example. Only a few years ago hijacking of planes was almost a daily phenomenon. Lately it is very rare because we undertook measures, defensive and also offensive. Now I can tell you, I do not boast but merely state a fact, we undertook measures in El Al planes, and El Al planes are now the safest in the skies. Because we undertook measures, we overcame this. We do our best in Lebanon too, against the terrorist bases.

Sometimes people preach to us: Why do you go up to Lebanon and hit those bases? I will ask this question: What should we do? Use only so-called retaliation, wait between attacks upon the civilian Jewish population in our country, in other words, condemn an unknown number of our citizens to die? Because in between there will be death. So we do not use any more the so-called retaliation principle. And as far as children are concerned, we always remember the famous verse of our great poet Bialik: "Revenge like this, the revenge for the blood of a child, Satan himself has not yet created." Nobody can take revenge for the blood of a little child. Nobody. We don't want to return it, we want peace and security for our people and for our children.

So we hit them and this is the most sublime, most legitimate national self-defense. Until we overcome, and overcome we shall. We will unite and resolve not to have this curse — especially in free, democratic countries.

But beware. Don't give, my dear friends from Europe, or your governments, comfort and support to this terroristic, horrifying, inhuman, barbaric organisation called the PLO. It is bent on genocide, bent on the destruction of Israel and her children and people.

Comment from the floor concerning the freeing of terrorists: *They* [*the Israeli Government*] *have released 80 dangerous terrorists and they are going maybe to release more* — *it is your government* — *please tell us why.*

Thank you. Yes, you asked a question. It was a very hard decision. We wanted to save a man, who was not in the hands of any government, who was tortured, who could have been killed any minute. Yes, it was a great sacrifice. It was not a precedent, don't take it as a precedent. And, please let me finish my remarks.

Freedom Fighters and Terrorists

Ladies and gentlemen. I promised you a certain revelation to prove my thesis about the difference between the methods of fighters for freedom and the methods of terrorists. Of course all of you remember the great operation, and even greater tragedy, at the King David Hotel in 1946*.

Since then, for 33 years, we contended that we issued a warning, we gave enough time to evacuate the hotel so that no one would have been hurt. There were denials: First, that the warning was not given at all. Secondly, that it didn't reach the men on the spot.

Three weeks ago Lord Janner made a speech in the House of Lords. He told the august assembly that he got a letter from a Dr. Crawford. Dr. Crawford wrote to him about the British general, Dudley Sheridan:

"In 1946 he was head of the hospital in Palestine here in Jerusalem. He was a frequent visitor to the King David Hotel. He was there on the very day of the explosion. And he wrote me that the warning was passed on to the officers in the bar and in rather jocular terms, implying that it was a Jewish terrorist bluff. But despite advice to ignore the bluff he decided to leave and thus was out of the hotel when the explosion occurred.

*The King David Hotel housed the headquarters of the British Army in Jerusalem at the time. It was bombed by the Irgun Zvai Leumi after advanced telephone warning.

I kept this letter for many years but, unfortunately," so writes Dr. Crawford, "after the death of my wife in 1970 and my own severe illness in 1971, I sold my house and went into a flat. And because of limited space I unwisely threw away a lot of my accumulated papers and correspondence. So the letter is no longer available. And Brigadier Sheridan has long since died. I hope these facts will be of some help to you.

Many of my friends knew the story at the time. But few have survived. My sister-in-law will remember it clearly, as she was friendly with the Brigadier. She lived with us at that time. If you think it worthwhile I could contact her."

Lord Janner finished his speech saying, "I did ask him to contact her and she wrote a letter confirming what Dr. Crawford said."

Ladies and gentlemen, from my teacher Jabotinsky I learned the famous slogan of Thomas Masaryk, "Truth prevails and must win."

Since 1946 the debate went on. And now you have this letter proving that the officers got the warning. Unfortunately, tragically, they didn't heed it. But we gave that warning for half an hour because this is the difference between a fighter for freedom and a terrorist. A terrorist kills civilians. A fighter for freedom saves lives and fights on at the risk of his own life until liberty wins the day.

Second Session
Subject:
STATE SUPPORT FOR INTERNATIONAL TERRORISM
Morning, July 3, 1979
Chairman: Ambassador Chaim Herzog

PREFACE

Political violence has always been a fact of life. Nor has terrorism — violence systematically directed at innocent civilians for political ends — been exclusively a phenomenon of our time. But the recent fantastic growth in international terror movements and incidents, the enhanced prestige of terrorists, and even the spectre of internationally-sponsored terrorist states, are the direct result of the *state support* extended to terror movements. This support has taken a number of forms: arms, money, training, sanctuary, the use of diplomatic pouches and passports, and political backing in international forums.

Yet the democracies of the West have exhibited a curious reticence about the support given by the Soviet Union, Cuba, East Germany, Libya, Iraq, Syria, South Yemen, and other members of the Soviet and Arab blocs. Despite the unquestionable evidence available of that support, little attention has been given the problem of sovereign state involvement. Fear, either of economic blackmail (in the case of the Arab states), or of political intimidation (in the case of the Soviet Union), has kept the West from focusing directly on this problem.

The Jerusalem Conference offered a forum at which the overwhelming evidence of such support would be publicly presented. Speakers detailed the collusion of governments and noted ways in which such support could be discouraged. Many felt that until the real backers of terror movements are shown that such support will cost them dearly, they will continue to aid and abet the architects of terrorist crimes. All agreed that the indispensable first step in combatting international terrorism is massive exposure of the central role played by certain governments in its alarming growth.

CHAIM HERZOG was Israel's Ambassador
to the United Nations from 1975-1978. He
had also served as Chief of Israel's Military
Intelligence, as Israeli Defense Attaché in
Washington, and as Military Governor of the
West Bank. Mr. Herzog has been a television
and radio commentator, and contributes
regularly to newspapers in Israel and abroad.
He is the author of several books, including
*Israel's Finest Hour, Days of Awe, The War
of Atonement,* and *Who Stands Accused?*

CHAIRMAN'S OPENING REMARKS

Three years ago next week, it fell to my lot to face the
Security Council of the U.N., when the African bloc introduced a resolution condemning the rescue operation at
Entebbe. It is perhaps appropriate in opening this assessment
on state support for international terrorism, that I recall those
moments when for the "crime" of rescuing innocent people
hijacked by terrorists, the Security Council was convened to
condemn Israel, the Security Council which has never once
been convened to condemn terrorist activities.

I opened then with these words, which are no less valid
today than they were then:

"Mr. President, from a purely formal point of view,
this meeting arises from a complaint brought against
the Israeli government. However, let me make it clear
that sitting here as the representative of the Israeli government, as I have the honor to do, I am in no way
sitting in the dock as the accused party. On the contrary,
I stand here as an accuser on behalf of free and decent
people in this world. I stand here as an accuser of the
forces of evil which have unleashed a wave of piracy and
terrorism which threatens the very foundations of human
society. I stand here as an accuser of all those evil forces
which in their inherent cowardice and abject craven attitude see blameless wayfarers and innocent women and

children — yes, even babes in arms — a legitimate target
for their evil intentions. I stand here as an accuser of the
countries that because of evil design or lack of moral
backbone, have collaborated with these bloodthirsty
terrorists. I stand here as an accuser of all those in authority throughout the world who for reasons of cynical
expediency have collaborated with terrorism. I stand
here as an accuser of this world organisation, the United
Nations, which has been unable, because of the machinations of the Arab delegates and their supporters, to coor-
dinate effective measures in order to combat the evil of
world terrorism. I stand here as an accuser of those
delegations to the organisation which for reasons of
political expediency have remained silent on this issue,
an issue which is bound to affect each country in this
organisation. In so doing, they have themselves become
accomplices.

"In the dock before us are the representatives of all
those countries who stood and applauded the entry into
the hall of the General Assembly of a gun-toting terrorist
who, according to the President of Sudan, personally gave
the order to execute the American and Belgian diplomats
bound hand and foot in the basement of the Saudi
Arabian embassy in Khartoum on March 1, 1973. Yes,
sir, before us stands accused this rotten, corrupt, brutal,
cynical bloodthirsty monster of international terrorism
and all those who support it in one way or the other,
whether by commission or omission. Facing them today
are the ordinary decent human beings throughout the
world who seek nothing more than to live a life free from
terror and from intimidation, free from the threats of
hijackers, the indiscriminate bombs of terrorists, and the
blackmail of criminals and murderers.

"In more ways than one, this organisation is in the
accused stand because never has the issue been clearer,
never has the issue been so clear-cut. There will be no
excuse in history for this body or for the constituent
members of this body if it fails to condemn terrorism.

The issue before this body is not what Israel did in
Entebbe Airport; the issue before this body is its own
future in the eyes of history."

The Essential Support of States

I have no doubt that during the course of the remarks here,
much attention will be directed to the activities of those
various states which support terror. It is quite clear to us today
that without the active support of states, terrorism would have
little chance in the world today, and could certainly be
curbed. There comes to mind the central role played by Libya.
Qaddafi's regime has for years been the world's most un-
abashed proponent of revolutionary violence. And from the
number of times that Libya has been linked to terrorist groups
and incidents (including Carlos' raid on the OPEC conference
in Vienna), it would appear that Col. Qaddafi has been one of
the world's least inhibited practitioners of international
terrorism.

Tripoli's focus has been on nationalist formations, whatever their ideological coloration or leanings. Thus the recipients of Libya's favours have been numerous and varied. In
addition to some of the more militant Palestinian splinter
groups, it includes the I.R.A. and a number of less widely-
known guerrilla movements based in the Philippines, Ethiopia,
Somalia, the People's Democratic Republic of Yemen, Chad,
Morocco, Tunisia, Thailand and Panama.

Moscow's posture has been more ambiguous. Basically,
the Soviets have had serious misgivings about the utility of
transnational terrorist activity. They have repeatedly warned
that excessive violence can tarnish the reputation of those
involved, and have stressed their belief that such tactics are not
only generally unproductive, but can lead to unforeseen and
possibly uncontrollable adverse consequences. At the same
time, however, the Kremlin's broader interests — including,
importantly, those stemming from its continuing adversary
relationship with Peking — have denied it the option of a
straightforward hands-off policy. Thus, after a period of hesi-
tancy, the Soviets began channelling funds, weapons, and

other assistance to fedayeen groups through a number of intermediaries in 1969. All indications are that they continue to do
so today. Similarly, they have continued their long-standing
program (the more innocuous aspects of which are publicly
associated with Moscow's Patrice Lumumba University) of
bringing young revolutionaries from all parts of the Third
World to the Soviet Union for training and indoctrination.
And like Carlos, some of these individuals have subsequently
cropped up on the transnational terrorist scene.

Nonetheless, one thing is clear. However much the
Soviets might wish otherwise, their efforts to gain some handle
on extremist activity have, together with their pursuit of less
congruent objectives, done more to aggravate than to contain
the current rash of transnational terrorist activity. The hard
fact is that it is difficult to translate assistance into leverage or
control when there are other available sources of support.
Indeed, as the Soviets should by now have learned, any assistance provided to an extremist group under these circumstances risks simply increasing the recipient's potential for
autonomous action.

Unabashed Hypocrisy

In recent months, when listening to President Nyerere's
violent fulminations against the Organisation for African
Unity, and his rationale for the Tanzanian invasion of Uganda,
I could not but think back to that dramatic debate in the
Security Council when the Tanzanian delegate, one of those
leading the attack on Israel, expressed himself as follows:

"Therefore — and I say this in all solemnity — we
view the Israeli action against Entebbe not only as a threat
against Uganda but as a threat against the sovereignty,
independence and territorial integrity of African States.
We consider this a very dangerous precedent in international relations. We consider it to be an even more dangerous precedent insofar as the rights of smaller nations
and less powerful nations of the world are concerned.

"The representative of Israel more or less challenged
my position and said, perhaps by implication, perhaps

directly, that my Government and I myself preferred expediency to principles. He gave what I consider to be a long lecture on principles. But I want to assure the representative to Israel that we in Tanzania attach the greatest importance to principles.

"In all humility, I also beg to submit that we are not discussing here the international situation in Uganda or the likes and dislikes of people insofar as the Government of Uganda is concerned. It is not Uganda which is being discussed here; we are discussing an action against Uganda; and nothing would be more hypocritical, I submit, than to transform the victim of aggression and make him the principal culprit and the principal villain of our deliberations."

In my reply to him, in which I rejected out of hand his insinuations, I asked him:

"Would Africa have looked better if Palestinian terrorists, in connivance with President Amin, had slaughtered over a hundred men, women and children?

"Would Africa have looked better with the blood of those innocent victims bespattering the soil of Africa?

"Who has besmirched Africa? Israel, for exercising its right to save its citizens in accordance with international law? Or that racist regime in Uganda, waging an heroic war against a defenseless old lady of seventy-five years?"

The Deliberate Failure of the UN

Finally, I cannot open this discussion without referring, in passing, to the miserable efforts of the U.N. Two years ago, under threat of a world-wide strike by the airline pilots, the General Assembly adopted a wishy-washy, inconclusive resolution, which we maintained was insufficient and ineffective. I regret to say that the bulk of the airline pilots' associations failed to take a firm stand and insist on a resolution which was clear, unequivocal and with teeth.

In 1972, following the murder of the Israeli athletes at Munich, the Secretary-General introduced a draft resolution on the subject of terrorism to the General Assembly. That draft resolution has now been discussed, since 1972, at every meeting of the General Assembly, and has not yet been approved. It has by now been emptied of all content. Its title alone is a joke, an international joke, which only emphasizes the impotence of the U.N. Let me read it to you:

"Measures to Prevent International Terrorism Which Endangers or Takes Innocent Lives or Jeopardizes Fundamental Freedoms, and Study of the Underlying Causes of Those Forms of Terrorism and Acts of Violence Which Lie in Misery, Frustration, Grievance and Despair and Which Cause Some People to Sacrifice Human Lives, Including Their Own, in an Attempt to Effect Radical Changes."

The list of the sponsors of this draft resolution as it is today is also an education in itself: Algeria, Burundi, Congo, Democratic Yemen, Egypt, Ethiopia, Ghana, Guinea, Kenya, Laos People's Democratic Republic, Lesotho, Libyan Arab Jamahiriya, Mali, Morocco, Niger, Nigeria, Sudan, Togo, Tunisia, Uganda, United Republic of Tanzania, Yemen, Zaire and Zambia.

The first four operative paragraphs of the resolution as it is today, in the seventh year of discussion of the resolution, reads as follows, after a preamble which opens with the words, "The General Assembly, deeply perturbed over acts of international terrorism which are occurring with increasing frequency and which take a toll of innocent human lives,

"1.   Expresses deep concern over increasing acts of international terrorism which endanger or take innocent human lives or jeopardize fundamental freedoms;

2.   Urges States to continue to seek just and peaceful solutions to the underlying causes which give rise to such acts of violence;

3.   Reaffirms the inalienable right to self-determination and independence of all peoples under colonial and racist regimes and other forms of alien domination, and upholds the legitimacy of their struggle, in particular the struggle of national liberation movements, in accordance with the purposes and principles of the Charter and the

relevant resolutions of the organs of the United Nations;
4. Condemns the continuation of repressive and terrorist acts by colonial, racist and alien regimes in denying
peoples their legitimate right to self-determination and
independence and other human rights and fundamental
freedoms."

You will see in the title, let alone the resolution, all the if's
and but's and maybe's of the terrorist organisations and of
their supporters in the Soviet bloc, the Arab bloc and part of
the Third World. The fact is, the incontrovertible fact, that the
U.N. has not yet been able to pass a resolution with teeth in it
on the subject of international terrorism.

The working paper on the underlying causes of international terrorism is a most revealing document. Unfortunately, I do not have the time to read it and the various
Addenda. The burden of the document is an examination of
the all-embracing "Underlying Causes" which has been used to
vitiate every attempt at a resolution or a convention. Under
the major heading:

"Desire for Domination, Exploitation, Expansion,
Hegemony, Imperalism, etc., which results in:"

(a) causes of a political character (there are 8 such
causes), and
(b) causes of an economic and social character (there are
6 such causes)

We find in the draft report of the Ad Hoc Committee on International Terrorism dated April 5, 1979, that:

"It was suggested that one more cause should be added
to the list in the working paper, namely, the connivance
of states with regard to groups and organisations of
Fascist, neo-Fascist and Zionist countries, including
racism, racial domination, policy of apartheid and
genocide."

With the infamous resolution passed by the General Assembly
on November 10th, 1975 in mind, one can see how any U.N.
organ will react to justify any act of terror, for instance,
directed against Israel.

In July 1976, during the Entebbe debate, the distinguished delegate of the Federal Republic of Germany, Baron Rudiger von Wechmar, took the seat next to me at the Security Council. This was the first time that the Federal Republic had done so in a debate of the Security Council when it was not a member of the Council. He announced the German government's intention to propose a convention against the taking of hostages. It was introduced by Foreign Minister Genscher at the Assembly in September 1976. It has not yet been passed or adopted. Again, the same foot-dragging, the same reservations, the same objections, the same seemingly innocuous introduction of wording designed to exclude terrorist activities from the operation of the resolution, by the subtle or not-so-subtle means to which one becomes accustomed in the U.N.

These few examples are sufficient to assure us that the last place to look for support and comfort in this struggle against international terrorism is the U.N. Only a firm, unequivocal stand taken by the free world, and particularly by the United States, which will outlaw terrorists and will impose sanctions for harboring or aiding terrorists has any chance of curbing the activities of the terrorists. The bills introduced by Senators Ribicoff and Heinz in the U.S. are indicators of what type of legislation could be introduced so as to create a sanction which would deter countries supporting terrorism. It seems to me that it is important that this Conference, commemorating as it does one of the great historic blows that ever was struck against international terrorism, should produce some practical suggestions to guide governments in their decisions on this issue.

Organizing to Fight Terror Outside the UN
It is utterly unrealistic to expect any positive development to emerge from the U.N. on the subject of terrorism, as indeed on many other subjects. The only hope is for the free countries led by the U.S. and the Nine to bind themselves in a convention outside the U.N. against terror which provides

for international sanctions, a convention by which they will be bound.

We are discussing what is, we believe, the greatest tangible threat to civilisation today. Recently, the C.I.A. confirmed that a nuclear pack capable of being carried on a man's back is now a reality and the implications thereof are mind-boggling.

Europe is in the throes of a serious terrorist threat which is growing. Latin America has it too. Across South Asia and the Middle East there sweeps a new danger for our Western society — an extreme form of Islam, violently orthodox and fanatic, which has affected many countries, Iran and Pakistan, and threatens many more. This threat becomes a grave one when we contemplate the fact that it is linked to a potential to acquire the most modern technology. It is a function of the impact of the 20th century with untold wealth on medieval societies. Pakistan is today by all means of subterfuge constructing facilities for nuclear weapons with Libyan financial aid. France aided Pakistan in this project as it is aiding Iraq in its nuclear development. Herein lies the great danger facing our free world.

It therefore behoves all free societies to band together in order to give meaning and teeth to their opposition to terrorism and to outlaw now these elements who would bring our society to the brink of disaster and those countries which aid and comfort them.

There is no room for compromise. If free society does not awaken to the danger, that danger will threaten its very existence. We owe it to ourselves, to our children and to our future generations.

RICHARD PIPES is Professor of History,
and former Director of the Russian Research Center at Harvard University. He
is widely recognized as a leading expert in
Russian history. Prof. Pipes is the author
of many studies in this field, including
several important works on the Russian
Revolution; among his books are *Formation
of the Soviet Union* and *Russia Under the
Old Regime*. He is now completing a multi-
volume biography on the legal Marxist
Peter Struve.

THE ROOTS OF THE INVOLVEMENT

The philosophical origins of modern terrorism may be found
in the *Catechism of the Revolutionary* by the Russian Nechayev,
who over a hundred years ago spelled out exactly what the
function and morality of a terrorist should be. It is generally
believed that Russian terrorism failed, that the terrorists did
not achieve their purpose, and that in 1917 power was seized
by a group — the Bolsheviks — who were hostile to terrorism.
The more I study the history of the Russian Revolution, the
more skeptical I become about this commonplace assumption.

The roots of Soviet terrorism, indeed of modern terrorism,
date back to 1879. This year, therefore, marks the hundredth
anniversary of the establishment of terrorism as an organized
political movement. It marks the founding of that organization
which is the source of all modern terrorist groups, whether
they be named the Tupamaros, the Baader-Meinhof group, the
Weathermen, the Red Brigade or the PLO. I refer to the establishment in 1879 of a Congress in the small Russian town of
Lipetsk of an organization known as *Narodnaya Volya* or The
People's Will.

This small organization initially had hardly more than
thirty members. Early in its existence it passed a death sentence
on the then reigning Czar, Alexander II (known as the Czar
Liberator because in 1861 he freed the Russian serfs). After a

succession of failures, on March 1, 1881, it finally succeeded in murdering the Czar.

Why do I take the year of 1879 of which we are today "mourning" the first centenary, and maintain that it represents something really new in history? Surely we have had innumerable political murders in the past. But those murders were of individual political leaders. The new development lies in the following distinction: the murder of political figures in the past had been carried out by individuals against individuals, by those who felt that a particular man in power represented or embodied political or social evil. These political assassins were not organized, they had no program and they had no vision beyond the assassination of those individuals who in their minds embodied this evil.

The People's Will organization was the first to consider the enemy to be *the whole system*, and by system again I emphasize it meant not only autocracy, but also capitalism, religion, law and everything else which kept the body politic intact. They had no particular hostility towards Alexander II personally; some of them indeed admired him for liberating the serfs. But he was regarded as an essential part of an inherently evil system, and had to be destroyed.

This was an innovation. I think there was nothing like it before in history, but there has been a great deal like it since.

Legacy of Successful Terror

After the assassination of Alexander II there was a revulsion against terrorism, and for about 20 years there was a hiatus when the movement lay dormant. It was revived in 1902, and was active for the next 5 years until it was finally broken by Prime Minister Stolypin. Thousands were killed, many of them innocent bystanders. I do not not subscribe to the distinction by some that modern terrorism differs from previous terrorism in that it takes no account of civilians and innocent bystanders. That is not the case. Several anti-czar revolutionary groups very happily killed anybody who came in their way. In a celebrated attempt on the life of Prime Minister Stolypin in 1907, they set off a bomb in his villa which killed 50 people, including people who were just there accidentally hoping to see the Prime Minister. This type of action was carried out repeatedly.

The successor, then, in method and partly in ideology, to the *Narodnaya Volya* movement was the party of the Social Revolutionaries (the S.R.'s). In the early years of this century the S.R.'s launched attacks on the Imperial Government with the deliberate purpose of destroying the awe in which the population in Russia held the regime. They felt that as long as people feared the government, and believed it to be omnipotent, there was no possibility of revolution. So the murder of government officials or supporters of the government was an important step in causing the numinous glow surrounding the government to evanesce. The S.R. campaign succeeded to a remarkable extent. Almost all contemporary observers note that after 1905 the traditional loyalty and belief of the Russian peasant in the monarchy were broken. There was a great deal of contempt on the part of the peasant for the regime. This facilitated the events of 1917.

It should be noted that not only did the terror campaign demystify Russian rulers in the eyes of the people, but it also caused the government to overreact. From 1879 onwards the Imperial government introduced a series of extremely harsh countermeasures meant to prevent terror, but which had the effect of alienating moderate groups in Russia. In the long run this made it impossible for the regime to ever secure the support of moderately conservative and liberal elements in Russian society, so it was left to fall, isolated and alone, in 1917.

Terrorism in Russia thus succeeded beyond the wildest expectations of its supporters. The Bolsheviks were essentially beneficiaries of this process, even though as Marxists and Social Democrats they rejected terror as a means of coming to power — this despite the fact that Marx himself, when he learned about the exploits of the People's Will in Russia, called these terrorists "splendid fellows" and agreed that possibly in Russia one could come to power without going through all the phases which he had outlined for a socialist revolution in the West. Lenin, apart from a brief flirtation with terror in his youth (he was brought up in a People's Will environment), believed as did most of his colleagues in the Jacobin policy of applying terror only after power was seized. It was not a means of coming to power, but a means of breaking the will of the opposition after power had been seized. But he was able to seize power in October 1917 only because the state's authority had collapsed after a progressive breakdown in which terror played a major role.

This experience left an indelible imprint on the minds of the Soviet leadership. This cannot be overemphasized. Nearly all the elements of Soviet global strategy are essentially an adaptation to foreign policy of methods which had been learned by the Bolsheviks and their allies when they were in the underground fighting the Imperial regime. If you want to understand what Soviet foreign or global strategy is, you must study the history of the Russian Revolution. That is the only way you can understand not only their strategies but even the language which they adopted toward the "capitalist-imperialist" West. All of this was nurtured in the experience of the period 1879-1917.

A Two-Faced Policy

The Soviet attitude to terror as a means of foreign policy strikes me as both favorable and unfavorable. It is negative, on the one hand, because the Soviet government feels itself vulnerable to terror internally. I disagree with the contention that the West is vulnerable to terrorism, and the Soviet regime or totalitarian regimes are not. I think the contrary proposition is truer. In fact I think the Soviet regime is far more vulnerable to terror, internal terror, than are democratic societies, because their entire internal authority rests on the impression which they create of omniscience and omnipotence; if that image of omniscience and omnipotence is successfully challenged by terrorists, the Soviet regime will be threatened with exactly the same loss of internal support and respect which caused the downfall of the Imperial regime. Their tolerance of terror, therefore, is much lower than ours.

The open encouragement of terror by the Soviet government as a means of political action abroad could turn against that government itself, especially because it could be picked up as a weapon by the minority populations inhabiting the Soviet Union, who could launch a war of national revolution inside the Soviet empire using this instrument. For that very reason the Soviet Union, while using terror abroad, nevertheless prefers not to *identify* itself with terror openly (another reason, of course, is the desire not to jeopardize trade relations and other benefits from the West). Nonetheless it also encourages and employs terrorism because terrorism is a handy and relatively cheap weapon in their arsenal to destroy the Western societies, both directly, by supporting terrorist movements in the Western world, and indirectly, by striking at what they perceive to be the sources of the West's power in the Third World.

Concrete examples of Soviet support of terrorist organizations have been given by others. It always has been very striking to me that these terrorist groups, among whom there are many anarchists who detest the Soviet Union as much as they do the Western capitalist countries, have almost *never* struck at Soviet objectives. This is to me added evidence that the Russians exercise a very considerable controlling influence over these movements.

The Soviet Union has enjoyed great success with terror and profited from it in many ways, just as the Bolsheviks did before 1917. We must expose its support of terrorism as widely as possible, and make the public aware of Soviet complicity. The Soviets should be held accountable for these actions. It must be made absolutely clear that these activities of theirs will no longer be tolerated.

Understanding the Full Threat

In closing, let me say a few words about the general nature of the terrorist threat. In addition to all the dangers which were mentioned yesterday by various speakers, terrorism threatens the very principle of statehood which is so indispensable for civilization's survival. Sociologists and political scientists in the late 19th century sometimes defined the state as an institution that enjoys the monopoly on violence. By this they did not mean that it has a license to engage in violence, but that if any violence is to be perpetrated, either in the form of an external war or of punishment of criminals, the state and the state alone would do so. Hence in the 19th century it was taken as axiomatic that guerrillas are not armies and that political murders are not executions, that they are guerrillas and murders. This has been effectively challenged by the modern terrorist, thus threatening to bring down the state and its institutions through the reversion to totalitarianism, or perhaps to something that is even worse — a reversion to the Dark Ages, when the mass of mankind was dominated and held in abject terror by warring gangs of armed men, responsible to no one and moved only by superior force.

But what about terror? Are there any objective criteria by which we can judge what is legitimate terror and what is not? I personally believe that it is illegitimate to use terror anywhere at any time as a means of fighting what is perceived, rightly or wongly, as political, national, or economic oppression. It is legitimate, in my opinion, only as a means of fighting terror itself, whether it emanates from the state, as was true for example in Nazi-occupied Europe, or from political organizations dedicated to terror. It goes without saying that subduing terrorism — and it seems to me the job is easier than it appears on the face of it — requires will power and cooperation and understanding such as this conference is trying to achieve and publicize. If such public understanding and cooperation are achieved, terrorism will vanish quickly, and with it the counterterrorism which I believe to be legitimate. Unless this is done, we shall see an ever increasing wave of terrorism and countertorrism, leading us inexorably to two unpalatable alternatives — totalitarianism or anarchy.

BRIAN CROZIER is Director of the
Institute for the Study of Conflict in
London. He is the author of *The Rebels: A
Study of Post-War Insurrection, A Theory
of Conflict, Strategy of Survival* and *The
Minimum State*, as well as biographies of
De Gaulle and others. Mr. Crozier's works
are required reading in defense colleges and
institutes in a number of countries. He
writes frequently for American and British
magazines on political and strategic subjects.

SOVIET SUPPORT FOR INTERNATIONAL TERRORISM

The Soviet Union is deeply involved in supporting terrorist
groups in many countries — through the provision of arms,
weapons and training. There are of course gaps in the publicly
available evidence of Soviet involvement; the contrary would
be surprising in a field in which clandestinity is essential to
success. But the evidence that *has* come to light is sufficiently
abundant and authentic to put the facts beyond all doubt.

Nor is this support in any sense ideologically surprising,
for although Lenin would probably not have supported such
romantic or "adventuristic" efforts as the late Che Guevara's
attempt to stir up revolt among Bolivian peasants, the advocacy
of violence and direct methods of revolution runs like a leit-
motif throughout his works. Many, though by no means all,
terrorist groups style themselves "Marxist-Leninist," whether
or not they are critical of the brand of "socialism" practiced
in Brezhnev's USSR. In any event, ideological purity is visibly
not a qualification for Soviet support. Although Soviet spokesmen have condemned hijacking (presumably because the
Soviet Union itself has suffered the inconvenience of this form
of terrorism), the organs of Soviet power — in particular, the
International Department of the CPSU's Central Committee,
and the KGB — support many terrorist groups (sometimes
styled "national liberation movements") for a variety of
reasons, including the following:

1. Terrorism contributes to the enfeeblement and destabilization of non-Communist regimes.
2. By supporting groups or governments that are overtly critical of the USSR, the subversive apparatus of the Soviet Union creates a dependency and need for further support. In time, the Soviet Union may hope to bring such groups or governments under their influence, and eventually under their control.

Promoting Terrorism in All its Forms

Some observers or analysts would contest these opening statements on the grounds that Soviet support for "pure" terrorist groups is relatively small and that those groups which have received sustained Soviet support are really "freedom fighters" or "national liberation movements," but such semantic pitfalls should be resisted. It can be shown, for instance, that a number of "pure" terrorist groups have received direct or indirect Soviet subsidies; as for the "freedom fighters" or "national liberation movements," all or nearly all have practiced or continue to practice "pure" terrorism — that is, acts of violence in which innocent members of the public are the sufferers, whether deliberately or through callous disregard for the risks of death or injury on the part of the perpetrators. The fact that some terrorists in receipt of Soviet help may abandon terrorism in favor of guerrilla war or even full-scale war (as in Indochina during both wars) does not absolve the Soviets from the charge of having supported terrorism. Moveover, many terrorist groups revert to terrorism after a phase of guerrilla activity; indeed, the incidence of terrorist acts (as distinct from guerrilla incidents) serves as a reliable "barometer" of insurgent success or failure. Graduation to a guerrilla phase is a sign of success; reversion to terrorism, of failure.

Another point needs to be made. Although the "pure" terrorism of such groups as the Baader-Meinhof gang in Germany or the Red Brigades in Italy causes much disruption, inconvenience and suffering, it does not seem, in the end, to be capable, in itself, of causing the disintegration of a society. On the other hand, terrorism which is a phase in a "revolutionary war" is ultimately far more grave and deadly. A commitment to terrorism of this kind implies sustained assistance (of the kind the Soviets gave the Vietnamese Communists in both Indochina wars), and is therefore far more important than assistance to groups which indulge in terrorism for its own sake, in that it may lead to profound and lasting strategic change.

Historical Perspective on Soviet Support

Even in the relatively brief historical period since the end of World War II, which is the main focus of attention of this Conference, Soviet involvement in terrorism is long-standing. The left-wing terrorist groups in Greece and in Indochina in the last phases of that war were ultimately under Soviet control. The Vietminh was created by the Comintern agent, Ho Chi Minh. In 1948, only three years after the war had ended, Stalin sponsored insurgencies throughout South-East Asia, in all of which terrorism played a major part.

In the intervening decades, Soviet involvement in terrorism has been both direct and indirect. The distinction is largely academic. It suits the Soviet leaders that gullible observers abroad should blame others — Czechs, East Germans, Cubans or, for instance, Portuguese Communists — for terrorist outbreaks that would never have taken place without Soviet directives and the facilities available to the Soviet subversive apparatus. Not all Communist parties are necessarily or invariably at Moscow's orders, but many continue to be, and parties which at times have been openly critical of the Soviet Union (for example, the PCI in Italy) have been willing on occasion to do Moscow's bidding in the field of terrorism. It is known, for example, that the Italian Communist Party acted as a conduit for the funding of Venezuelan terrorists in the 1960s.

Portugal and the former Portuguese territories in Africa provide one of the most striking examples of a protracted Soviet support for terrorism. The Portuguese Communist Party, which has been consistently and totally subservient to Moscow, set up a clandestine Communist party in Angola in 1955. In turn, this party created the Popular Movement for the Liberation of Angola (MPLA) in preparation for the rebellion against Portuguese rule that was launched in 1961. It was learned many years later that from the start, MPLA terrorists and guerrillas were trained in vast camps in the Soviet Union. Similar circumstances applied to the Front for the Liberation of Mozambique (FRELIMO) and the African Party for the Independence of Guinea and Cape Verde Islands (PAIGC). As with all such insurgencies of the "People's Revolutionary War" type (e.g., Indochina, Algeria, etc.) the key factor in the final outcome was the morale of the Portuguese themselves. Although the Portuguese Communists probably did not themselves set up the Armed Forces Movement which toppled the Caetano regime on April 25, 1974, they were involved in it from the beginning. In anticipation of the anti-Caetano coup, the Party decided in May 1973 to abandon the terrorist campaign it had launched nearly three years earlier (October 1970) through a clandestine organization, the Armed Revolutionary Action (ARA). Both the decision to start terrorism and the decision to halt it must have originated in, or at least have been cleared by, Moscow. It is true to say that in Alvaro Cunhal, leader of the PCP, the Soviets had their own "man in Lisbon." The fall of the Caetano government paved the way for the Communist victories in Portuguese Guinea, Angola and Mozambique, even though a more direct attempt at a Communist takeover in Portugal itself failed in November 1975.

Soviet Training Camps for Terrorists

Through the long years of the Portuguese African insurgencies, the subversive organs of the Soviet State trained many hundreds, and probably thousands, of terrorists and guerrillas from these territories. The main training camps are known to be located in Moscow itself, in Baku, Simferopol, Tashkent and Odessa. Between 1964 and 1974, it was possible through the revelations of numerous African defectors from the terrorist training system to build up a reasonably detailed picture of Soviet facilities in this domain. Candidates for training come in two streams: the orthodox Communist stream and the National Liberation stream. Trainees in the orthodox stream consist of members of Moscow-line Communist Parties from many countries who, on arrival in Moscow, are given six-month training programs in the Lenin Institute. The National Liberation entrants are initially offered academic courses through the Patrice Lumumba People's Friendship University in Moscow, and those selected for terrorist training are later dispersed to one or other of the camps already mentioned. In one stream or another, the trainees come from Latin America, Africa, the Arab world, the Middle East, Western Europe, South-East Asia and Australia. Subjects taught include: agitation and propaganda, target practice and bomb-making, sabotage, street fighting and assaults on buildings, and assassination techniques.

By far the most notorious "student" in the Patrice Lumumba University course in terrorism was "Carlos" (alias "The Jackal"), whose Communist father had named him Ilich after Lenin, and whose real name was Ramírez Sánchez. Recruited by the KGB in his native Venezuela, Carlos was sent to Cuba in the 1960s and was trained in terrorism and guerrilla warfare under the KGB Colonel Victor Simonov. After his intensive Soviet training, he was expelled from Patrice Lumumba, allegedly for various misdemeanors. But it has since become clear that he has continued to work to Moscow's orders.

Direct and Indirect Forms of Russian Involvement

As a rule, Moscow *identifies* itself with terrorist groups only when they may be successfully labeled as "National Liberation Movements" and where local Communist interests are unlikely to be damaged. The Soviet attitude in this respect is purely opportunistic. Thus, it suited the International Department that the PCP should indulge in terrorism between 1970 and 1973. In other places, Soviet support for terrorists may be clandestine, especially where it is thought useful that the local Communist Party should criticize revolutionary violence, in an attempt to pose as a sober and responsible organization with the aim of persuading the public of its worthiness to participate in government.

A striking illustration of this proposition occurred in Chile during the Allende regime. As partners in the ruling coalition, the highly disciplined Chilean Communist Party cultivated an image of moderation. In particular, it was highly critical of the violent excesses of the extreme left MIR. Meanwhile, in secrecy, the KGB was training the Miristas in terrorism in camps situated in southern Chile. In other camps, North Korean instructors were training young terrorists from the most extreme faction in Allende's own Socialist Party.

Similarly, the Uruguayan CP maintained a critical distance from the terrorist Tupamaros, although it was learned later that Moscow had provided arms and other assistance through their Cuban satellites.

The KGB and North Korean training schemes in Chile were of course collusive, and this was not the first occasion on which the Soviets had drawn upon North Korean skills in this department. In 1971, for instance, a group of young Mexicans recruited by the KGB for training at the Patrice Lumumba University was despatched for further training in North Korea, sent back to Moscow for a final briefing, then on to Mexico, where they attempted to launch a campaign of terrorism and insurgency. The group numbered about 50, calling themselves the Movement of Revolutionary Action (MAR).

Although the Soviet training scheme for terrorists in Chile became known while it was still in progress, this was an exception to the general rule. More often, a group which claims and is generally believed to be independent of Moscow is seen later to have received Soviet help. I have already cited the example of the Tupamaros. A more arresting one was that of the Red Army Group in Germany, better known as the Baader-Meinhof gang. Although the leaders of this notorious terrorist organization were openly critical of the Soviet Union, it was secretly subsidized by the East Germans (whose Ministry of State Security is at the direct orders of the KGB). The RAG evolved out of a journal of the extreme left entitled *Konkret* and edited by Klaus Rainer Röhl, whose wife was Ulrike

Meinhof. Both were secret members of the Communist Party
from 1956 to 1964, and Röhl received about $250,000 in
subsidies through East Berlin and Prague.

Another striking example of indirect Soviet involvement
in terrorism came to light with the seizure at Schipol Airport
in Holland in October 1971, of a large consignment of weapons destined for the (then) anti-Marxist wing of the Irish
Republican Army — the Provisionals — in a deal negotiated
with a Czech agency.

Two more examples — one direct, the other indirect —
may be given of the continuing Soviet interest in Irish terrorism. The direct case was the financing by the USSR of an "Anti-
Imperialist Festival" held in Dublin and Belfast in August
1974. Ostensibly, the "Festival" was sponsored by the Official
Sinn Fein, the political wing of the IRA; but it was in fact
convened by the Communist Front.

The indirect example occurred on March 28, 1973, when
the Irish security authorities apprehended the s/s *Claudia*, in
which they found five tons of arms, ammunition and explosives. A smaller quantity of arms was found in July that year
in the ship *Manchester Vigour*. The *Claudia* shipment, at any
rate, consisted of Soviet arms, probably from Libya.

That country benefited in 1976 from what appears to
have been the biggest arms deal in history — probably of the
order of $12 billion. Arms in such quantities are of course
massively beyond the needs of Qadaffi's armed forces, and
the surplus serves, among other things, to feed terrorist groups.
Indeed, apart from the IRA, recipients of large-scale shipments
of Soviet arms channeled through Libya include the Black
September Organization (the offshoot of Al-Fatah, responsible
for the murder of Israeli athletes at the Munich Olympic
Games in 1972), the Japanese United Red Army, the Popular
Front for the Liberation of Palestine, the Arm of the Arab
Revolution (Carlos's group), the Baader-Meinhof gang, and
terrorist or guerrilla groups in Turkey, Iran, Yemen, Lebanon,
Eritrea, Chad, Chile, Uruguay, Nicaragua and the Philippines.
Although Moscow officially disapproves of hijacking, Moscow's
protégés, Libya and North Korea, have consistently defied

international law by providing havens for skyjackers. Shortly after the Entebbe hijacking (which tragically inspired the founding of this Institute) in June 1976, Moscow reiterated its disapproval of air piracy. Yet the skyjackers belonged to the PFLP and the Baader-Meinhof gang, both of which have received Soviet arms and money.

The Soviet Role in Arab Terrorism

The degree of Soviet involvement in Arab terrorism has aroused much controversy. I know of no evidence that the Soviets mastermind individual acts of terrorism by any Palestinian or other Arab group. But there can be no doubt about general Soviet aid and sponsorship. I attach particular importance to the Soviet decision, in August 1974, to invite the PLO to open an office in Moscow, for experience shows that this "honor" is rarely conferred and indicates a long-term commitment. Thus Moscow's decision in November 1964 — only a month after Khrushchev's overthrow — to invite the Viet Cong's political wing (NFLSV) to open an office in Moscow was the prelude to a massive commitment of Soviet arms to the Communist side, sustained until the defeat of the Americans and their South Vietnam allies in the 1970s. At that time, the NFLSV already had offices in various capitals; similarly, the PLO already had an office in East Berlin, and was represented elsewhere.

Nor is Moscow's support for Arab terrorism confined to the Palestinians. For instance, two Syrians arrested in Holland in September 1975 for plotting to hijack a train and take Soviet Jews as hostages revealed that they had been trained, along with scores of other Arabs, in terrorist techniques in a village camp outside Moscow.

A graver case of Soviet support for Arab terrorists was the insurgency in the Dhofar area of Oman. The rebels of the Popular Front for the Liberation of the Occupied Arab Gulf (one of several changes of name fitting the initials PFLOAG) were armed with Soviet weapons and mainly trained by Cubans in South Yemen (PDRY). It is gratifying to add that they were defeated by the Sultan's forces, with some British assistance, at the end of 1975.

One more example must suffice in this necessarily selective compilation: the Curiel network. Henri Curiel, an Egyptian, worked for the KGB, probably under the control of Boris Ponomarev's International Department. He built up an organization named Solidarité, which had connections with no fewer than seventeen illegal organizations, including the Popular Revolutionary Vanguard in Brazil, the Movement of the Revolutionary Left in Uruguay and Chile, the Quebec Liberation Front and the African National Congress in South Africa. Curiel was murdered in mysterious circumstances last year.

Having, in the best journalistic traditions, stated my conclusions at the start, I need only add that the evidence I have presented seems to me to be overwhelming.

AHARON YARIV was Israel's Chief of
Intelligence for nine years (1964-1972) and
today is the Director of the Institute of
Strategic Studies at Tel Aviv University.
In 1972 General Yariv was appointed a
special adviser to the Prime Minister. He
later served as Minister of Information in
the Labor government.

ARAB STATE SUPPORT FOR TERRORISM

Mr. Chairman, participants, ladies and gentlemen, the Arab
states have a tradition of political violence, or what we call
terrorism. This goes back into Arab and Muslim history to the
well known phenomenon of the assassins, *hashishin*; the term
"fedayeen" was already used in Arab history centuries ago, but
there is also no lack of examples of the practice of political
violence among and within Arab states. I only have to mention
the massacre of fifty military cadets in Syria by another terrorist group, and other assassinations in Syria during the last
year. There are many other examples of high Arab dignitaries
or cabinet members who have been murdered by agents of
another Arab country. I'm not speaking about PLO assassinations, but about assassinations engineered by fellow Arab
regimes, one against the other.

The support of Arab states to international terrorism expresses itself in various ways: First, in the direct support to
non-Arab terrorist organizations; second, in their broad-scale
unceasing support and continuous manipulation of the Palestinian Arab terrorist organizations which constitute the PLO;
third, in the links between the Arab states and the Eastern
Bloc countries, as well as other Soviet satellites, such as Cuba.

The PLO — a Major Instrument of Arab States
I emphasize Arab state support for the PLO as an essential
element of their support for international terrorism, first

because of the central role the PLO plays in international terrorism — in terrorist acts outside the Middle Eastern arena, such as skyjackings and assassinations. Between 1968 and 1979, there were about 240 incidents of international terrorism in which the PLO was involved. Abut 140 of these incidents were launched against non-Israeli targets.

The second reason I mention this is because of the PLO's links to terrorist groups all over the world. A report published by the *New York Times* on June 26, 1978, says: "U.S. intelligence agencies, drawing largely on information from foreign intelligence sources, have linked terrorists from 14 countries with international operations of the Popular Front for the Liberation of Palestine." This is only one constituent terrorist organization of the PLO, one that is very prominent in international terrorism. West Germany, the Netherlands, Brazil, France, Venezuela, Britain, Colombia, Turkey and Italy are some of those countries mentioned among the 14. The third reason is that without the help and approval of the Arab states the PLO could by no means play the role in international terrorism it plays today. The Arab states are well aware of the central role the PLO plays in international terrorism, and they know the PLO would definitely not be able to play such a role without them. These are three important reasons why we should look closely at the Arab states' support for the PLO in its terrorist activities, within and outside the Middle East.

The Arab states do not support the respective Palestinian terrorist organizations which make up the PLO for so-called ideological reasons alone. The support is also given in order to exploit this or that organization of Palestinian terrorists in maneuvering for a prominent or a dominant role in the Arab world. It is also given so as to exploit the terror group in machinations against fellow Arab countries. Finally support may "buy security" — as Saudi Arabia heavily supports the Fatah and therefore buys Fatah protection from other terrorist organizations.

But whatever the reasons may be, this Arab state support is essential to the PLO and to its role in international terrorism. Let us look at what this support consists of. First, *sanctuary* —

a place where the terrorist organizations can conduct recruitment, maintain their training camps, their logistic bases, their operational bases and their various headquarters. Such sanctuaries exist in Syria, Iraq, Libya, South Yemen, Kuwait and Algeria. Special attention should be paid to Lebanon, which now, mainly under Syrian protection, provides most of the *lebensraum* for Palestinian terrorist organizations. It is these sanctuaries, in Lebanon particularly, which permit the Palestinian terrorist organizations to let other terrorist organizations benefit from their experience and facilities. It was these sanctuaries (again especially in Lebanon) that started the PLO off on its central role in international terrorism. This is where the Japanese Red Army terrorists were trained for the Lod massacre. This is where Turkish and Red Army members were initiated into intensive training in terrorist tactics. And so on. And the price the Republic of Lebanon has had to pay for becoming this main sanctuary for PLO terrorist activity is well known.

Secondly, there is substantial *financial support* to the PLO as such, as well as to each of the terrorist organizations. Thirdly, *weapons and munitions* are often supplied by the Arab countries. Although the PLO organizations now have their own conduit, they still rely to a large extent on supplies from Arab countries. I don't have to underline the well known fact that the Soviet Union and other Communist bloc countries play an important role.

Diverse training courses as well as special instructors have been and are being placed at the disposal of the terrorist organizations. Mass media in the Arab states do not fail to contribute their share to the PLO and its terrorist activities by providing *publicity*, that vital adjunct to political violence. For Palestinian Arab terrorist activity outside the Middle East, which can be defined as international terrorism, the Arab states provide the following: passports and other important official papers; the use of the diplomatic pouch, not only for mail but also for weapons and explosives. A diplomatic pouch does not necessarily have to be literally a "pouch." A crate can also be a diplomatic pouch. Intelligence and miscellaneous on-the-spot operational assistance is also given by Arab states to various Palestinian terrorist organizations for their activities outside the Middle East.

Arab diplomatic representatives very often assist Palestinian terrorist organizations in making useful deals with the governments of respective host countries. It is this kind of support which permits PLO terrorists, among other activities, to cooperate closely with other Arab terrorist organizations in operations like the hijacking of the Lufthansa plane to Mogadishu, the massacre at Munich, etc. The Arab states also provide a haven for terrorists once they have completed some spectacular international terrorist act without of course taking any legal steps or punitive measures against them.

And lastly, but not least, the Arab states provide the Palestinian Arab terrorist organizations with worldwide political support. This also includes the blocking of the adoption of really effective anti-terrorist measures on a large international scale. This is a direct contribution to international terrorism.

Arab Confirmation

In addition to what has been mentioned so far, I would like to quote a few statements from the Arab press concerning Arab states' support to the PLO. In an article published on March 6, 1979, in the official Syrian newspaper *Teshrin*, we read: "The March Revolution (meaning the Syrian revolution) has nurtured the Palestinian revolution from its inception and Syria was the first to emphasize that the gun and resistance are the way of Palestine. When the first shot was fired in the beginning of January 1965, Syria was the channel through which the world heard about the first fedayeen activity in the heart of the conquered land" — that was prior to 1967, please note. "The Syrian revolution is the lung which enables the resistance to continue to exist and to act, and it is the base which enables the resistance to build itself and to reinforce its victories."

As to Libya, Prime Minister Jaloud declared on March 14, 1979, "If the Palestinian people cling to the gun the hope of liberating Palestine will be realized", and lest one assumes the term "gun" has been not used literally, there follows: "Palestine cannot be liberated through speeches, but rather by more bombs and explosives."

As regards Saudi Arabia, Abu Mazzin, one of the top Fatah leaders, in an interview to the Lebanese newspaper, *Al-Nahar wa Araby wa Douli*, which appears in Paris, on September 30, 1978, proclaimed the following: "I want to emphasize that we are getting three times as much support from Saudi Arabia as we are getting from other Arab countries. This support is not only material but also military."

Support to Non-Arab Terrorists

In addition to what I have mentioned so far I shall give a few examples of direct Arab state support to international terror. Under the guidance of the Marxist-oriented government of the Popular Republic of Southern Yemen, Arab-American and West German and Japanese terrorists are being trained in Southern Yemen for terrorist activity. On March 14, 1979, the Egyptian newspaper, *Akhir Saah*, published the following news item concerning Iraq. "Intelligence sources report that Iraq is becoming a haven for terrorists. The four German terrorists who were freed by Yugoslavia are in Baghdad. They have been given passports, presenting them as officers in the Iraqi army. The man responsible for the activities of these terrorists is Gerhard Lang who has been residing in Baghdad for a long time." The gist of this report was repeated by West Germany's Minister of the Interior, Herr Gerhard Baum, in an interview to *The Guardian* on October 27, 1978.

Libya has probably been playing the most important role among Arab states as far as direct support to international terrorism is concerned. It played host to an international terrorist conference in 1971, and again to a conference of Latin American terrorist organizations just recently. Libya supports Moslem terrorists in the Philippines, it supports the South Moluccans, it supports the IRA. It was and probably continues to be the supporter of the Iranian Marxist-oriented terrorists and many others.

I have shown how far Arab states are directly involved in international terrorism, and how much, whether by intention or in fact, they are in tune with what is being done by the Soviet Union and its satellites.

I think that the pretexts of the Palestinian Arab refugees' plight, and of the so-called "Occupied Territories," should not and cannot be accepted as an excuse, and much less as a justification, for aiding and abetting international terrorism. The Arab states should be exposed, their complicity recognized, their responsibility proclaimed, and they should be made to account for it. Should this not be done, loudly and clearly, then the possible combination of international political violence and oil blackmail, whether by price or by embargo, may wreak havoc on the free world.

LORD CHALFONT is a distinguished
British author and journalist, and a former
Minister in the Labour Government of
1964-1970. He is the author of several
works, including a biography of Field
Marshal Montgomery, an analysis of American military power (*The Sword and the
Spirit*), and is a frequent contributor of
articles and reviews to *The Times* and
professional journals.

OUR MAIN PROBLEM: THE CLIMATE
OF APPEASEMENT

It is, I think, clear from the mass of evidence concerning state support for international terrorism, that its principal target is liberal democracy on the Western pattern. So far, this challenge to the political institutions of the free world has not been met. In a very real sense the terrorists have succeeded, since in many cases they have literally frightened democratic govern-ments into attitudes of accommodation and appeasement. Captured terrorists, instead of being imprisoned or executed, are often deported to the very countries which have paid for their recruitment and training, there to be received as heroes and allowed to prepare for their next operation. Neither the international community collectively nor the nations of the free world individually have shown much sign that they recog-nize the threat of international terrorism; and still less that they have any idea how to deal with it.

A Deliberate and Organized Assault
The first important point to be made is that international terrorism consists of a series of carefully planned and ruth-lessly executed military operations. It is true that quite often they are aimed at "soft" targets — at air passengers, school buses, unarmed politicians and unprotected businessmen; but they constitute, nevertheless, an assault upon the security of

sovereign states. As in any other military situation, it is necessary to identify and define the threat clearly before attempting to establish defenses and formulate countermeasures against it. Organized terrorism threatens democratic societies at two levels. The first and most obvious is the direct attack on the institutions and foundations of liberal democracies — the murder of elected leaders, the despatch of letter bombs through the post, the destruction of shopping centers, trains and motor vehicles, piracy in the air, and the planting of explosives in hotels and on the beaches of holiday resorts — the pattern is one of a deliberate and organized attempt to weaken the whole fabric of free societies and to destroy the confidence and the quality of life of those who live in them.

The secondary effect of terrorist activities is to provoke certain minimal defensive measures which, while they may improve security, tend themselves to inhibit freedom of action and erode the quality of life. We have all come to accept as a feature of everyday life the security precautions at airports, the screening of letters and packages and the restriction of public access to parliament and government buildings. Yet these are, in fact, intolerable invasions of privacy and diminutions of personal freedom which are normally accepted in free societies only in time of war; and it is here that the key to the problem lies. International terrorism is, indeed, *at war* with liberal democracy, and it is upon that premise that we should be organizing our countermeasures against it. In the organization and preservation of a civilized system of living, the classic and essential conflict between the demands of freedom and order is normally resolved with a marked and justifiable bias towards freedom. When, however, the civilized system of living is threatened with destabilization and destruction by hostile forces — whether external or internal in origin — there is a strong argument for reversing the priority and placing the demands of order and security before those of individual freedom (temporarily at any rate, and until the threat is eliminated or at least contained).

If the normal principles of military operations are applied to the terrorist threat — and I believe that with certain obvious reservations they can and should be — it would be necessary first to establish, as far as possible, the capabilities and intentions of the enemy by means of accurate and coordinated intelligence; then to secure the full cooperation of the citizens of the threatened communities through an effective and vigorous information system; and finally to assemble and deploy overwhelming military force, at the appropriate places and times, with the aim of crushing the enemy and preventing him from renewing his threat.

Effective Use of Intelligence

In any military operation, accurate intelligence — the ability to see what is "on the other side of the hill' — is of crucial importance. Without it commanders are blind. All intelligence consists, basically, of discovering the intentions of the enemy and his ability to carry out those intentions, early enough to frustrate them. An effective intelligence operation has three elements — the *collection* of information, its processing or *collation*, and finally its quick *dissemination* to those who need it for operational purposes. The first phase, the gathering of intelligence, should not be an insuperable problem for the West, which has at its disposal some of the most experienced and efficient services in the world — the Israeli and British intelligence services are still in the top five, and even the CIA, damaged and demoralized as it has been by an orchestrated and systematic attempt to destroy it in recent years, is still able to give a reasonable account of itself.

It is in the matter of collation and dissemination of intelligence, however, that the free world has yet to establish a fully effective system of coordinated intelligence. The science and technology of data processing have reached a level at which it is technically possible to process and store in a central memory bank every available piece of information which exists about the personalities, organization and methods of operation concerning international terrorist organizations, and to make that information instantly available, on time, to any counter-terrorist organization, anywhere in the world, authorized to have access to the central data bank. Some countries have already begun individually to make effective use of the computer in anti-terrorist intelligence. The United States makes extensive use of electronic data processing, the results of which are available to the Special Assistant to the Secretary of State appointed to combat terrorism, whose activities involve both contingency planning and coordinating action once a terrorist incident develops. Other countries, including West Germany, have established a similar organization. What is needed is that *every* country threatened by international terrorism should have an anti-terror bureau or section at a high level in its government, and that there should be close and systematic international cooperation between them.

There are, of course, certain real barriers to this kind of international intelligence operation. Some national intelligence services are noticeably less secure than others. To put it more bluntly, some of them leak like sieves and no director of intelligence in his senses would trust them with anything more sensitive than the weather forecast. The barriers are not, however, insuperable. It would be possible, through a sophisticated system of classification and a fairly selective application of the "need to know" principle, to organize an international intelligence network against terrorism without too much fear of compromise.

The Value of Public Opinion

Having set up an effective intelligence system, it is important to establish a sympathetic and supportive climate of public opinion. One of the principal instruments in achieving this ought to be, of course, the free press and communications media of the West. The depressing fact, however, is that our newspapers, radio and television have probably done more than the terrorist organizations themselves to make organized political violence glamorous and successful. The first essential point to be grasped is that terrorism would be impotent without publicity — it depends for its effect upon dramatic impact in order to compel and hold public attention. Terrorists have occasionally shown great sophistication in manipulating the media.

Some of the results of all this have been striking and disturbing. The FLN in Algeria discovered that if you killed ten Frenchmen in the desert, no one noticed; but kill *one* in the casbah and it would be front page news the next day in every Paris newspaper. Perhaps the most illuminating case history in this context is the SLA — The Symbionese Liberation Army — which sprang into prominence in California over the case of Miss Patty Hearst. For months the SLA received massive exposure on television and in the press; their tape recordings were broadcast over the radio networks in circumstances of maximum drama; a massive operation, involving a great number of police and FBI agents, was mounted to search for them. Yet this terrifying organization never consisted of more than a dozen people, and its experts, apart from the sensational abduction of Miss Hearst, were no more than small time criminals. It had been amplified into an important political phenomenon almost entirely by the attention of the media.

It has to be admitted, of course, that violence makes good copy. A machine gun attack on a bank makes exciting reading. In a free press journalists report, and editors will always print, what they believe to be exciting for their readers. Yet the matter cannot be allowed to rest there, because it is arguable that in this particular context the freedom of the press is being consistently abused, or at least manipulated cynically and irresponsibly.

False Symmetries

There are, of course, a number of journalists who actively sympathize with the aims and activities of terrorist movements, especially those dedicated to the destruction of capitalist societies. Others assist less consciously in the promotion of terrorism by accepting terrorist organizations at their own value and adopting the kind of newspeak which George Orwell made so familiar in his *1984*. Terrorists are referred to as "commandos," "urban guerrillas," or even "freedom fighters"; an organization dedicated to the violent overthrow of an elected government becomes "The Patriotic Front"; IRA murders in

Northern Ireland are reported as "executions," and the brutal torture of soldiers and civilians as "trials" or "interrogations." At the same time there is a tendency to search for some kind of bogus intellectual objectivity and to regard the terrorist on the one hand and the policeman or soldier on the other as two sides of a morally symmetrical confrontation. It is possible to read in publications of otherwise impeccable respectability the phrase "state violence" used to describe military or police action against violent subversives and terrorists. One of the results of this reluctance is the sheer inability to distinguish between the right of a violent minority to attack the institutions of a democratic state, and the right of the state to defend itself against such an attack as demonstrated by the frequent television appearances of terrorists, or the spokesmen of the political organization which sponsor them, disseminating their violent propaganda with the same freedom as a candidate for parliament addressing his constituency.

As a result, many reasonable people, especially among the young, have failed to understand the true nature of the terrorist threat which threatens their survival. This failure of understanding creates a climate of opinion in which it is difficult for political leaders and the commanders of security forces to act decisively in a terrorist situation; and it is in this special context that the balance between freedom and order must be subjected to constant reappraisal. The press and other communications media of the free world should, as a matter of great urgency, reexamine their attitudes to subversion and international terrorism. They should realize that their freedom is conditional upon the larger freedom of the society in which they exist; when the larger freedom is destroyed, their own freedom disappears with it. This is not to suggest that news of terrorist activities should not be reported; but that it should be reported coldly and factually, deprived of its excitement and glamor. Gunmen and bombers should not be interviewed respectfully as though they were delivering an address on the state of the nation; and those who seek for some totally fallacious moral symmetry in their editorializing should remember the words of Sir William Haley, a former editor of *The Times* and Director-

General of the BBC: "Some things are evil, cruel and ugly, and no amount of fine writing will make them good, or kind, or beautiful."

The only alternative to some kind of self-regulation in these matters is interference by the state; at this very suggestion, great cries of outrage will be heard emerging from the newspaper offices and television studios. Yet, in wartime, the free nations of the world willingly accept a degree of press censorship designed to prevent damage to national security; and unless newspaper editors, and those who control our radio and television programs are prepared to give evidence of a greater sense of responsibility than they have shown in the past, the pressures for some kind of legislative regulation over the reporting of terrorism and the interviewing of terrorists are bound to increase.

The Inadequacy of Traditional Measures

If it should prove possible to construct an effective anti-terrorist intelligence system and create a favorable climate of national and international opinion in which to implement effective anti-terrorist measures, we must ask, of what should these measures consist? Principally and immediately, this is a matter for the central or federal governments of those countries threatened by terrorism. It has been suggested at the Ditchley Park conference that the actions of democratic governments should follow three fundamental guidelines: First, exceptional measures of law enforcement should be kept to the lowest necessary level; secondly, all such measures should be specifically described as temporary deviations from the norm; and thirdly, that they should be tightly framed so as to ensure that the civil liberties of the people as a whole should be affected as little as possible.

At first glance, all this looks unexceptionable. It is certainly conceivable to preserve that precious balance between freedom and order. Yet I wonder whether it takes sufficient account of the modern level and scale of internationally organized terror. It is significant that the Ditchley formulation is consistent with one of the golden rules of traditional internal

security operations, "the use of minimum force." It is important to remember, however, that much of this approach derives
from the old-fashioned threat to public order — the assembly
of protestors and rioters would meet with a platoon of soldiers
armed with wooden clubs, exhibiting a banner inscribed in the
appropriate language with the words "Disperse or Fire." This
is not quite enough to deal with such organizations as the PLO
or the Red Brigades; and it is perhaps relevant to comment
that whereas internal security operations, in their classically
limited form, have always called for minimum force, war has
always implied the use of maximum force, irresistibly applied.

There are a number of measures open to national governments. The power of arrest and detention without trial for
limited periods is clearly a potent weapon, as is the power to
prevent known terrorists from entering the country, and the
practice of proscribing named terrorist organizations and making membership of them a criminal offence. The withholding
of information about acts of terrorism is arguably something
which also falls within the category of criminal activity. But
perhaps the most controversial of the measures open to
governments is the imposition of the death penalty for murder
committed in the course of terrorist activity. Quite apart from
the argument about whether this would constitute a deterrent
— which is for all practical purposes the same as those surrounding the issue of capital punishment for ordinary criminal
offences — there is a separate argument in the case of terrorism.
It is that when a convicted terrorist is put in prison he immediately becomes a potential catalyst for further acts of violence
designed to bring pressure for his release. It is significant that
a great number of people who have consistently opposed
capital punishment in ordinary criminal law are disposed to
support it in the case of political murder.

An International Anti-Terrorist Force
In the development of countermeasures, however, as in the field
of intelligence, the greatest and most urgent need is for effective international cooperation. There is a strong argument
for the establishment of an international anti-terrorist force.

Already there have been isolated examples of international cooperation. The West German force which flew to Somalia for the Luftahsa captives was helped by the British Special Air Service; after the murder of Hans Martin Schleyer there was close collaboration between the West German and Swiss police. It is at least worthwhile examining the possibilities of extending this cooperation in an institutional form using the national anti-terrorist squads of countries like West Germany, Britain and Israel as the nuclei of a permanent force. There should certainly be clear international agreement on such matters as extradition. The cause of political terrorism in Northern Ireland was given aid and comfort in May this year when a San Francisco judge ruled that an IRA suspect could not be extradited to Britain on the grounds that his alleged crime — the bombing of an Army barracks in Yorkshire — was a political crime. This judgment was apparently based upon the argument that a state of civil uprising existed between Britain and the IRA, a concept which has some startling implications. If this doctrine were held to apply to IRA gunmen, it would presumably apply equally to the Symbionese Liberation Army, the PLO, or even the American Weathermen. Every civilized country in the world would suffer if politically motivated crime were to be given the protection of legal respectability.

There are many other aspects of international terrorism which demand concerted action by the liberal democracies of the West such as economic and diplomatic sanctions against countries which offer support and sanctuary to known terrorists. There may be an argument for reviving a proposal, made just before the beginning of World War II, that there should be an International Criminal Court to be granted jurisdiction over crimes of international terrorism, superseding national judicial processes. It is, of course, easy to propose measures of this kind; but no one, I think, would underestimate the difficulties of implementing them. In the first place it is difficult to reach agreement between countries on a precise definition of international terrorism, and as all nations are not equally threatened by it the development of countermeasures tends to be a matter

of politics rather than of law. Most countries think they have
more important things to worry about than other peoples'
terrorists; and when terrorism strikes at *them* they tend to
take the easy way out in an attempt to buy a solution, however
temporary it may be.

The One Approach to Prevent Disaster

Clearly any progress towards international anti-terrorist cooperation is going to be difficult, slow and complicated. It is going
to require the combined wisdom and expertise of politicians,
lawyers, academics and publicists. Yet there can be no doubt
that it is one of the major problems facing the democratic
community of nations. Even in its present form it is a serious
and persistent menace; and it is virtually certain that it will
become even more threatening in the future. The international
links between terrorists may become institutionalized and
formalized far more quickly than the links between those who
are threatened; terrorist organizations may acquire more ready
access to precision guided ammunitions or even to nuclear
weapons; national governments may employ terrorist organizations as surrogate forces in some kind of alternative to conventional warfare. Indeed, it is possible to argue that the
developments which have made international terrorism possible
may eventually result in a fundamental change in the world's
political structure.

If this threat is to be eliminated, the democratic countries
of the world must act with a great deal more courage, resolution, and even ruthlessness, than they have shown in the past.
Of course they will be attacked and reviled by those who have
a vested interest in the success of international terrorism, and
by those who are so ideologically or intellectually confused
that they can perceive no moral distinction between the activities of the burglar and the policeman. When the Government
of Uruguay acted decisively to crush the Tupamaros they pro-
voked a wave of protest from the "human rights" industry
which had maintained a discreet silence during the Tupamaros'
reign of terror. In an interesting article in *Encounter* magazine
as far back as 1973, two American writers pointed out that the

imperatives of ecological safety had imposed upon the world the necessity for international cooperation in such matters as energy conservation and preservation of the environment. They went on to ask a question which is relevant to any analysis of the problems of international terrorism. *How long will it take for governments and peoples to realize that the effects of modern terrorism are as contagious as smallpox, as poisonous as air-pollution, and as dangerous to non-immunized societies as measles was to the American Indians?*

The Institute under whose sponsorship we meet here in Jerusalem was founded to keep alive the memory of one great, unforgettable anti-terrorist operation which demonstrated that Israel, at least, has realized the truth of this. I hope profoundly that this conference will lead to some positive action which will inject some of the spirit of Entebbe and Jonathan Netanyahu into the international community and persuade it to recognize the real significance of international terrorism for the future of the community of free nations.

RAY S. CLINE is Executive Director of the
Center for Strategic and International
Studies at Georgetown University. He has
served the United States government for
more than thirty years. Among his posts
have been those of Deputy Director for
Intelligence at the C.I.A. and Director of
the Bureau of Intelligence and Research at
the State Department. Dr. Cline is the
author of numerous works on intelligence
and foreign policy, including *Secrets, Spies
and Scholars, Washington Command Post,*
and *World Power Assessment*, 1972.

THE STRATEGIC FRAMEWORK

It is high time for the scholars and statesmen, who live in
nations that have some right to call themselves free, to come
to grips with the brute fact of the widespread adoption of calculated terrorism as a preferred instrument of policy by a
finite, known number of modern states. The truth is that the
use of physical and psychological force, involving intimidation,
political coercion, assassination, and the wanton destruction of
property, has become part of the arsenal of geopolitics and
will be an important ingredient of international conflict in the
1980s. Terrorism is one of the weapons with which states
organized on the principle that political power grows from the
barrel of a gun attack their enemies. Open societies built on
the moral imperative of preserving the political and economic
freedoms of individual citizens are the main target.

Time is not on our side! Terrorism is a part of a larger
war! We, the open societies, are the target! It is later than we
think! In terms of geopolitical conflict we are approaching
what may well come to be known as the fateful eighties.

The inhumanity of man to man since time immemorial
and, especially, in recent years, the flood of TV images of
brutality and suffering into our very living rooms, have tended
to deaden our sensitivities to the home truth that terrorism
today is more than an intrinsic, inescapable consequence of

the flawed character of mankind — that it is instead a form of low-intensity warfare.

Terrorism is intended by those who finance it, arm it and ideologically inspire it, to weaken and ultimately dissolve the fabric of civilized behavior in open, pluralistic societies. Open and pluralistic societies, by my definition, are those in which government provides guarantees for minorities to live with mutual respect for cultural and ethnic differences and wherein, by one political process or another, the making of important decisions reflects the views of an informed electorate. Let us make no mistake about it. These open societies for all their superior qualities of life are in a minority — only 20 percent — in the world, and they are under attack. One of the most insidious forms of attack is the calculated use of terrorism by some states to undermine social order in others — and the others are ours! I mean not only our host country, Israel, which lives daily under terrorist threats, but also the United Kingdom, Italy, Germany, and the United States. If this Conference brings this fact to the forefront of political consciousness, it will succeed.

Moscow's Upsurge of Terrorism

What I hope to contribute to this discussion is to put the information about the extraordinary surge of terrorist activity in the past 10 years into a strategic framework that makes sense in terms of the posture and policy of the United States and its closest friends and allies. First, let me say, however, that the 10-year span of terrorism is no accident. It began in 1969 when the Soviet KGB persuaded the Politburo of the Communist Party of the Soviet Union to accept the PLO, the Palestine Liberation Organization, as a major political instrument in the Mideast and to subsidize its terrorist policies by freely giving it money, training, arms, and coordinated communications. These things constitute the infrastructure of terrorism; they are for terrorists what the automotive industry, the spare parts and repair garages, and the petrol stations are for the motorists. They are in fact the life blood of terrorism, the indispensable ingredients of an international geopolitical apparatus. This phenomenon is quite distinct from the anarchic, sometimes aimless acts of violence of equally malevolent but much less dangerous individuals or independent small groups. The Soviet Union has provided the logistic support and political rationale that tie the terrorists together strategically in ways they themselves may not fully realize and which American scholars, journalists, and political leaders have failed to focus on. This 1979 conference in Jerusalem ought to mark a turning-point in public understanding of this important fact. Soviet support to international terrorism makes it a geopolitical fact of enormous import for all free societies.

These are what in Toynbee fashion we might call times of trouble, an era of too rapid technological and social change, in which settled societies are beset by barbarians within and beyond their own boundaries. All this welter of disorder is what the late Chinese Communist Leader Chou En-Lai hailed as a "great disorder under Heaven — an excellent world situation."

Terrorism is escalating to become part of the struggle for international power. It is becoming a form of surrogate warfare, whereby small groups with direct and indirect state support are conducting political warfare on a broad scale that ultimately can alter the balance of world power without resort to the kind of organized warfare against which most of our military defence efforts are aimed. It could be the Achilles' heel of the open societies unless we begin to grapple with what it does to us strategically as well as emotionally.

Russia's Substitute to Traditional Warfare

It is not surprising, therefore, that the strategic thinking of Communist states, as exemplified by the Soviet Union's policies and actions, calls for manipulation of terrorism as a suitable substitute to traditional warfare which has become too expensive and too dangerous to be waged eyeball-to-eyeball on the battlefield. By overtly and covertly resorting to nonmilitary techniques and exploiting low-intensity operations around the world, the Soviet Union is preparing the ground for what it calls legitimate "revolutionary action."

While it is true that the Soviet Union as a matter of doctrine traditionally has deplored the use of violence, i.e., terror for purposes other than establishing a one-party Communist dictatorship, Soviet ideologists have always been a little ambivalent toward revolutionary violence that weakens the fabric of non-Communist societies even when Moscow is not the immediate political beneficiary. Since the military occupation of Czechoslovakia in 1968, and the commitment to provide aid to the PLO in 1969, Soviet practice has increasingly favored the kind of civil disorder that characterizes Iran today, obviously hoping to be the ultimate winner. Moscow is evidently playing roulette with international terrorism, calculating on picking up some of the chips on the board from time to time and someday walking off with the whole board and everyone's chips. At times the actual promotion of specific terrorist operations has been no more than a largely unintended byproduct of Soviet dabbling in troubled international waters at particular stages of its history. In the past decade, however, Soviet attitudes vis-à-vis terrorism and the supporting role played especially by Bulgaria, Cuba, Czechoslovakia, East Germany, North Korea, and Vietnam have hardened into a system — an international trouble-making system. The coordinated aid provided by these countries to various Communist and non-Communist terrorist movements in both developed and developing countries is something for which Moscow must increasingly be held accountable. If we do not see this problem clearly, we cannot begin to solve it.

The True Face Behind the Mask
Clearly, to be sure, the Soviet Union has attempted to voice opposition to terrorist activities to which it itself is vulnerable, especially when the opposition is mainly rhetorical, as in the case of the UN General Assembly Resolution 2625 (XXV) of October 24, 1970, which asserted, *inter alia*, that terrorist and other subversive activities organized and supported by one state against another state are a form of unlawful use of force. Soviet endorsement of Resolution 2625 has not ended practical Soviet support of those operations that

attempt to tear down the fabric of Western society and to weaken other non-Socialist governments. The Soviet Union, by use of selected proxies like Cuba, Libya, South Yemen, and North Korea, and of course the ubiquitous PLO, has been able internationally by and large to have its terrorism cake and eat it too, with pious disclaimers of responsibility. This state of affairs must not be permitted to continue.

Despite the Soviet public posture of propriety, the circumstantial evidence that emerges shows the existence of a carefully developed terrorist infrastructure which serves Moscow's foreign policy objectives. The International Department of the Central Committee of the Communist Party of the Soviet Union (CPSU), the Soviet Security Police (KGB), and the Soviet Military Intelligence (GRU) have played a major role in this effort.

The International Department of the CPSU, headed by Boris Ponomarev, has been the most important Soviet Agency for the support of terrorism. It established, for example, the Lenin Institute in Moscow (also known as the Institute of Social Studies, Institute of Social Sciences, and International School of Marxism-Leninism) which is responsible for supervision of the curriculum of revolutionary thought and practice and serves as liaison with the Central Committee of the CPSU. Selected members of Western and Third World Communist parties following the Soviet line have been training there in psychological warfare and propaganda as well as in armed and unarmed combat and "guerrilla warfare."

The CPSU had also built Moscow's Patrice Lumumba Friendship University to serve as a base for indoctrination and training of potential "freedom fighters" from the Third World who are not Communist party members. More specialized training in terrorism is provided at locations in Baku, Odessa, Simferopol, and Tashkent.

Both the KGB and GRU have attempted to construct, or at least to influence, various terrorist movements. V.N. Sakharov, a defecting KGB officer, has revealed that the KGB sought to form terrorist cells in Saudi Arabia and the smaller Arab states in the Persian Gulf and in Turkey. Similarly, clandestine Soviet efforts have been made to penetrate and control the Palestinian movement since at least the early 1970s. Also, KGB members have established links with the IRA through the British and Irish Communist parties and the Marxist wing of the IRA (Official). In fact, through Libya, arms have reached all sides in the Irish terror and counter terror warfare except the UK forces of law and order. Moreover, since the KGB virtually controls the Cuban Intelligence Service (Direcion General de Intelligencia, or DGI), it is able ultimately to influence the activities of a number of Latin American and African vaguely Castroite terrorist groups like the Sandinistas in Nicaragua and the dominant revolutionary parties in Angola and Ethiopia.

In view of the fact that "détente" and "peaceful coexistence" do not, by Soviet admission, cancel Soviet policies or actions aimed at achieving a position of predominance regionally and globally, the global exploitation of terrorism calls for a realistic strategy on the part of the United States and its endangered friends and allies to deal effectively with this challenge. "Peaceful coexistence," properly understood, is a Soviet recipe for ideological warfare — i.e., what I prefer to call a steady state of "coexistential conflict."

Terrorism and Geopolitics

To be more specific and deal with the real world of national behavior in a disorderly world, there are 160 independent, self-governing nations in the world. Many of them are newly constituted and politically fragile. Many of them — 100 or so — are relatively small, that is, with populations of less than 10 million, about the size of one of the world's larger cities.

Thus there are not so many really powerful nations directly involved in international conflicts. The smaller nations are usually obliged to observe rather than to act, and in time fall in line with the pattern created by the balance of power among the major powers.

Yet all of the nations, large and small, are getting more and more mixed up in each other's business — economically, politically, culturally, and in terms of military security.

This is because the earth — this planetary spaceship on which all of us live — is shrinking in relation to the rapid growth of population supported by its resources and in terms of the speed of travel and international communications.

The two nations by far the most powerful in the world — the United States and the USSR — confront each other across the north polar wastes, with their central regions separated just by the range of an ICBM. The distance from Washington to Moscow is about that range, 7,000 miles. In naked military destructive power terms the world is still remarkably bipolar. In the broader configuration of geopolitics there is also a core of bipolar antagonism between closed or totalitarian nations and open society.

The United States and the USSR exercise an extraordinarily strong influence on all of the world's approximately four and one-half billion peoples, scattered around the roughly 52 million square miles of the globe's total populated land surface. The other three-quarters of the globe is covered by water — the world's oceans, on the surface of which move most of the economic resources exchanged in trade between one region of the earth and another.

In this context it is easy to recognize that the United States and the whole Western Hemisphere are outclassed in terms of territory, economic resources, and population. The U.S. must go across the oceans to get almost anywhere. It must reach out to its friends and allies on the periphery of the Eurasian continent and Africa. In these transoceanic links rest the basic prosperity as well as the military security of the United States and the global trading system of the free world.

Tension and instability are strategic facts of life on the entire periphery of Eurasia and indeed along the 4,500 mile border between China and the USSR, between Peking-controlled Tibet and India across the Himalayas, and in Southeast Asia, where a tremendous clash of strategic forces has just taken place. In this latter region the United States and its friends in the area suffered a tragic defeat; it is not yet clear exactly who won — the North Vietnamese, the PRC, or the

USSR, all of whom are still engaged in bitter military conflict over Cambodia and China's borders with Laos and Vietnam.

Peripheral clashes appear inevitable when adjoining zones are dominated by powers with different cultures, different social and political systems, and markedly different world views. The recent Vietnam war is a classic case. Current conflicts over religion, oil, and politics are wracking the Mideast. In fact this struggle is spilling over into central and southern Africa. There Soviet advisors and Cuban troops installed in Angola and Ethiopia threaten to cut the continent in two by exploiting Rhodesia's troubles and linking up Africa and Eurasia on a line stretching from Angola through Yemen to Afghanistan. Looking at the world in a broad geopolitical way, a great British geopolitical writer of the early 20th century observed that any nation ruling the heartland of Eurasia (between the Urals and the Rhine) was likely to reach out to try to dominate the Rimlands, the periphery of Eurasia, and hence the whole world island, and eventually, because of superiority in population and resources — the whole world. Napoleon and Hitler both had the domination of Central Eurasia in mind — and failed. Stalinist Russia and — I regret to say — Brezhnev's Russia also dreams this dream. Unless we take this fact seriously, the 1980s may be the climax — a fateful climax — to the struggle so clearly forecast by Sir Halford Mackinder many years ago.

Now no communist system has ever made economic achievements comparable with those of the open societies, primarily because of over-centralization of decision-making at the top and inadequate incentives at the bottom. If the USSR, however, can gradually acquire political and economic domination of resource-rich states like Iran and the African states of the region surrounding Rhodesia, the Soviet economic difficulties will have been solved with that power that grows from the barrels of guns. And the guns of terrorists are even now softening up the target areas in the Mideast and Central Africa from which the energy resources and rare minerals come to fuel the industries of West Europe, Japan, and the United States.

The Key Strategic Question

The crucial strategic problem for the rest of this century
for the United States and for other open pluralistic societies is
that, as I said before, they constitute only about 20 percent of
the peoples of the world, whereas the vast central heartland of
Eurasia, comprising about a quarter of the earth's land surface
and containing a third of its population, is now occupied by
states organized on the model of the Leninist-Stalinist dictatorship, and irreconcilably opposed to the very existence of open
societies. The point that must not be forgotten is that these
states do not seek political freedom for their people, but
instead constantly proclaim their intention to destroy or at
least cooperate in the destruction of the open societies that
best embody political rights and liberties as we know them.

How the totalitarian states think of bringing about our
destruction is the key strategic question. Let us leave aside
China, whose effective power is limited because of poverty and
overpopulation. Peking's leaders' main strategy seems to be to
urge the United States to confront the USSR, their ideological
rival and neighboring enemy, with which they say war is
inevitable.

The real key to the 1980s is Soviet strategy. This strategy
is clear, despite the tactical flexibility and rhetorical camouflage that a dictatorship can employ in pursuit of its strategic goals. Essentially, Brezhnev's strategic thinking revolves
around the doctrines enunciated years ago by Lenin and
Stalin.

Lenin said: "War is a continuation of politics by violent
means." Of course, this means politics is a continuation of war
by less violent means!

Lenin also said: "Politics is the concentrated expression
of economics." Of course, this means politics is the science of
dividing up wealth and material resources.

Terrorism — the Spearhead of Russia's Expansionism

Stalin made clear shortly before his death in 1953 the fundamentally economic character of Soviet strategy, predict-
ing: "... the sphere of exploitation of world resources by the

major capitalist countries (U.S.A., Britain, France) will not expand but contract, ... the world market conditions will deteriorate for these countries and ... the number of enterprises operating at less than capacity will multiply in these countries." Today, of course, we must add Japan and West Germany and others to that list. The struggle for access to critical raw material resources like oil, gas, and rare minerals such as chrome and cobalt is at the heart of Soviet-American conflicts in the Mideast and Southern Africa. It is no accident that terrorism, guerrilla war, and Cuban supported revolutionary war are the order of the day in just these areas.

To come more up to date, Soviet Communist Party Chief Brezhnev said in December 1972, shortly after formally inaugurating the era of "détente" during Nixon's visit to Moscow: "... The world outlook and class aims of socialism and capitalism are opposed and irreconcilable." And in February 1976: "... The international situation of the Soviet Union has never been more solid."

He concluded, "In this volatile situation, we act as we are bid by our revolutionary conscience, our Communist convictions," confident, he said that "capitalism is a society without a future."

Area by area, nation by nation, the Communist leaders hope to make what the Russians call an irreversible gain in the correlation of forces — what we would call a decisive shift in the balance of world power. The selective use of terrorist activities in critical regions of peripheral conflict is becoming a crucial, risk-free part of the Soviet strategy of making that irreversible shift before the democracies wake up to what is happening. It cannot be allowed to happen. That is why we are here — to say, "Wake up, America, wake up America's friends and allies."

It is not for me to tell you how to deal with the phenomenon of terrorism when we have wakened our minds and consciousness to the dangers. But a central problem is the extraordinary recent weakening of the intelligence services of the leading free world nations, especially the American CIA, which 15 years ago was the best intelligence system in the world. I cannot, then, refrain from saying: the essential means to combat terrorism is better intelligence and better intelligence coordination and exchange of information among the free nations, especially those represented at this Conference. After 30 years in intelligence service in America, including close liaison with the services of the countries represented in this meeting, I must say intelligence is the key to the terrorist problem. If the later sessions of this conference do not stress intelligence as part of the solution to our problem, then I am afraid we will be wasting our time, and indeed contributing to the problem.

QUESTIONS AND ANSWERS

Chairman (Ambassador Herzog): We are left now with approximately 20 minutes for discussion of questions from the floor.

Professor Mordechai Abir: Gentlemen, in the review of the Arab states which support terrorism, a notable and very important omission was made. It was not mentioned that one of the focal points of Arab terrorism has been Egypt, and I am saying "has been" and not "was." I don't want to elaborate because the facts are generally known, but I want to mention that the classic example of using terrorism as a means of foreign policy was the case of Egypt. Egypt also organized in 1970 the famous conference of Al Azhar. The subject of this Islamic conference was the defeat not only of Jews and Zionism, but the whole Christian world. The minutes of this conference are preserved in very bad English in a 900-page volume. For the time being I don't want to abuse your patience and I am content to mention these facts. Thank you.

Moshe Cantor, Israel: Most of the distinguished participants pointed out that international terrorism is practically a war against liberal democracies — in fact, it is one of the dirtiest wars that have ever been waged, and it is fast becoming a terrible disease and epidemic. I have three questions: One, why are the attacks against international terrorism so delicate? Two, for how long shall innocent people pay with their lives? Three, how many more examples of the success of terrorism will the free world need to understand the dangers and take massive steps necessary to stop it?

Walter Eytan, Israel: Dr. Cline and other speakers have spoken of the crucial importance of intelligence in the fight against terrorism. That is absolutely true, of course, but everything depends on the use which governments make of the intelligence available to them. Governments which have intelligence available to them and do not make use of it are in fact giving state support to terrorism, which is the subject we have been talking about this morning. There has been case after case all over Europe in which terrorists who have been caught have been in one way or another allowed to get away. They're like hot potatoes. Everybody wants to get rid of them. The most notorious case that I can think of was that of Abu Daoud in France, where you had the extraordinary situation that one arm of the Government, thanks to good intelligence, grabs him and within 48 hours another arm of the Government lets him go. We must account for this implicit support on the part of the governments of the free countries, who have thus given not only indirect but in fact direct encouragement to terrorism, including terrorism on their own territory.

Jacques Soustelle: I just wanted to underline the necessity, in my mind, to link the problems of terrorism in this part of the world to those of Africa. It is quite obvious to me that there is a general offensive of the Soviet-led system of terrorism against Europe through Africa, because it's quite clear that should the natural resources of Africa, and the lifeline of oil tankers around Africa, fall into the hands of Soviet-controlled governments, then Europe would be in a very dangerous situation. I think, therefore, that we should be conscious of that necessity and mention it in the documents which will be written at the end of this conference.

Nicholas Kitry, U.S.A.: Given some of the statements last night and today I really hope that I could impose on you with some definitional request. As we all know part of the problem in responding to international terrorism is that the term itself remains vague and you have a major disagreement, nationally and internationally, as to what it's all about. To be more specific — there is in the history of international law a great amount of sympathy and support for political offenders. In the 19th century it was viewed that political offenders are different from regular offenders, and they are to be given certain recognition. I wonder if we could at least try to draw some lines for the benefit of the participants here, between what you might consider internal or domestic war, guerrilla warfare, urban guerrilla, coups d'etats, and terrorism.

Unidentified Speaker: My suggestion to you gentlemen of the panel and those who head the Jonathan Institute is that from this Jerusalem Conference we should establish a non-stop source of media in order to pump our ideas, our information into the world's free press. Deception is one of the main tools of terrorists. They mix humanitarian, human and civil rights ideals with their true aims. I wonder how many people in the free world are conscious that the danger, as Dr. Cline very well put it, is at their own doorstep, and that it might materialize any day. If this Institute will constitute such a center for effective psychological warfare, maybe the media would be successful in influencing leaders and legislators not to have that which General Herzog so precisely described to us — the mock attempts of the so-called international society at the United Nations to delay vital international legislation that was first initiated in 1972. Thank you.

Chairman (Ambassador Herzog): I will allot three minutes to each panelist to try to answer some of the questions. There are some questions, such as the very important one about the definitions within the framework of international law, which incidentally have been keeping the United Nations going now for a long, long time. We could never sum it up or even attempt to discuss it at this meeting. But it is a very important point which could be dealt with in great depth within the

framework of the activities of the Institute. So please, start
from left to right, three minutes if at all possible.

Prof. Richard Pipes: I just wanted to say that we shall never
defeat terrorism unless we take a global and strategic view of
it. If we simply try to deal with individual terrorist groups,
even on an internationally coordinated basis, without taking
account of the absolutely crucial role of the Soviet Union and
without taking account of the support by other states, either
at the behest of the Soviet Union or acting parallel to the
Soviet Union, then we shall fail.

One has to understand that from the Soviet point of view
terrorism is only one of the instruments at its disposal. If we
reread the articles of the Commintern in 1919 and the
Communist Party Program of 1924, we shall find everything
that has happened in recent years clearly delineated. One has
to understand that we are talking about subversion, terrorism,
guerrilla and revolutionary war; we're also talking about the
denial of strategic materials which is a more recent phenomenon. We have to deal with this globally, and in my view it can
only be done if the Western alliance calls a special session to
rethink the problem of the Soviet Union which has changed
in many respects since NATO was formed in 1949.

Lord Chalfont: I'd just like to say a word on the question as
to why the defense against terrorism in the West is perhaps so
moderate (I think the speaker used the word "delicate".) I
think the reason is that most Western countries do not, as
many of us have said earlier, realize that they are in fact at
war. International terrorism has declared war on liberal democracy and they are therefore taking the view — a civilized and
compassionate view, and one incidentally based upon ages and
ages of the doctrine of internal security as it was once called —
that you use the minimum possible force in meeting a threat
to internal security. Secondly, as Hugh Fraser made quite clear
on the first evening, if in meeting the threat of terrorism you
are lured into taking measures which make your regime more

repressive and more terrible than anything that the terrorists can impose upon you, then they have won their battle.

I think these are the reasons why so far the response has been so moderate. I also suggested earlier this morning that I think the climate of public opinion has not yet been sufficiently mobilized. I think that it should be. If people will realize that this is a war, and that it is a war that is going to intensify, then I think it possible that the response might become less moderate. We might have to reverse our priorities. In the classic conflict that always takes place in any compassionate society between freedom and order, we may have to place more emphasis on order and security, and perhaps temporarily rather less emphasis on individual freedom in combating terrorism.

One final thing: I'm certainly not going to attempt a legal definition of terrorism. That is a matter for international lawyers. I would only remind you of a classic formulation of this problem: I would find it very difficult to define an elephant, but I know one when I see one.

Dr. Ray Cline: Let me conclude by saying that if the nations very closely allied with the United States all cooperate more effectively and recognize the need for mutual security (and I include Germany, Italy, and Great Britain in that number), we have the strength to meet these challenges very readily. I calculate that with 10 states and the United States cooperating closely we would dispose of sufficient economic and military power that could be politically brought to bear against these incursions. What we need to do is to understand the problem and join together to meet it.

Aharon Yariv: In reference to the question of the omission of Egypt: When I spoke about the Arab states' support for international terrorism, it was not a question of omission, it was a question of emphasis. The emphasis was on international terrorism, and I did not enlarge upon terrorism in the Middle East. Therefore I chose examples of those countries that were more pronounced in their support of international terrorism.

I think that a very good example of state support for terrorism is the example of the Egyptian government's full support of the fedayeen war that was waged against us prior to 1956. And we can also mention Egyptian training of Palestinian terrorists, mainly from the Fatah, in the not too distant past. I emphasize the not too distant — frogmen, intelligence, commandos, rocket-firing, etc.

Chairman (Ambassador Herzog): Thank you very much. I want to take this opportunity to thank the panelists for a very stimulating and educational session, and let me sum up briefly. It is quite clear that *international* terrorism exists because it is state supported, and it is impossible to envision the growth of international terrorism without this massive state support. It is furthermore clear that there are two main groups of states supporting terrorism — the Arab states and the Soviet bloc, but there is in addition to that, as was mentioned by Walter Eytan from the floor, the traditional problem, the weakness of the Western states which at times almost becomes connivance. To combat international terrorism effectively, democratic countries must deal with the supporting nations as well as with the terrorist groups themselves, and there must be strengthening of intelligence cooperation.

For this there must be a no-nonsense convention with teeth in it which would bind the free countries of the world. I agree entirely with Dr. Cline that 10 countries would be enough. The key lies with the United States because the sanctions which it can apply are so much more telling than those that may be used by other countries. The free countries must also legislate and organize themselves domestically, and in this struggle they must enlist the support of the mass media. Again, it was made quite clear that we are fighting for the survival of our society, for the open societies of the world as we understand them.

I can never forget the feeling of horror which overcame me at the United Nations when it dawned on me that only some 30-35 countries out of 152 member states are democracies such as we understand the word. In the final analysis we are a minority fighting for the existence of our system, and in this there is no room for compromise. If free society does not awaken to the danger that faces it, terrorism will threaten its very existence. Thank you very much.

Third Session
Subject:
THE THREAT POSED BY TERRORISM
TO DEMOCRATIC SOCIETIES
Afternoon, July 3, 1979
Chairman: Ambassador Gideon Rafael

PREFACE

As a number of speakers noted, terrorism poses a dilemma for all free societies. It is, before all else, a deliberate murderous attack on those very societies. It kills the innocent. It puts intolerable pressure on governments to concede politically, either by changing policies or yielding on fundamental principles. It destroys the delicate web of life. It undermines morale, imposes huge security costs, and softens up countries for more conventional kinds of takeover. Yet in combatting terrorism through police and judicial measures, the democracies must be careful to strike the proper balance between protecting their citizens from terrorist violence and protecting the very freedoms Western societies cherish. What kinds of measures have been employed? Which, if any of them, have proved effective? These are some of the questions that had to be addressed.

Speakers also had to deal with the looming threat of terrorism on a global scale. Above all, the terrifying prospect that at some point terrorists would acquire nuclear weapons

was of great concern. The likelihood of
terrorists manufacturing such weapons on
their own was held to be small, but experts
agreed that there was a real danger that a state
supporting terrorism would supply terrorist
groups with such weapons. It was stressed
that the civilized nations must ensure that
such "crazy states" as Libya and Iraq are prevented from acquiring a nuclear capability.

Finally, the problem of "terrorist states"
— that is, states set up for, and run by, terrorist organizations — was examined. Such a
development would increase the probability
that other terrorist groups (linked by ideology,
sympathy, or simply *modus operandi*) would
receive support including the most advanced
weapons. Indeed, the establishment of "terrorist states" was viewed as constituting a "quantum leap" for global terrorism that might well
make Qaddafi's Libya seem pale by comparison
and would present intolerable dangers to the
entire international order.

GIDEON RAFAEL is one of Israel's senior
diplomats. Among his posts have been Ambassador to Great Britain (1973-1977),
Israel's permanent representative to the
United Nations (1967), and Director General
of the Foreign Ministry (1968-72). Mr. Rafael
contributes regularly to Israeli newspapers
and foreign affairs periodicals.

CHAIRMAN'S OPENING REMARKS

There would be no need for a conference of this kind if the
subject to be discussed would read: The Threat Posed by
Democratic Society to Terrorism. But as matters stand, the
title of the discussion this afternoon reflects justly the anxieties gripping thoughtful leaders and an enlightened public,
conscious of the menace of terrorism to democratic freedoms
and civil liberties.

The Antithesis of Democracy

If democratic governance is recognized by the freely expressed
will of the majority of the people, then terrorism is the crassest
antithesis of democracy. It is the attempt to subjugate and pervert the will of the people and its elected leadership by a
minute bunch of reckless people resorting to terrifying threats
and unbridled violence. They say that they kill for the cause.
What is that cause? Liberty from oppression? Freedom from
want? Justice for a people? If that would be their cause, how
could they plot the extermination of another people, terrorize
their own kinsmen and stuff their war chests with oil money
from Saudi Arabia, to finance the assault against the regimes
of these countries? Their cause is killing. Their vocation is
violence.

They are not the avant garde of a popular upsurge, but a
fiendish fringe which worships violence and despises humanity.

They are part of an international demolition squad disguised as freedom fighters, presented by perverted publicity as glamorous guerrillas, idolized by a disoriented community of alienated adolescents. They are the outlet for uncontrolled savage passions. They are the proxy weapon to wage war by stealth in behalf of militant governments anxious to escape the risks of open warfare.

Submission Breeds More Violence

And what are we doing to ward off this spreading fury? We reel in revulsion at the sight of the macabre spectacle and return sickened and resigned to our routines, hoping against hope that it wouldn't happen again. But it does happen — and the happenings become more and more hideous. It is said that violence breeds violence. It may be so. But surely submission to violence generates even more violence.

If these destructive forces are allowed to rage unchecked, they will sap the very foundations of modern society. They threaten to pervert man's mind who will be driven to see, as the Bible says, "the shadow of the mountains as if they were men." Solzhenitsyn has said so aptly in his undelivered Nobel Prize address: "Any man who has chosen violence as his method has chosen falsehood as his principle."

International terrorism strikes on land, air and sea, wherever it can find an easy prey. It causes airliners to be transformed into flying fortresses, embassies to be turned into citadels and public places to be guarded like military installations. All travelers have become *a priori* suspects of crime and are subjected to the indignity of security frisk and search. At a recent visit to the White House, I was stunned by the elaborate measures and unavoidable security checks needed to protect the seat of power of the mightiest nation in the world against a handful of ruthless outlaws. The terrorists neither respect national sovereignty nor international boundaries, not even those of Arab countries which support and shelter them. They live beyond the human pale.

The malignancy of terrorism not only accounts for growing numbers of victims, slain and maimed men, women and children whose only offence was to travel in commercial air-liners, blown up in midair, or to live in peaceful villages and be massacred in their sleep.

The exchange of hostages taken at gun point for con-victed terrorists apprehended in action perverts the funda-mental process of law which is meant to secure the individual liberty of the citizen and protect the democratic freedoms of society.

Terrorism and extortion are of the same breed. They grow in the same contaminated soil. Economic coercion, whether practiced in the form of boycott or price and produc-tion manipulation by OPEC, is but the other side of the terror-ist coin. It is blackmail exercised by recognized governmental institutions. The jacking up of oil prices is just another form of hijacking. It is meant to hold to ransom the economy of the Western industrialized world. And the more the hostages woo for their freedom, the higher the price soars. The fetters will not be removed by pleading and persuasion, but only by con-certed action. A time bomb cannot be made harmless by coax-ing it out of action; it has to be defused.

The Need to Act

From whatever perspective we view the situation created by the terrorist rampage it looks bleak, morbid and menacing. We cannot confine ourselves to the role of the melancholic specta-tor. This "epidemic insanity", to use the term of Emerson, is spreading. It must be checked by worldwide quarantine meas-ures. The individual has no means to organize effective counter-action, but he can help create a climate of resistance which will impel the powers that be, to take action.

What should be done? First we should decide what should not be done. We must refuse to be deceived by counter-feit ideologies. We must free ourselves from false romanticism. The perpetrators of the crime of Munich, of the carnage at Lydda airport, the assassinations of the editor of El-Ahram in Cyprus, of Aldo Moro in Rome, those responsible for the slaughter in a remote hill station in Japan, whether they call themselves Red Army Youth or Black September, are not knights in shining armor, but thugs in bloodstained fatigues.

Mankind is desperately struggling in this age for the preservation of its human image against the outrage of violence and brutality, for the sanity of the human spirit against the spread of depravity and degeneration and for the protection of its freedoms against rampant encroachment. If humanity wants to remain free, sane and human, it must liberate itself from the scourge of the new "liberators."

And what should the governments do? They must deny staging areas to the terrorists from where they have easy and protected access to their targets. Front organizations which serve them as camouflage and cover should be disbanded. The governments should be far more insistent in their refutation of states which assist the outlaws and glorify them when they return from their killing sprees. They should heighten their vigilance and perfect their measures of surveillance.

Like-minded governments should join in an "Alliance to Combat Terrorism" — ACT; an alignment of nations willing to subscribe to a common code of international conduct. Such a charter should lay down the guiding principles, prescribe the measures to be adopted, jointly and individually, and specify the mutual obligations, national and international, of the contracting parties. Such a convention is overdue. Since it cannot be worked out within the framework of the United Nations, the governments that care and count should urgently convene a special conference open to all states which are prepared to outlaw and combat international terrorism. This is the time to ACT. The democratic world urgently needs a visible and tangible manifestation of its determination to protect its liberty.

The session of this afternoon will give us the opportunity to hear the views on this crucial issue from a number of distinguished speakers, eminent in public and academic life. They will give us their assessment of the implications of rampant terrorism for the functioning of democratic society. I would hope that the speakers and the participants in the debate might also wish to discuss proposals how to cope with the plague of terrorism, and how to immunize modern society from its disruptive effects.

JOHN DANFORTH has been a U.S.
Republican Senator from Missouri since
1977. Before his election to the Senate he
served eight years as the Attorney General
for the State of Missouri. Senator Danforth
earned his Law and Divinity degrees from
Yale University in 1963, and is an ordained
Episcopal priest.

TERRORISM VERSUS DEMOCRACY

My specific role today is to discuss the effects of terrorism on
the democratic societies in which we live. In order to perform
this role, I want first to say a few words about the common
characteristics of democratic societies. Then it is my intention
to discuss the effects terrorism and the methods used to combat it have on democratic values. Finally, I will make some
comments which I hope will be helpful in thinking about the
future.

Democratic societies, of course, differ widely in the precise structures of their governments. Some are parliamentary
in their organization, others rely on separately chosen execu-
tives. Some build upon written constitutions, others point to
long traditions which provide the framework for ongoing governmental action. Yet, with all the variations in form, democratic societies share fundamental assumptions about the
nature of man and the purpose of government.

Democratic societies share a common respect and concern
for the individual person. An individual, no matter who he is,
has a special value just because he is an individual. He has his
own worth — his own dignity. That worth and dignity shape
our way of thinking about the purpose of government. A
population consists of individuals, each with his own distinct
worth. Therefore, it is foreign to the nature of a democratic
society to think of persons as "the masses" or "the proletariat."

They are persons, each of whom is unique and each of whom possesses his own set of hopes and dreams.

Government in a democratic society, by its nature, respects the dignity of its citizens. The state exists to serve and protect the individual, which is the precise opposite of the relationship that exists in a totalitarian regime. Totalitarianism, the total claim of the state on the lives and loyalties of its subjects, is in flat contradiction to the values of democratic society. The purpose of democratic government is not to bully people — to push them around for its own ends — but to provide individuals with the necessary structure so that their oppurtunities for personal fulfillment are enhanced. In the words of the United States Constitution, a function of the government is to "insure domestic tranquility." Thus, the democratic state restrains antisocial behavior and prevents those outbreaks of destructiveness which would make a decent life impossible for the individual citizen.

While democratic governments must preserve order within their countries, they do not possess unlimited power to do so. They themselves are restrained, and this sets them apart from totalitarian regimes.

A totalitarian state can maintain order quite efficiently by the exercise of unrestrained power. By contrast, a democratic society must preserve order without abridging the individual rights of its citizens.

Effects of Terrorism on Democratic Societies

This tension between insuring domestic tranquility and avoiding excessive governmental power is heightened by the growing frequency of terrorism. On the one hand, violent extremists so disrupt the orderly workings of society that effective governmental action is a necessity if we are to enjoy the fruits of civilization. On the other hand, we must be watchful lest, in dealing with the actions of terrorists, the values of a democratic society are weakened by governmental excess.

Clearly, terrorism cannot be ignored on the theory that to deal with it effectively threatens the civil liberties of our citizens. A well-advanced sensitivity to civil liberties is an essential ingredient in a democratic society. Yet unchecked terrorism is, by itself, a threat to the values of a democratic society. Therefore, not to check it, and effectively, is to invite the destruction of a set of values which were centuries in the making.

Terrorism is the antithesis of democratic values. As democratic societies hold a common respect for the unique worth of each individual, terrorism rejects that concept of personal worth. Terrorism is inherently indiscriminate and arbitrary in its actions. Any innocent civilian killed will serve its purposes. It does not matter who the next victim is. All lives, combatant and, preferably, noncombatant are equally expendable. No matter whether violence produces dismemberment, maiming or death; no matter whether the victims are young or old, male or female; all serve the purpose of the terrorist.

When a locker in a busy airport explodes, it does not matter to the terrorist who may happen to be walking by. When an airplane is hijacked, it does not matter to the terrorist who is in that airplane.

Persons are, to the terrorists, not persons at all. They are not separate and distinct human beings, each possessing his own special value. They are only things — objects — numbers to be counted in some body count when the anonymous phone call is made claiming credit for the most recent outrage.

As terrorism is the antithesis of a democratic society's concept of man, it is obviously the antithesis of a democratic society's concept of the social order.

Unlike a democratic government, which depends for its authority on the consent of the governed, terrorists depend on no consent at all. They exist by stealth in tiny bands, sneaking from one secret hiding place to another to scheme about their next maneuver. With tiny followings, they reject the democratic process. They cannot operate openly. They do not appeal to the public. They hide from it. They are accountable to no one except themselves.

As terrorists destroy lives, their aim is to destroy democratic institutions as well. Their goal is to shake the faith of citizens in their government, or to trigger a repressive military or police response which, in itself, destroys democratic institutions.

Public cooperation with democratic institutions can be seriously weakened by terrorist activity. In Northern Ireland, citizens who under normal circumstances would be willing to cooperate with police and prosecuting officials have refused to do so. The effectiveness of the jury system in criminal prosecutions has been seriously compromised by jurors who fear reprisals at the hands of the terrorists.

Terrorism, then, is far more serious than the ordinary variety of criminal activity. It is destructive of democratic institutions which have taken centuries of persistent effort to develop. For this reason, effective measures to combat terrorism are imperative.

Combating terrorism has not been undertaken without cost to democratic values. Most of us flew to Israel to get to this Conference. In order to board our planes, we passed through metal detectors, or were subjected to body searches. Our luggage was X-rayed or searched by hand. These were minor inconveniences, but they were invasions of the personal privacy free people have grown to expect in our normal lives. They were necessary procedures to combat what had become an epidemic of aircraft hijackings.

In the United States, thousands of citizens visit the Capitol each day. As a precaution against terrorists, they must have their briefcases and handbags inspected by police officers.

Of necessity, the government of Italy has responded to terrorism with emergency measures. Police have been given the power to wiretap without written authority, to interrogate suspects without a lawyer present, and to hold them for investigation for extended periods of time.

In Northern Ireland, traditional police and court procedures have been altered to meet emergency conditions. Suspected terrorists have been locked up for indefinite periods of time. In some cases jury trials have been dispensed with, and presumptions normally existing in criminal cases have been modified.

Placating Terrorists

The extent to which democratic governments have gone beyond modification of criminal justice procedures, and have altered governmental policies to placate terrorists is speculative. It is understandable, of course, for political leaders to want to avoid conflict and attain peace by making alterations in public policy. There is always the possibility that such changes in public policy may be justified on their own merits — that a change in political direction has been long overdue. Yet to change policy in order to placate terrorists and buy civil peace is a dangerous process which leads in the end to the encouragement of more disruptive activity and to the further disintegration of democratic values.

We in the United States are not beyond criticism in this regard. Some time ago, I was puzzled by the policy of our Administration with respect to Rhodesia, and especially with respect to what I saw as a bias to guerrilla forces operating from bases in neighboring countries. My inquiry to a very high Administration official was greeted by a response which was disarmingly frank. "That," said the official, referring to the guerrilla forces, "is where the guns are."

I also think it is possible to argue that there have been instances within the United States where our government has overreacted to incidents of violence in the name of a political or economic cause.

One recent situation which exhibits some of these characteristics is the strike by independent truckers. I do not mean to characterize as terrorism the relatively few random acts of violence that accompanied this strike. Nonetheless, there was some violence and the government did respond to the entire situation by modifying its diesel allocation system to improve the situation for these truckers. The Administration also urged states to modify their rules on the size of trucks they permit to use their highways.

The *Washington Post* described the strike and the Administration's response as follows:

"The Carter Administration moved yesterday on several
fronts to try to end the increasingly violent nationwide
strike by independent truckers.

"In separate actions, the Department of Energy suspended
a federal regulation giving farmers priority status in the
purchase of diesel fuel, and the Federal Highway Administration urged governors in a number of states to consider
lifting temporarily weight and length limits on trucks
using their highways."

When a government tailors its foreign policy according to
"where the guns are," when violence in a truck strike appears
to yield a change in governmental policy, then the values of a
democratic society have been compromised, and the strategies
of those who use force to accomplish their purposes have been
validated.

The Democratic Dilemma

This brings us to the basic question I want to raise today. How
can we combat terrorism effectively without either adopting
undemocratic, police state methods ourselves, or meekly
accommodating ourselves to extremist demands made upon us?
To answer this question, I offer the following suggestions.

First, it has been said that democracies are especially
vulnerable to terrorist acts. Totalitarian regimes, it is said, are
better equipped to monitor the activities of dissident groups
and to suppress them before they become a serious threat. The
openness of a democracy is, it is said, its weakness.

Let me suggest that the openness of a democracy may in
fact turn out to be its strength. So long as a vast majority of a
population believes that it has a stake in its system of government, so long as normal channels of political participation are
open to all, those who resort to violent measures will not gain
widespread support. A terrorist cell will not develop into a
revolutionary movement if citizens have freedom to express
their views and advocate change within existing political and
social institutions. Therefore, it is both consistent with our
traditions and essential to our future that our legislatures and
our courts be readily accessible to all our citizens.

Second, the first duty of any government is to preserve order and defend its own existence. Chaos and constant terror cannot be permitted in a civilized world. Therefore, it is the duty of any government to use such measures as are necessary to maintain order. In appropriate circumstances searches, seizures, electronic surveillance and detention may have to be used to protect society from destruction.

The challenge is to make sure that such use of the state's police power is not excessive and does not degenerate into the abuse of power. If this challenge is to be met, anticipation and careful planning should supplant sudden reaction to unforeseen emergencies. To the greatest extent possible, governments should consider how to deal with terrorist activities before a crisis is at hand. An appropriate number of police and military officials should be carefully selected professionals who are specially trained in emergency procedures. Above all, a society itself should be given ample opportunity to foresee the problem of terrorism and to discuss in dispassionate terms the options for dealing with it. Such an opportunity for rational planning can be a major contribution of this Conference.

Finally, in an era when terorrism is on the increase, a democratic society must resolve that it will continue to stand firmly for its own set of values. To abandon those values in the face of a threat, or to accommodate ourselves to the strident demands of those who resort to violence is to give the terrorists the victory they seek, and to encourage similar outbreaks in the future.

The traditions of democracy have deep roots in the history of Western civilization. Over the centuries, men and women have struggled to develop and nurture those traditions. From them stem our concepts of the nature of man and his relation to the state. No stern terrorist effort, however well planned and executed, is sufficient to destroy a democratic society.

Our challenge is to maintain those traditions ourselves, to resist the temptation of responding to terror with naked and unchecked power, to reject the suggestion that our decisions be made to appease the enemies of democracy, and to preserve the values of a democratic society for generations to come.

DAVID BARRETT is head of the New
Democratic Party, one of the main oppo-
sition parties in Canada. He was leader of
Her Majesty's Loyal Opposition from 1970
to 1972, when his party won the elections
for the first time. From 1972-75 he was the
Premier and Minister of Finance of British
Columbia.

THE THREAT OF TERRORISM
IN A BROADER CONCEPT

Ladies and gentlemen, I am honored to be sharing the platform with such a distinguished group of jurists, writers,
scholars and statesmen. I hope that my perspective, both as a
Canadian politican and also as a social democrat, will contribute to the usefulness of these proceedings.

Eight months ago the New Democratic Party of Canada
was host to the fourteenth post-war congress of the Socialist
International. Terrorism was a subject of much debate among
the congress participants because terrorism is, by its very
nature, abhorrent to the goals of social democrats.

Private Power
Firstly, it is private power, be it at the highly publicized level
of skyjackers, assassination squads and political kidnapping or
at the less publicized level of protection rackets, loan sharks
and the urban criminal terrorist when they usurp "public law"
and become a law unto themselves. Private power in the form
of private armies is readily challenged by all of us who believe
that power comes out of the ballot box, and not the barrel of
a gun. But private armies are not restricted to the political
variety. I will have more to say about this later, but it should
be sufficient at this point to underscore my basic premise as an
egalitarian and as a social democrat. When the terrorist

unsheaths his gun, there is no consensus or equality in decisions which follow.

I quite deliberately chose organized crime, however unorthodox, as one of my first examples of private power because that is the usual context in which a North American leader experiences terrorism. As a preliminary definition, then, terrorists can be described as a minority group, in some cases a few individuals, who seek the fulfilment of their goals through indiscriminate violence, whether physical or psychological. Organized crime in North America perfectly fits that description. And just as in the world community where there are governments that negotiate away the rights of a people — because that in fact is what is traded off in democratic societies where terrorists demands are met — so too there have been governments that allow multi-million dollar crime to operate either outside the law or at the fringes of the law. The same definition applies — a minority group using indiscriminate physical or psychological violence to pursue its own ends.

Media Sensationalism and Double Standards
In the context of popular conceptions of terrorism, I would like to turn my attention for a moment to the media. In this regard, it is worth remembering the words of a noted thinker, a Canadian by birth, Mr. Marshall MacLuhan. He coined the term the "Global Village." Because of the vast technological advances made since World War II, we are now aware of political events almost as they happen around the globe. Every evening, the mass media bring intense and immediate news coverage into the living rooms of western democracies.

In recollecting my thoughts for this speech, I was struck by the number of occasions I could recall in which banner headlines and sensational publicity surrounded the more notorious acts of terrorists. Notable by its absence was sober and factual reporting of both the actual events and of the measures taken to combat them. The media have a public responsibility in the event of a terrorist act just as the public official does.

We should also be aware of a double standard. The sufferings inflicted by terrorists make front page news and readily shock us. The sufferings endured by minority groups, on the other hand, that amount to a daily cultural and economic deprivation are less newsworthy and it is comparatively easy to treat these sufferings with indifference.

Unfortunately, to this day, terrorism is regarded as a hot news item that makes instant celebrities out of usually desperate men and women. An audience that has been subtly conditioned to expect sensational news becomes a weapon for exploitation in the arsenal of the terrorist.

Terrorism Provokes Reactionary Response

This brings me to the second aspect of terrorism which is also inherently at odds with social democracy and that is, of course, violence. Violence not only begets immediate and, in the case of terrorists, indiscriminate cruelty, it also fosters the most undesirable and reactionary attitudes in society.

Such was the case almost a decade ago when Canada abruptly underwent a set of terrorist kidnappings. The attitude of the government of the time was a reference point in modern Canadian history. Members of the New Democratic Party argued that the police had the powers under the criminal code to capture the terrorists. Despite this argument, the government proclaimed the War Measures Act. The police were able to arrest without charge, and civil liberties were suspended right across the country. Eventually, discovery of the two groups involved occurred, but it should be noted it occurred through normal police work and it was not the result of any capricious arrests or searches carried out under the authority of the War Measures Act. Five years later, the Conservative Leader of the Opposition, Mr. Robert Stanfield, joined the growing number of Canadians who in sober reflection realized that the proclamation of the War Measures Act, in response to the 1970 terrorism, was wrong.

In mentioning the above example of Canadian political experience, I want to note the full dimension of the threat posed by terrorism to democratic societies. On the one hand, I see the real terror of those who take the law into their own hands. I see the justification for the full weight of the law falling on these individuals who flaunt the authority of the state for their own terrorist ends. On the other hand, governments must make sure that the cure is never worse than the disease. The scar on Canada's record of civil liberties which occurred ten years ago is a classic illustration of how the state, in an attempt to combat terrorism, overstepped its boundaries and actually threatened its own citizens. Democratic governments cannot legitimately establish consent by the use of force.

Social Alienation Begets
a Wider Form of Terrorism

Finally, it follows from this point of view that it is misleading to talk of terrorism as a "threat to civilization" — except in the sense that all violence, including war and state violence, is incompatible with a truly social and civilized condition. It is incorrect to equate the continuing existence of particular states, which may be democratic in name only, with the survival of a society.

The noted historian, Hannah Arendt, has pointed out a connection between terrorist violence and protest against the anonymous character of modern society. She was attempting to explain whatever it is — a tension of industrialization perhaps that seems to be the inevitable result of man purchasing his goods and services rather than producing them himself. I suspect this terrorism is more widespread than the public manifestations that the media report. It includes, for example, those members of society who "self destruct." Like other forms of terrorism it has its innocent victims, in this case, the battered spouses and children of those whose anger and frustration with the meaninglessness of their own lives spill over into domestic conflict.

What spawns this alienation which leads to a more subtle but nonetheless violent form of terrorism? What morality, for example, could have motivated an automobile company to proceed with the manufacturing of a car whose gas tank was proven, prior to the car's production, to blow up upon impact? What kind of alienation would have allowed a corporate board of directors to proceed with production of a nucle-ar reactor when adequate safeguards could not be guaranteed in the plant's construction? The kind of alienation that is involved in the priorities of these corporate decisions surely qualifies as a starting point for an enlarged definition of terrorism. There is, after all, every hallmark in this respect that is associated with terrorism: private power, indiscriminate violence, and innocent victims. It is perhaps not as public as in the usual connotation of terrorism, but its wake of human suffering is just as great.

Eliminating Social Alienation

But there is a more important consideration here and that is the recurring question as to what can we do to check this alienation that inevitably begets terrorism. As free citizens, men and women should have a share in all vital decision making processes thus enabling them to participate in putting the inevitable technological changes at the service of a society which is worthy of mankind.

In conclusion, I would like to recall the debates that took place at the Fourteenth Socialist International Congress held in Vancouver. They represent the thinking and contributions of some leading world statesmen, including the Chairman of the Congress and the Nobel Peace Prize winner, Mr. Willy Brandt. The conclusions of the Congress on overcoming terrorism are as follows:

1.   By seeking constantly to improve and extend democratic processes and institutions;
2.   By an unremitting struggle for social justice, democratic rights and peaceful co-existence around the world;
3.   By refusal to aid, in any way, groups which resort to or condone terrorism;
4.   By refusal to depart from constitutional and democratic principles or to allow infringement of civil liberties or to resort to unnecessary measures of response.

I hope in this brief elaboration of my perception and

experiences, I have made these conclusions sound more than just pious, diplomatic rhetoric. They have a great deal of meaning for me because of the large scope in which I view the presence of terrorism in democratic societies. In any form, it cannot be justified and should be combatted.

ROBERT MOSS is the Editor of *Foreign Report*, the private intelligence bulletin of *The Economist*, and a columnist for the London *Daily Telegraph*. He is a visiting lecturer at many universities and defense academies around the world, including the Royal College of Defense Studies in London and the NATO Defense College in Rome. Mr. Moss is the author of *Urban Guerrillas* and *The Collapse of Democracy*, and a regular contributor to major American magazines and newspapers.

THE TERRORIST STATE

If there has been a conspiracy of silence about the involvement of the Soviet Union and other governments in international terrorism, that is perhaps understandable. For those who vest their hopes for the future in a one-sided détente with the totalitarian leadership in Moscow, it is not comforting to be reminded that, in their efforts to weaken the Western democracies and achieve global hegemony, the Soviets are willing to make use of any and all weapons.

The best example of this is Iran. During 1978 the Carter Administration chose to ignore the mounting body of evidence on the covert participation of the Soviet bloc, Libya and the PLO in the campaign to overthrow the Shah; press reports that detailed Soviet backed propaganda operations, the training of Iranian terrorists in Palestinian Arab camps, or the vital role that was played by the PLO as an intermediary between Ayatollah Khomeini's entourage and Moscow were frequently shrugged off in Washington. The result is the chaos in Iran today, in which a special PLO unit — whose members were selected by the KGB residencies in Baghdad and Beirut for specialist training in security techniques in the USSR — now functions as the nucleus of a new secret police, a revolutionary SAVAK. While it is by no means certain that the pro-Soviet Left will emerge as ultimate victor from the bloody power-struggle that continues to rage in Iran today, what is absolutely certain is that the West has lost an irreplaceable ally. The effects of that loss can be observed in the spectacle of angry queues of American motorists at the gas-pumps, in the way that the Iraqis are bidding to occupy the strategic vacuum that the fall of the Shah has opened up in the Gulf, and in the great fear of revolution that now guides the policies of the Saudi royal house.

Thanks to Western inertia, Iran under Khomeini has already joined the ranks of the terrorist states. Two Palestinian Arab terrorists, members of the so-called "Black March" Organization, who were arrested after an abortive assault on Brussels airport earlier this year, were found to be traveling on Iranian passports. Iranian radicals became a popular source of false documentation for international terrorists after a Leftist student group occupied the Iranian consulate in Geneva in June, 1976; Baader-Meinhof terrorists traveling on passports that were stolen at that time were intercepted at Orly airport in Paris and on the Canadian/U.S. border last year. But no independent organization can match the resources available to a government. There are reports that the revolutionary regime in Iran, sworn to support the Palestinian Arab terrorist movement, has promised to provide the PLO with American-made planes for its Libyan-trained pilots to fly in a future phase of the campaign against Israel.

This is an example of how the number of outlaw states opposed to the norms of the international community has been expanded — and could expand still further — through the failure of Western governments to come to grips with the reality of the Soviet bloc's involvement in revolutionary terrorism and to take appropriate preemptive action.

Expedient Intermediaries
I do not believe that we can effectively contain international terrorism without adopting effective countermeasures against the terrorist states that provide the training, arms, finance, propaganda backup, sanctuaries and, in some notable instances,

strategic guidance and the resources at the command of their secret services.

The states that provide official backing for international terrorism include (a) the Soviet bloc countries, Cuba and North Vietnam; (b) the radical Arab states — Libya, Syria, Iraq, South Yemen, Algeria; and (c) Iran. There is a powerful lobby that is calling for the most dangerous imaginable new addition: an independent Palestinian Arab state. I shall turn to this question in a moment.

The Russians have an obvious and compelling interest in using any instrument that can help to weaken the NATO alliance and erode the fabric of the Western democracies. Terrorism has its place in the long-term Soviet strategy for overcoming the West, along with subversion and disinformation, the breakneck expansion of the Russian war machine, and the systematic attempt to deprive the West of automatic access to its major sources of energy in the Gulf and of strategic raw materials in central and southern Africa.

No doubt there is a constant debate in the Kremlin over how much support it is expedient to give to terrorist causes. For the KGB to be exposed as playing a key part in terrorist operations in Europe, for example, would not assist the advocates of treaty arrangements that favor Soviet interests. Nor would it help West European Communist Parties that are seeking to acquire an image of democratic respectability for electoral purposes. However, the Russians can rely on intermediaries, or on cut-outs — radical Arab states that pass on Soviet-made weapons to terror organizations, for example, and intelligence services that are subject to some degree of KGB control — to do much of the work for them. This may explain how Soviet-made Strela missiles came to be in the hands of Joshua Nkomo's ZAPU guerrilla movement, which used them to shoot down two civilian airliners from its bases in Zambia. Western analysts believe that what happened in that instance was a rather complicated transaction. The Russians supplied Strelas to Libya, which in turn passed some of them on to the PLO, which in turn played the part of benefactor to Nkomo's regime.

Guidance and Organization

There are signs that, over the past year or so, the most aggressive faction in the Soviet leadership — the group that centers around Mikhail Suslov, Boris Ponomarev and certain elements in the KGB — has seized on the political uncertainty that stems from Brezhnev's failing health to promote a more adventurist line in dealings with the international terrorist movement. There is a great deal of evidence of the direct role that is played by the Soviet Union and its satellites in training foreign terrorists. I might add a few details about the current courses that are being provided at the military academy at Simferopol in the Crimea. Courses specially tailored for the Palestinian Arabs — including techniques of river crossings and all types of sabotage — are provided at Simferopol for mixed groups (usually numbering about 60 trainees at a time) including Fatah, Saiqa, the PFLP and the PLF, whose differences seem to be submerged on these occasions for the sake of self-improvement. Political indoctrination in the glories of the Soviet revolution begins even before the trainees leave Lebanon; it is usually provided by Abu Khaled Hussein of Fatah's political department.

At the Russians' behest, the East Germans have played a growing role in coordination and intelligence for the international terrorist network, and a great deal of documentation on terrorist targets has been centralized at the Ministry of State Security in East Berlin.

The background support offered to the terror international is now well-documented. A more difficult question to answer is: to what extent have the Soviets (or their surrogates) "tasked" terrorist organizations to attack specific targets of Soviet rather than, say, Palestinian Arab interests? This question deserves to be pondered.

The terror groups also figure in Soviet contingency plans for industrial sabotage against the West, to which a series of important intelligence defectors, including the Czech General Sejna, the KGB Department V specialist, Oleg Lyalin, and the East German SSD officer, Werner Stiller, have all borne witness.

A Quantum Leap in Terrorism

Fatah, as the largest of the Palestinian Arab groups, is not under the guiding influence of any particular Arab government. Together with the openly Marxist factions of the PLO, like Naif Hawatmeh's group, Fatah is the Soviet's favorite, and its leaders make regular visits to the capitals of the Soviet bloc and maintain close contacts with Russian embassies and KGB *rezidenturas* in the Middle East. Indeed, it is hardly an exaggeration to say that Fatah has emerged as an immensely valuable surrogate just as the Cubans in Africa have emerged as a surrogate for the Soviet armed forces. The current role of the PLO in trying to establish a new security *apparat* in Teheran is one example. Another was the role of the PLO in assisting Idi Amin's State Research Bureau in Uganda. A less well-known case is the role that the PLO has also been playing in recruiting Latin Americans for the international terrorist cause. It has long-standing associations, for instance, with Argentina's Montoneros, whose leaders come from the converging stream of anti-semitic ultra-nationalism and Marxist extremism.

One of the PLO's major attractions for the Russians is that it appears to them as the group that can put a knife to the throats of the conservative Arab rulers of the Gulf — threatening them with a fate analogous to that of the Shah unless they adjust their policies to the radical current, while continuing to prepare the bases for a potential Leftist revolution in Arabia.

The PLO is also helping to add to the turmoil in Turkey, which just happens to possess NATO's largest land army in Western Europe. Turkish General Ergun Gokdeniz has confirmed the substance of my earlier report on PLO support for the Marxist Left and the Kurdish revolt in Turkey, commenting that the PLO "have been trained for wars of liberation to be fought with Marxist-Leninist methods."

The recent track record of the PLO in coordinating international terrorist actions and providing a substitute, in some cases, for the KGB, demolishes the naive hopes of those who maintain that the creation of an independent Palestinian

Arab state would provide a "political solution" to the violent assault on Western societies in which it has served as a motor.

The creation of an independent Palestinian Arab state on the West Bank under PLO domination would not simply constitute the addition of one more terrorist state to the already lengthy list: *it would represent a quantum leap in the capabilities of the international terrorist movement.*

Can anyone seriously believe that the rulers of such a state would be so absorbed in their internal economic problems and their traditional infighting that they would abandon the attack on Israel — and also Jordan? There is truth in the proverb, *l'appétit vient en mangeant,* and it is arguable that satisfaction of part of the PLO's demands would merely serve to encourage its leaders to demand, even more intensely, the whole of their original claim.

Arrangements for demilitarization would be liable to be overthrown with full Soviet backing. It is possible to imagine Soviet cargo planes and helicopters moving in arms on the pretext of an Israeli reprisal for terrorist actions. It is also possible to conceive of a direct appeal to Moscow from the new Palestinian Arab leadership to put troops on the ground to make a West Bank state an inviolable sanctuary for terrorism.

Renewed Resolve

International terrorism can neither be understood nor effectively combatted as an isolated phenomenon. It has its place in the spectrum of pressures that are now being exploited by the Soviet Union and other interests in the effort to undermine Western societies. One of the forms of pressure most intimately related to terrorism is disinformation — the attempt to deceive and mislead Western public opinion — which is being pursued today through covert Soviet influence over the media and covert financing by radical Arab governments, notably those of Libya and Iraq. A climate conducive to terrorism is one in which the terrorists are depicted as representatives of a legitimate political cause, while the societies they attack are depicted in pejorative abstractions, their leaders ridiculed and dehumanized. This involves the colonization of the dictionary by the far Left — a process that is indeed well advanced when the murderers of women and children are described as "freedom fighters."

Lenin said that "the purpose of terrorism is to terrify." It is a simple definition, but an apposite one. To contain terrorism — or for that matter, to cope with the abuse of the "oil weapon," Soviet expansionism in Africa, or the Soviet race for strategic superiority — Western societies must first resolve not to be terrified and to hit back instead with all the relentlessness that the challenge demands. Yoni acted in that spirit at Entebbe, and it is in that same spirit that we must seek to increase the cost to the terrorist states of continuing to engage in their present assault on the civilized world, to the point where they may one day be compelled to abandon it.

PROF. MORDECAI ABIR is an authority
on Middle Eastern affairs and specializes in
the Arabian Peninsula and the politics of oil.
He is a consultant to the Foreign Relations
and Defense Committees of the Knesset,
Israel's Parliament. His books include *Oil
Power and Politics* (1975) and *In the Direction of the Gulf* (1968). His latest work is
The Red Sea and Ethiopia.

THE ARAB WORLD, OIL AND TERRORISM

In the Muslim Middle East the borderline between countries with "non-terrorist" and with "terrorist" ideologies is very vague; indeed, the former can hardly be said to exist. The history of our region is replete with terrorism long before the word itself existed. The very word "assassins" comes from the *assasseen* organization, the *hashishin*, an Ismaili branch which succeeded in inspiring fear all over the Middle East in the 11th and 12th centuries by sheer communal and personal terror.

Islamic Terrorism and Marxist Ideology

More recently, the targets of such Islam-based terrorism have included not only Western "imperialists," but those people and organizations who were willing to accept this "imperialism" and go along with the government. For example, the people who were the predecessors of the Moslem Brothers assassinated the grandfather of the Egyptian Deputy Prime Minister, Butros Ghali, in 1911, because of his collaboration with the "imperialists." The assassins promoted the idea that an ideology can be forced on a community through terror. We should remember that after the end of colonial rule democratic institutions could not take root in the societies of the Middle East, and how completely alien these institutions were to the people of the region.

In the 1960s and 1970s puritan Muslim ideology was replaced, ironically, by an extreme Marxist ideology. This ideology emerged originally from a single organization called the Kalmiyun Arav, which later branched off into all sorts of smaller groups. Although the founders of the Kalmiyun Arav were mainly Palestinian Arabs, it did not remain purely a Palestinian Arab organization, just as the Muslim Brotherhood did not remain an Egyptian organization.

The ruling party of the People's Democratic Republic of Yemen, for example, is Kalmiyun Arav-oriented. Hence the very close relationship between South Yemen and anything that happens in the terrorist international, especially in the different branches of the Popular Democratic Front and its related organizations.

Arab Extremism and Soviet Designs

Let us consider the relation of these Arab extremist groups to Soviet strategy in the area. I have long claimed that the Soviet presence in the Gulf of Aden was not merely defense-oriented, but definitely aimed also at the supply of oil from the Gulf. Before 1973 that was not a readily accepted position, but things have changed. Significantly, the appearance of the Soviet flotilla in the north-western part of the Indian Ocean nearly coincided with the unsuccessful attempt by the Israeli tanker, "Coral Sea," to navigate the Bab-el-Mandab straits (it was attacked by Palestinian Arab terrorists). Both events demonstrated the two potential means of interdicting the supply of oil to the West in the future: Intervention by regular armed forces or subversion by surrogate groups.

In an era of nuclear weapons, each superpower is careful about using even conventional weapons on the seas, so that the Soviet presence may be seen as a show of the flag in an area that is extremely crucial for the West. The Soviet Union, however, is definitely assured of having sufficient proxies on the spot, be they the Sons of the Arabian Peninsula, the Front for the Liberation of the Gulf, the Front for the Liberation of Oman, the Young Saudis, the Young Yemenis, etc. There are about twelve such organizations which all derive their ideology from the same source — the Kalmiyun Arav. They have developed from groups of "intellectuals" who believe they have discovered ultimate truth, who claim to know what is best for their own people, and who are ready to force this truth, not only on their own people, but also on the countries which surround them.

The target of these groups — as of the Soviets — is the oil of the Gulf. Their aim is first to overthrow those regimes considered friendly to the West, or "moderate," among the oil-producing countries. The second aim is to fight "Western neo-imperialism" in the area. "Neo-imperialism" — because to this day, during the most fantastic oil extortion by the Arabs, the West is still held to be utilizing and "exploiting" the wealth of the Arabs and of their neighbors, and the only way to overcome that, according to such people, is to establish their own mastery over the area.

The first victory for this group was the revolution in Libya in 1969, which changed the balance of power within OAPEC, the Organization of Arab Petroleum Exporting Countries. Even more devastating for the West was the oil embargo of 1973-1974, not so much because the price of oil was quadrupled (after all, oil was underpriced for many years), but simply because it showed the West for what it is: a group of countries which were spineless, leaderless, and unable to react. It was precisely this view of the West which has been guiding the countries and organizations that use terrorist activities in the region. They know that they can get away with it.

Two factors prevented successful subversion of Western oil interests on a wide scale in our region. The first was the willing adoption by Iran of the role of mini-superpower and policeman of the area. With an army of nearly half a million and an impressive air force (nobody knew just how weak it was from within), it instilled fear in the supporters and organizers of subversion such as Iraq and the People's Democratic Republic of Yemen, both proxies of the Soviet Union.

The second factor, strangely, was Saudi Arabia, not because it had any military strength, not because of its economic strength, but because everybody believed at the time, and until very recently, that the United States was so much involved in the area that it would not permit anything to happen to its friends here. In the meantime, I regret to say, the credibility of the United States in the world has become next to nil, and among the Arab countries, after the Iranian fiasco, it has shrunk even lower. In the Arab press that comes across my desk, the possibility of the United States doing something is not taken very seriously, to say the least.

Regional Instability

The probable watershed of events in our region is the Khomeini revolution in Iran. Not because, as some would have it, this signals the beginning of a general Islamic revivalism in the area. Far from it. Iran is a Shiite country, and has followed a path of its own. What happens in Iran may influence some other Shiite communities but will not have such an impact on, for example, the Sunnis of either Saudi Arabia or Syria. What is significant is that the country which had been the self-appointed guardian of the Gulf against the radicals, against the Soviet Union, has utterly abandoned that role and appears increasingly anarchic and subject to centripetal ethnic tugs.

It is important to stress that the area which supposedly holds nearly 60% of the proven oil reserves of the world (these figures should be taken with a grain of salt, because all figures about proven oil reserves have "proven to be unproven") contains enormous asymmetries. It is a region where tiny countries, the twentieth century products of nineteenth century imperialism, without either a population infrastructure, or an economic infrastructure, without armies to speak of, and with politically archaic regimes, are holding an enormous treasure, not a treasure merely because it is valuable, but because it is the lifeline of the West and the lifeline of the Third World — indeed of the whole world.

And let us remember that it is *not* only the advanced nations of the West that suffer. Perhaps we speak too much about the problems of the West in this regard. In a recent conversation with the Kenyan Minister of Education, I learned that he was forced to give up two-thirds of his budget because his country had to pay — not the recent rise in the price of oil — but the previous rise in the price of oil. The Third World countries are suffering, and suffering terribly, because of the oil extortion. My heart bleeds less for the West than for these countries on the edge of disaster.

Direct Soviet Aggression

The real danger, in this unstable region full of such asymmetries, is that the Soviet Union, which will be a net oil importer by the 1980s (importing about two million barrels a day at that period), will become increasingly aggressive in the region.

There are two possible directions for the future. The first is that of direct Soviet aggression. By 1973, the Soviet proxies in the area had stopped subversive activities, and stopped supporting all of the organizations that I mentioned above, because OAPEC was doing the Soviet Union's work for it in damaging the Western economies, and the local proxies were afraid of a more overt attack leading to a strong reaction by the West.

After 1977-78, however, Iraq and its allies renewed their subversion in the area in the hope of creating an oil colossus in the area. And, indeed, there is nobody left anymore to put an umbrella over Kuwait. Kuwait was protected until recently by Iran on one side and by Saudi Arabia (with the United States) on the other. I mention Kuwait, not only because Iraq has a historical claim to Kuwait which it has tried to make good on three occasions, but also because annexation of Kuwait by Iraq is still a most realistic possibility. If this happens we will be faced with an oil producer even more important than Saudi Arabia. Moreover, in contrast to Saudi Arabia, Iraq which has nearly 13 million people, is dedicated to revolutionary extremism, has an economic infrastructure, and is very rapidly building up its armed forces. It has between eight and nine divisions of which three are armored divisions. Worst of all, this is a country that is also furiously attempting to obtain its own nuclear capability. So one possible direction of events centers on Iraq, a powerful oil producer, which might support subversion and aggression on a scale we have not known.

Radical Arabs Are an Independent Threat
The second direction that we can contemplate is the possibility
of radical Arabs working within OAPEC. There is no necessity
anymore to annex by force if you can coerce by psychological
terrorism. An example of this is what happened at the recent
Baghdad Conference, where the radical powers put certain
facts of life before the other Arab countries concerning their
view of the Israel-Egypt agreement. OAPEC can today be
manipulated in any way that powerful countries such as Iraq
would wish.

I do not believe that the extremist organizations in this
region are just proxies of the Soviet Union — at least in one
sense. They undoubtedly further the work of the Soviet Union,
but they may not always realize that they are proxies. After
the fall of the Shah and the rise of Khomeini, what can we expect in the Gulf? It is important to understand that in the
Persian Gulf and in the Arab world generally, it is not simply a
question here of two kinds of regimes — pro-Western or pro-
Communist. These are not the only alternatives. What these
regimes aspire to be is pro-Arab, pro-Muslim, because the big
and lasting dream of this region is that of pan-Arabism, the
dream of Gamal Abdel Nasser and others, to revive the golden
days of the Arab Empire, and to renew the position of the
Arabs in global decision-making in the family of nations.
And according to the philosophy of the aggressive Arab
countries, this can be accomplished only through the undermining of the Western economies and Western power, which is
regarded as an enemy, a new "colonialism" which stands in the
way of the Arab Empire and its dreams. It is naive, and indica-
tive of ignorance of the Arab world and its mental makeup, to
presume that to be anti-Soviet in this region is therefore to be
"pro-Western." Nothing could be further from the truth, further removed from reality. Whether from a Soviet military presence, and state supported terrorist organizations, or from
economic extortion by radical Arab states — the threat to the
West's oil supply is grave.

EDWARD TELLER is a world renowned
scientist. He is the Director Emeritus of the
Lawrence Livermore Radiation Laboratory
where he works as a consultant. A physicist
by training, Professor Teller was a major
contributor to Project Manhattan which
developed the nuclear bomb and is known
as the father of the hydrogen bomb.
Professor Teller is the author of many studies
and books, including *The Structure of
Matter* (1948), *Our Nuclear Future* (1958),
and *The Legacy of Hiroshima* (1962).

THE SPECTRE OF NUCLEAR TERRORISM

We live in a rapidly changing world full of opportunities and full of dangers. One of the dangers is the topic of the discussion today, International Terrorism. It sometimes seems that this danger to the great majority of the peaceful people of the world cannot be overcome. Three years ago when the hostages of Entebbe were liberated, it was shown that a lot can be done.

A lot more needs to be done, and because the danger is international, the fight against this danger must equally be on an international scale. My special problem today is to discuss a question relating to a particularly horrible part of what the future might hold: the use for terrorist purposes of atomic explosives, explosives similar to those that were dropped on Japan in 1945. The problem is indeed difficult, but in facing it we must look at it in a realistic manner.

There has been a lot of loose talk that among terrorists a small group of ingenious people may put together an atomic explosive secretly, maybe in a garage. I am tempted to say that this is nonsense. Actually, I am almost justified to say that it is impossible. Too many skills are required. Too many risks have to be taken. To execute the operation in continuing secrecy is all but hopeless. Still, I don't dare say that something of this kind is absolutely impossible. It is extremely unlikely, and we should not worry about it, because there are greater, more real dangers.

What a small group of conspirators cannot do, almost any sovereign nation can accomplish, particularly if it has some cash. The secret of the atomic bomb is known to a million people. That does not mean that a million people know how to make an atomic bomb. It means that a million have some idea how to make it, and among these you can find experts in one or another aspect. If a government can hire a considerable number of these experts, allow them to cooperate, allow them to use experiments, it is highly probable that this effort will, in time, succeed. We don't know in how much time.

Proliferation Is the Real Danger

The real danger is proliferation of nuclear weapons. This is something we must stop, and furthermore, we should stop the next step: the possibility that a government, having made in secret a nuclear explosive, should then hand this nuclear explosive to selected agents, to selected terrorists.

What can be done to prevent proliferation? A treaty has been signed, but not by all nations. It is unlikely to be more effective than the Kellog-Briand Pact which outlawed war a few years before Hitler started on his dreadful march. Paper is *not* the solution.

It has been suggested that tests of nuclear explosives should be forbidden. That, too, runs into lots of difficulties. After so many years, after so much knowledge has become available, after so much thought has been given to the subject of atomic explosives, in a systematic manner or in fragmentary speculations, a government that makes a determined effort to make an atomic bomb, I believe — and I am only guessing — could make such an atomic bomb with considerable confidence that it actually will work. This is true particularly if the aim is to pass the bomb on to a terrorist group, and in case of failure the consequences could be limited. The risks they are taking will not be very great.

Otherwise, proliferation may turn out to be a somewhat lesser hazard because a country in possession of atomic weapons will be very reluctant to use them in open warfare, which would have unpredictable, and in all probability very dreadful, consequences to the very country that used the atomic weapons. This is the reason I am particularly afraid of the linkage between proliferation of atomic weapons and international terrorism.

The participants in this conference will not have any difficulty imagining occasions where a rich country and a radical country might make such weapons available to terrorists.

Controlling Nuclear Reprocessing

There is another proposal to stop proliferation; in my opinion it is not hopeful. It has been suggested that the burned-up fuel elements from nuclear reactors which contain plutonium, a nuclear explosive, should not be reprocessed, thereby making plutonium less available. However, there are plenty of small nuclear reactors which are not under international inspection. The danger from reprocessing in the case of big reactors, where supervision already exists, is much less than the danger from the numerous small reactors. It may make good sense to bring all reactors under international supervision. If this is not done, an attached small reprocessing plant may well be built and operated in secrecy.

But even this is not a satisfactory solution. A nuclear explosive does not require plutonium; the light isotope of uranium, uranium-235, can serve the purpose. Each year sees new and more practical methods on the separation of isotopes, and some of these methods can be, and in the course of time will be, applied to uranium. To stop nuclear explosions by trying to limit the availability of the explosive materials is something that should be tried, but it should be tried in the right way, and to eliminate reprocessing is not the practical approach.

I wish I could make a concrete and a practical proposal how to prevent the great danger of which we are speaking. I have none. But I want to speak of a series of actions that may lead toward a more secure world.

Avoiding Secret Development of Nuclear Weapons

We have been clinging to the idea that more secrecy means more safety. That idea does not seem to have a lot of validity. In the course of time, secrets invariably become known. To believe that we have more secrets than we actually do have can itself be a danger.

To move in the opposite direction might be more helpful. Let us try to open up, as much as possible, all of our activities — nuclear activities, military activities, all the rest. I do not mean to open up plans concerning the next two weeks, or even the next two months. What I am worried about is long-term secrecy, exceeding a year. If we could introduce rules whereby all of us (and, from my point of view, this must include the United States) should minimize long-term secrecy, eliminate as much of it as possible, that would be a step in the right direction.

The principles of the atomic bomb, for instance, are widely known if not officially known. It would be a step in the right direction to make public officially information that is, in fact, already known. We could reduce the validity of secrecy to periods of not more than one year, or at most two years.

If we pursued such a policy of openness, we would be in the position to take the next important step. We would be in the position to say that we are not going to help any country, that we are not going to give most favored nation status to anyone who does not go along with us in a policy directed toward openness.

Let me repeat: I do not feel I am in a position to make such a proposal in a concrete and clear way; I am only talking about possibilities we should consider. If such action should lead to greater openness throughout the world, then at least nuclear proliferation would not occur in secret; and if there is anything worse than nuclear proliferation it is secret nuclear proliferation. That is the kind of nuclear proliferation where the destructive instruments can be handed in small numbers, maybe singly, to a "reliable" group — reliable from the viewpoint of a subversively radical government; this group could then wreak enormous mischief.

The counter-pressure could and should be strong. It could hardly operate unless we managed to accomplish a great degree of openness in most of the world, at least in that part of the world not yet behind the Iron Curtain.

I do not know how that openness is to be achieved. Perhaps in fighting terrorists. To some extent, even the Russians might cooperate at some time.

Let us take another difficult case: Libya has great wealth; it is perhaps the most radical among the states of the world after the overthrow of Idi Amin. To restrain Libya might appear hopeless — but is it? In every case it is at least possible to try, and in many cases I think we might succeed.

The world as it is at present is very different from what it was a hundred years ago. With more knowledge, with more technology, with more science, with more understanding, the power of man has increased — the power to do what is good and the power to do what is evil. Terrorists have availed themselves of part of this power. We should hope that all of this power will never become available to them.

There is also the possibility of using power for good purposes. International united action against terrorism is absolutely necessary. In the case of nuclear explosives, it may be particularly difficult to prevent the action of terrorists; it may also be particularly important.

I do not imagine that what I have said is sufficient. The best I might hope for is that it points in the right direction. Human ingenuity is great, and it is not the exclusive privilege of terrorists to be ingenious. If the rest of us will give the most serious thought to the question of how to avert atomic terror, we may have made a small contribution toward a great cause.

Editor's Note: Illness prevented Professor Teller from attending the Conference as he originally planned. The above statement was read at his request by Mr. Peter Lubin.

THOMAS SCHELLING is Professor of
Political Economy at Harvard University.
He served for five years overseas and in
Washington in the National Security Council
before becoming Professor of Economics at
Yale University (1953) and at Harvard
(1958). His teaching and research have been
in national security, foreign policy, energy
policy, and nuclear non-proliferation.
Among his books are *The Strategy of
Conflict* (1960),*Arms and Influence* (1967),
Nuclear Energy and National Security
(1976), and *Nuclear Policy: Issues and
Choices* (1977).

CAN NUCLEAR TERRORISM BE NEUTRALIZED?

Like everybody else I will confine myself to twelve or fifteen minutes. To do that I am going to have to select some of the things I want to talk about. I will tell you about a few things I think could happen. I won't have time to tell you about some of the things I think are not likely to happen.

Let me begin by saying that this is a rather different subject from the one we have been discussing. I think it's rather disconnected from the kind of terrorist activity we have talked about. It is a different problem in its likely timing, its organization, even the kind of terrorism that might be involved. I cannot, as Mr. Crozier did, begin with facts. I'll let Edward Teller's facts be all the factual introduction we need. Most of what I will do is speculate. I would say that I will reason with you.

Professor Teller mentioned possible ways that some kinds of terrorist organizations might get weapons, specifically by transfers from countries that already have them. He said transfer would be comparatively riskless. I think that is not so, but nevertheless it can happen. Transfer might result from blackmail, rather than from a natural desire to utilize a front organization for terror. The weapons could also be stolen, although the news there is fairly good: The United States has deployed huge numbers of weapons around the world, in many different countries, including some countries where

military revolts took place. As far as we know the weapons are
still there. I don't think there is any evidence yet that any have
been stolen, American weapons or anybody else's. But at least
that possibility remains.

How Could Nuclear Weapons
Fall into the Hands of Terrorists?

I think there is quite another scenario by which we can
imagine weapons or fissionable material falling into terrorist
hands. If you imagine that the Shah had lasted ten years longer
and that the nuclear program he had planned two years ago
had been put into effect, by the end of another decade he
would likely have had an inventory of weapons-grade
fissionable material, at least if he or if some of his government
wanted to. Now suppose the revolution that just took place
were to take place then, with nobody quite knowing whether
the air force would be loyal and the army not; without quite
knowing whether the officers would be loyal and the enlisted
men not; with people rushing around knowing only that somewhere there was weapons-grade fissionable material, or that
somewhere there were weapons. If there had been weapons
they would have been located presumably where somebody
in the air force, in the army or in the navy would know where
to find them, or would already have access to them. It seems
quite likely, therefore, that weapons or weapons-grade materials would have disappeared. I don't know whom we would
have wished to have acquired them, but it is important
to keep in mind that the primary function of military force in
most undeveloped countries is either to overthrow the government or to oppose other military forces within the same
country. In Argentina it is the army against the navy, in
Indonesia it was some troops loyal to Sukarno against some
troops not loyal to Sukarno. Imagine if there had been
weapons-grade material somewhere in Lebanon over the last
few years. I don't know whose forces would have been in there
looking for it. Somebody might have found it. I just
mentioned that to suggest it is not an idle possibility that with-

in a decade the search for nuclear weapons by groups will be a major preoccupation in a significant number of countries.

How Might Terrorists Use The Nuclear Threat?
What would terrorists do if they got weapons-grade material? They would have to make a bomb. As Edward Teller told you, that is not easy. At least it's not easy for what he referred to as a small group of terrorists in a garage. Think of a large group of terrorists having as much money available as Howard Hughes might have given them. Or put it this way: Imagine if Israel's survival were so threatened that large numbers of Jews around the world were prepared to try to engage in nuclear deterrence in its defence, with their money, their skills, whatever loyalty and discipline they could muster. I guess that they could do it, and they wouldn't need to do it in a garage. But, if an organization did acquire nuclear weapons by building some, it would be a group of people that didn't look much like the Symbionese Liberation Army in California. It would be a group of people who have extraordinary discipline.

They would undoubtedly think carefully of what they would do with the weapons once they had them. It would probably take months for planning a strategic campaign. I don't think they would want to waste the weapon, or weapons, in any impetuous theatrics. They would try to think of something important to do. Let me speculate on what I think they would come to believe is the appropriate, most likely accepted use of a nuclear capability if they had it. They would ask themselves, how do nations that have nuclear weapons try to get some use out of them? I think they would first decide to try to make the weapon look like a military weapon, not a terrorist one. They would decide that the most effective threats to make would be deterrent threats designed to prevent action, rather than compellent threats designed to accomplish some quick action. They would probably decide — especially if they had only very few weapons, or if they preferred not to have to explode them in population centers, or if they were not altogether confident that the weapons would work — that success would involve never having to use the weapons. Just as success for the French, the British, the Americans, the Russians, presumably is measured in never having to use the weapons.

What would they threaten against? It seems to me the most likely, credible and acceptable threat would be a threat against somebody's military action. Whose military action? Here I would imagine a military action by some third party outside the theater who might want to intervene. For example, if the timing of terrorist nuclear weapons had been advanced by a about a decade, I imagine an ideal terrorist use would have been during the Yom Kippur War, when the Azores were very important for the resupply of Israel. The argument would be: we will pick a military target and try to deter military intervention by an outside power. We will try to find something that can be stopped by two, three, four or more governments or other organizations such that anyone can veto it. We can threaten a weapon against the Azores and maybe the planes won't be refuelled; we can threaten a weapon against Lisbon and maybe the Azores won't be available; we can threaten a weapon against Philadelphia and maybe the Americans won't want to use the Azores; we can threaten almost anything, and suddenly people all around the world discover that all they have to do is stop the Azores from being available to the United States and maybe the weapon won't go off. If this threat took the United States by surprise, it might find itself deterred.

Notice that this strategy would not cost the terrorists the weapon because they would not have to use it. It also would give them a kind of credibility, and it would put them very much in the position of being a kind of nuclear mini-state. Indeed, in a way, they would look less terrorist than the United States and the Soviet Union and France, because one thing you must keep in mind about nuclear weapons is that from the very outset they have been officially identified as weapons of mass destruction. All during the 1960s many of us memorized the phrases about the devastating retaliation that would be inflicted against the Soviet Union in the event of an attack on the United States. Success was measured in percent-

ages of population destroyed, and percentages like half were
what people were interested in. In other words, these are
essentially weapons of mass *terror* because the United States
and the Soviet Union have elevated them to that status.
Threatening to use them to destroy military targets might look
comparatively clean and non-terrorist, and in the process the
terrorists might elevate themselves to something very much
like a small state. Incidentally, I think delivery of the weapon
would be no problem. It might be hard to deliver one on short
notice to an Israeli target. It shouldn't be terribly hard to
deliver one by boat to some target in the United States. It
would frighten the wits out of the Americans.

Terrorists As A Nuclear Mini-State

When I say that the terrorists might become something like a
nuclear mini-state with a nuclear strategy of their own, it
is partly because they would be doing exactly what any nuclear
terrorist state would do. Imagine Syria or Iraq or Libya with
nuclear weapons. If they wanted to take credit for possessing
them, if they announced that they possessed them and had a
strategy for their use, I don't really imagine that they would
propose clean tactical use only against isolated military targets.
Again, taking their cues from the French, the British, the
Americans and the Russians, they would threaten massive retaliation against actions they would like to deter. And this retaliation could look fairly massive, because in retrospect Hiroshima
and Nagasaki still look to many people as something quite
massive.

Incidentally, the only uses of nuclear weapons in anger
that have occurred were, in a certain sense, terrorist. I think
the decision to bomb Hiroshima was a responsible decision,
that in all likelihood it saved Japanese lives. Nevertheless, you
must remember it reflected the decision of a nation that had
exactly two bombs, and was not altogether certain that both
would go off with the yield that had been promised. The
Americans discussed a nuclear demonstration in isolated
places, considered the possibility that a demonstration would
fizzle, or that those invited to see the demonstration wouldn't

understand it, or that by reporting unreliably they would minimize its effects. It was finally decided that the only thing that would shock the government in Tokyo to terminate the war was to hit a genuine target in the mainland of Japan. On the pretext that Hiroshima had a military-industrial capability a bomb was dropped there, and four days later another one was dropped. Our arsenal was gone. Historians still discuss whether it made all that much difference, but at least we went through the problem of what to do when you've only got two bombs and its terribly urgent to get a war stopped. And it might be that a mini terrorist nuclear state, a genuine terrorist nation state with very few bombs, will have to go through much the same kind of reasoning that the United States did when it was a puny, brand new nuclear power.

Preventing the Threat

Now what can we do about all this, besides worry about it or hope that it doesn't happen? One thing I would like to do is to contradict Edward Teller on the ease and safety with which Libya or Iraq could transfer weapons, if they had them, to a terrorist organization. It is important to try to get heads of state, even in places like Pakistan, to understand that the most likely targets for their own nuclear weapons are within their own countries. These are *very* dangerous weapons. If, for example, Sadat had nuclear weapons, I think he would discover that two things were absolutely intolerable. One would be to give them to his armed forces, and the other would be not to give them to his armed forces. Having them and not giving control to your armed forces is an act of such lack of confidence that the first thing they would want is having you out of the way. If you do give the weapons to your armed forces it is at least an implicit admission that, if absolutely necessary, authorization to use them will be forthcoming. As long as that is known, armies are very good at getting in a position where it's absolutely essential to use them. I hope that Sadat has the intelligence to recognize that the last thing he should want is a nuclear weapons capability. I just wish the governments of Argentina, Brazil, Pakistan, Indonesia and other places would come to that conclusion. I wish we could persuade them that these are dangerous weapons and they will sleep less well. A difficulty in doing this is that it's very hard to teach them a lesson. It's very hard to put the head of a state, the minister of defence, and the chief of staff of the armed forces in the same room and ask them to begin to discuss seriously the contingency that very soon they will be on opposite sides of a war.

What else can we do? I think, as several people have proposed, we've got to build up an intelligence capability to cope with this danger. I too deplore the loss of American confidence in the CIA. I put the blame differently. I believe that the loss of confidence was due to the squandering of a precious asset by the CIA, the confidence that at least the Congress, and sometimes the people, had in it. The CIA did not have the discretion, intelligence and good sense not to engage in the kind of excesses that, when brought into view, destroyed its credibility. Just as President Nixon may have destroyed the credibility of the executive branch as represented in the White House, I am afraid the credibility of the CIA has been appreciably hurt. Repairing this will take a long time. Nevertheless, intelligence is one of the lines of defence.

Another one may be weapons security. Here we face a dilemma. What do we do if Pakistan gets a nuclear weapon? I would hate to cooperate with them, to reward them for developing a weapon. On the other hand, I would like to cooperate with Pakistan and provide them the finest technology, so that if the weapons are stolen it will be hard to use them, or so that they can't be readily stolen. We have devices in the United States that make it less likely for stolen weapons to be used, or for weapons to be taken away undetected. We are likely to see nations in violation of the non-proliferation treaty, or those which have never ratified the non-proliferation treaty, acquire nuclear weapons. It may be that cooperating with them to help them keep those weapons will be on the one hand desirable, and on the other hand incompatible with what the treaty binds us to. That is a dilemma to think about.

An interesting question will be the role of the U.S.S.R. in all of this. One of the few things in which the U.S.S.R. has cooperated with the United States, and even badly wanted its cooperation (I think on the whole sincerely and genuinely), is suppressing the proliferation of nuclear weapons and nuclear weapon capability. But when the time comes for some country to make a nuclear threat, that country is likely to be either an ally of the Soviet Union or an ally of the United States. This is especially likely if there are several countries capable simultaneously of making nuclear threats against each other, particularly so if some country announces that it has weapons but will not engage in first use. It is hard to imagine a more vocal way of threatening first use than to announce that you have them and are not contemplating first use. It will become difficult to insure that we and the Russians will have a joint interest, let us say, in using the KGB if the CIA does not have the capability at that time to destroy the weapon as well.

The Anti-Nuclear Tradition
I don't really go along with the notion that terror states — that is, nations that support terrorist organizations — should be free of any kind of retaliation or sanction on our part. We should be prepared to declare in some fashion that any state that abets the acquisition of nuclear weapons by terrorist organizations is completely vulnerable to any kind of sanction that may be visited on it, that is, to declare it a kind of an outlaw. I have one proposal for what one may do about it. It sounds a little strange and very old fashioned, but one possibility would be to declare war. It might prove for a while to be a phony war, but it would be a serious action to take. It would put a country in a rather unusual and rather surprising position. Conceivably, one of the easiest ways to get a country outside of normal commerce, friendship, and navigation, would be to declare war on it.

Probably most important of all is to recognize that for a long time, since Hiroshima, and in some ways because of

Hiroshima, there has been a curse on nuclear weapons. Hardly anybody really thinks that they are merely another weapon. Even President Eisenhower, who used to say nuclear weapons were merely other weapons and who talked about the possibility of pinpoint artillery bombardment of nuclear weapons as though they were merely another type of larger explosive, even he deep in his heart understood that they were different; all of his negotiations on the test ban, surprise attack and so forth, were a recognition that nuclear weapons were different. They *are* different. Lyndon Johnson felt that they were different. Jack Kennedy felt that they were different. Most of us probably feel that they are different. This undoubtedly puts more inhibition on the use of these weapons than anything else we have. We are fortunate that perhaps because they were used in Hiroshima they weren't used in Korea. We now have a long tradition that these weapons are not to be used. We don't really know what would happen if one of them should ever go off again in anger. But it will be the most important event since Hiroshima when it happens. I just hope that the Russians, and the Pakistanis, and the Israelis, and possibly even the PLO, realize that.

QUESTIONS AND ANSWERS

Chairman (Ambassador Gideon Rafael): Ladies and gentlemen, I would now like to open the discussion to comments and questions.

Brian Crozier: I would have to exercise the greatest ingenuity to put these comments in the form of questions. But it is not impossible. I thought I ought to make a comment in the form of a question to Mr. Barrett, who raised two questions himself.

One was about the proper behavior of a state faced with a problem of terrorism. I would like to recall what happened during the Second World War which I had the fortune to live through in England. Now we understood that this was a war and that there was an external enemy. And so we realized that we had to sacrifice certain liberties for the duration of the conflict. I ask him, therefore, would he not agree that some such measures might have to be adopted if we recognize that we are faced with an internal war or with the threat from international terrorism?

The other point concerns the CIA. I think we met on the lift or elevator, and Mr. Barrett asked me, why hadn't I mentioned the CIA? Well, a lot of people have mentioned the CIA since then. The CIA has been destroyed in its operational capacity over the past few years by a tremendous smear campaign, by the irresponsibility of the media and the U.S. Congress. And it grieves me to say this.

Now the question is, can we do without the CIA in the kind of situation which confronts us? And if we haven't got the CIA what are we going to put in its place?

David Barrett: I don't offer the Royal Canadian Mounted Police, but by reputation they might be acceptable. First of all, there is the situation of a state that declares war. Secondly, over-reaction by a state to an incident, which then calls that a declaration of war, is more of a peril to that state itself; it shows a fragility of the state.

As to the CIA. I meant the self-destruction of the CIA, not by the media, the self-destruction at the Bay of Pigs, and other activities. For me, as a liberal free democrat, these extensions of state authority to a governmental agency to make decisions of action and preemptive strikes constitute a loss of liberty. Cooperation of intelligence, yes, certainly sharing intelligence . . . we would be mad not to. But to allow the delegation of the state's authority to a state agency is what I am opposed to, and I hope that I have made that very clear.

I once read an editorial in a newspaper when we had a serious problem of juvenile delinquency. The editorial said, "Let's do something. . . for God's sake anything." I don't subscribe to that way of thinking. I don't know the answer, but I'm not going to jump to the easiest, emotionally-impacted answer. I don't know the answer. I confess that. I live in a peaceful milieu and I can understand emotional responses to the situation. But I also have learned in my many years of working in prisons — I worked in prisons locking up people every night — that the simplistic answer from a distance about jails doesn't alter human behavior. It takes time, it takes thought. Teller's statement, I thought, was really brilliant: "It is not the exclusive talent of terrorists to be imaginative."

Let's be imaginative. I don't know what the answers are, but it is certainly not an immediate emotional response. We are dealing with each other as the family of man. I still have that hope. I don't think we're dealing with the complete loss of the potential of developing the family of man on the face of this earth. Perhaps it is too idealistic. It almost borders on being religious. Especially here in Jerusalem.

Professor Mordecai Abir: Mr. Barrett must feel here like Daniel, I think. May I say it is a pleasure to listen to him. But one thing confuses me, that is, I think something is confused in his theory.

There is a very obvious difference between the various forms of crime which he mentioned; for instance, the criminal negligence of the automakers or the perversion of the state's intent which can be accomplished by different agencies, and real terrorism. The former is illegal according to the law and can be taken to the highest authority of the land. We must distinguish this from a state or organization whose *official* ideology gives it the right to use terror against a civilian population, terror which is *not* against their law. Just read the Palestine National Covenant.

Robert Moss: First of all, Iran is a sign of the treason to itself of a large section of the media. I'll explain what I mean, because governments can't respond properly to a problem which is misrepresented. Remember all those articles about corruption and repression under the Shah that appeared for two years or so before he was thrown out? These had a decisive effect in isolating him from Western sympathy and depriving him of the support he should have got. And remember all the reports that arose when some Western correspondents were pushed around by the Shah's troops, about how brutal the Shah's regime really was, and all the bad prophecies being fulfilled.

Now I don't object to those complaints. But since the revolution, we know, leading journalists in Iran have been murdered on the orders of these so-called Islamic tribunals. I haven't seen any great display of liberal concern over this. And this worries me deeply. I think that the image that we are being presented of Iran to this day is still a one-sided and softened image. Iran is as close to a terrorist state as any of those we have been discussing. Its order to hunt down the Shah has been quoted earlier. I might mention that there are similar provisions in Soviet law for the hunting down and execution of Soviet citizens living abroad who commit "crimes" against the Soviet State. But that's a side issue.

So in my view, anything and everything that civilized countries can do to bring about a return of reasonable government in Iran is justified morally and sensible in practical terms, because we can't really have anything worse than the current setup in Iran today. I think that we should seriously consider whether any moderate forces have a chance of resurgence, given the revulsion of a large part of the Iranian people against their new masters and their foreign PLO secret police. And if such opportunities exist we should support them. Now that would be a genuine *liberation* movement.

Chairman (Gideon Rafael): I wish to thank the members of the panel for their tolerant presentation of an intolerable challenge, and the thoughtful and responsible way in which they covered such a wide range of problems. If I were to summarize them in a single sentence, I would say that the speeches both alerted us to the threat which an international network of well-organized terrorism poses to democratic society, and cautioned our societies not to destroy what they want to protect. I am sure that we will have that in mind in the continuation of our discussion tomorrow and in any conclusions at which we may arrive.

Paul Johnson addressing the Conference at the Opening Session. Seated right to left: Hugh Fraser, Senator Jackson, Shimon Peres, Prof. B. Netanyahu, Prime Minister Begin.

Fourth Session
Subject:
CURRENT RESPONSE OF DEMOCRATIC STATES
Morning, July 4, 1979
Chairman: Ambassador Asher Ben-Natan

PREFACE

How have the democracies responded to the challenge posed by international terrorism? Many speakers felt that to date Western societies have simply not met the challenge. Some countries yield at once to terrorist blackmail, freeing or deporting terrorists to welcoming countries out of fear of further incidents. The result has been more incidents, plotted and executed with impunity. The most deplorable development has been the permission granted by governments to avowedly terrorist organizations to open offices in, or send their official propagandists on missions to, democratic countries.

Meanwhile, the democracies wait for international forums to take action, but the total helplessness of the United Nations has been amply demonstrated by the history of its still paralyzed anti-terrorist legislation. Many of its member states, after all, themselves subscribe to the political use of terror, or have been manipulated and bullied by the Soviet and Arab blocs into so doing.

Nationally, the responses of individual countries to terrorism vary. Along with vigorous police and judicial measures in some countries, there are disturbing examples of pusillanimous behavior on the part of others, among them even some that are not directly faced with a problem of terrorism. The economic power of the Arab states and the political strength of the Soviet bloc both frighten some governments into a posture of capitulation or, at least, of refusing to face the problem squarely.

Noting that the "aim of terrorism is to terrify", participants stressed that the adoption of a new, aggressive posture would make it easier "not to be terrified." This would include the rebuilding of national intelligence networks and the sharing of information between the democracies. It would include diplomacy designed to forge an anti-terror alliance, capable of imposing economic and political sanctions on those countries which support terrorism. Finally, it would require in each of the democracies a body of enlightened citizens capable of serving as a nucleus for constant pressure on the respective governments *not* to yield to terrorists, or to tolerate sovereign states supporting terrorist crimes.

ASHER BEN NATAN was Israel's
Ambassador to France (1970-1975) and
Germany (1965-1970). Prior to that he
served in various capacities with the
Ministries of Foreign Affairs and Defense,
including six years as Director-General of
the Ministry of Defense. He is the author of
Dialogue with Germans (1974) and *Letters
to an Ambassador* (1973).

CHAIRMAN'S OPENING REMARKS

Members of the panel, ladies and gentlemen, we shall discuss
today the current response of democratic societies to international terrorism. Does submission to terrorism continue?
Are terrorists still released after having committed their outrageous acts?

When I spent 10 years as Israel's ambassador to Germany
and France, I had the opportunity to observe the ways of
terrorism and subversion at a ringside seat. By being a direct
object of terrorism, I also gained some personal experience. I
had the distinct honor to be very high up on Carlos' list which
was found after he murdered three French policemen. This
shooting down of the three unarmed policemen in France was
a very hard lesson for the French authorities who until that
day had treated the terrorists with, I would say, rather special
consideration.

The question is not only what to do with terrorists after
they are caught; the question is how to prevent terrorism in
the first place.

There was a time when certain governments preferred to
leave terrorist organizations alone as long as they did not
operate on their territory. That means that in certain countries,
there were people who were organizing, conspiring, and preparing acts of terrorism, and because their targets were not in
those countries but in another country, they were given a

certain freedom. Some governments thought that if their own policy toward Arab countries was favorable they might be spared terrorist acts. This was a fallacy — each realized finally that no one is immune.

This was the first lesson. Now, there was a second lesson: To combat terrorism effectively, you have to have the public with you. It is not just a battle between the government and a terrorist organization.

The more you have the public on your side, the better you are able to combat terrorism, and the less you must be worried about the freedom of maneuver so necessary if terrorism is to be effectively combated.

Much has been said about the threat to democratic societies by measures taken to combat terrorism, that such measures might disrupt the way of life and endanger the democratic system itself.

We haven't yet witnessed one democratic country whose political system has really been altered. I don't think that this has happened anywhere yet. We do have examples of democratic countries which, for a certain time, had to impose certain measures, without having demonstrated that this had any effect on the development of democratic life in those countries.

If it had not been so, Israel should have long ago ceased to be a democracy. We have lived with terrorism for 30 years. We have an open society. We have a democracy where everybody can say what they want — freedom of speech, freedom of expression. On Israel Radio and Television, you can defend the idea of a PLO state, and this is being done not only by Arabs but also by Jews. If you live in Gaza or Judea or Samaria, you can voice your opinion. There are Arab newspapers here which say whatever they want, criticize the government and support the PLO. And still this is a country where measures are being taken against terrorism, because if not, our life would be completely impossible.

I wanted to make this remark because this matter of constraints on a democratic system is, of course, something which is of concern to everybody.

Now, if today a terrorist knows that he can kill, and that he will be released, this is of course an open invitation. If there are no political consequences, if no steps are taken against the countries from which terrorists come and from which they obtain their weapons, and where they seek refuge after committing acts of murder, then it will be very difficult to combat terrorism. But though progress has been made in the last few years, at least as far as collaboration between the various police and intelligence organizations is concerned, it is not yet sufficient. I believe if there had been more such collaboration, terrorist acts would have become much more difficult to perpetrate than they are today.

But how can you combat terrorism if you permit in certain countries representatives of an organization which openly supports such terrorism? I am referring to the PLO. Some argue that by permitting the PLO in these countries, the PLO will no longer attack targets outside of the Middle East. Is that a reason for considering it an acceptable organization? If they say they are only killing people in Israel, murdering women and children, and throwing bombs indiscriminately, is that not terrorism? Is this acceptable? Because this is what is happening today.

There have been attacks of sabotage and terrorism committed here, claimed, organized and defended by the PLO, but the PLO can operate today freely in various countries. Their delegates can go and speak and defend their policy, and Arafat, with a gun on his hip, can speak at the United Nations. I think this is one of the worst developments that could have been expected. It poses grave questions for the current response of our democracies to terrorism.

JOOP DEN UYL was Prime Minister
of The Netherlands from 1973 to 1977.
From 1967 to the present, he has been
the Chairman of the Dutch Labor Party.
Earlier he served as Minister of Economic Affairs (1965-1966) and as
editor of the weekly *Vrij Nederland*
(1945-1948).

THE DUTCH RESPONSE

Mr. Chairman, ladies and gentlemen. I think that the best thing
I can do is to tell something of my experience in combatting
terrorism and of the conclusions we might draw from that
experience. I would like to be as factual as possible.

As you all know, the Netherlands has been faced with
much terrorist violence during the 1970s. As Prime Minister
during that time, I had to cope with six major acts of violence,
the taking of hostages in my country, and with four cases
of hijacking of Dutch civil aircraft.

In those years the Dutch government developed a
certain strategy of dealing with terrorist acts. The essence of
this strategy, as I see it, could be formulated thus: The duty of
governments is to save the lives of captured innocent people,
without giving in on any essential point to the terrorists. It
is also our duty to prove that terrorist crimes do not pay.

In my view, the essence of the problem with which we
are dealing in this conference is, just how can we prove that
terrorist crime does not pay? In some ways I think I differ
from opinions that have been formulated during the last
two days of this conference, and that will become clear.

Though I do not think that what we achieved in Holland
in the fight against terrorism is anything to be particularly
proud of, I do think that, compared with some other countries, we did not do badly. We developed certain rules and

procedures which I think have some meaning in dealing
with the question: How can democratic societies combat
terrorism effectively and continue to be democratic societies?

Dutch Measures Against Terrorism

May I illustrate this by referring to the well-known terrorist acts of the South Moluccans in the Netherlands.
These are 35,000 people who came to Holland in the
years 1949-50, after Indonesia became independent.
This population had a unique relationship to the Dutch
colonial government. In Holland they were longing to go
back to the islands from which they came. They founded
the Republic of the South Moluccans in Holland, and they
sought to persuade international opinion and the Dutch
government to intervene in the affairs of the Republic
of Indonesia to get their own state established. The essence
of the problem of the South Moluccans is their longing to
have a.state of their own.

At the end of the 60s and the beginning of the 70s, they
proceeded to violent action. In 1970 they attacked the Indonesian Embsssy and took the Indonesian Ambassador as a
hostage for one day. In 1974 they captured a train with
about 50 people for a few days and they attacked the Indonesian consulate in Amsterdam. In 1977 they again
captured a train and took hostages in a school in the same
area.

I do not want at this moment to describe the actions
and counteractions of the government at that time; it is well
known that the last act of the terrorists in 1977 ended with
an act of the Dutch government in which six of the terrorists
and two innocent hostages were killed.

How would you characterize the behavior of the Dutch
government? How did Dutch society respond to terrorist
acts?

First, there has been a growing conviction and a growing
consensus in government, parliament, and among the people,
that one should not give in to the demands of terrorists.

When I say that, it is stated very simply. In practice, it does not exclude, in my opinion, negotiations with terrorists on minor points just to save the lives of the hostages. That demands a great deal of inventiveness and patience on the part of the government.

During all those years, I found that patience and willingness have paid off in a very fruitful way. We have negotiated on minor points just to save the lives of hostages. And I think that in dealing with terrorists and with terrorist acts, any democratic, humane government is obliged to try to save those lives, and the situation is one in which it has to choose between the devil of giving in to the demands of the terrorists and the deep sea of having lost the lives of innocent people.

We have succeeded in having terrorists surrender. We have brought them to trial; we have given them a fair but severe trial; and they have been sentenced, where killing was involved, to fifty years in jail. But, at the same time, we have set up committees to study the problem. I don't know if I still am permitted to use the words, "the social roots" — the concept is under attack, I have understood — but we have committees to study the social roots of this type of terrorism of the South Moluccans.

We have tried to demonstrate to the public and to the group involved, the South Moluccans, how cruel terrorist acts are, precisely because they hurt innocent people, and how counter-productive they are, how illogical and how stupid.

I wish to emphasize that terrorist action, until now, has proved to be counterproductive. It is our duty to demonstrate and to show that terrorists cannot force a democratic government to be swayed from its own policies. That should be the way to respond to terrorism.

Effectiveness of Current Democratic Measures
Against Terrorism
Now, of course, we have done what we should have done. We have improved the arsenal of the police; we have established a special unit to combat terrorists; and we have

improved our intelligence as much as possible. We have not felt it necessary to introduce special legislation. After thinking it over, our conclusion was that we did not need it, that anything that could be done should be done under the law as we had it.

I know that in other countries they have tried to pass new legislation, and I won't condemn any type of new legislation, but it is my conviction and my experience that, at least in a democratic society like the Netherlands, we did not need this to be effective in our combat against terrorists.

I think I differ somewhat from Ambassador Herzog's remark that what has been done up to now in the international field in the fight against terrorism has not been impressive.

There have been a series of conferences and measures taken in the international field. A year ago at the Bonn Summit the heads of state of the United States, France, Japan, West Germany, Italy and the United Kingdom agreed that their governments would immediately stop all flights to any country that refuses to extradite or prosecute hijackers, or does not return the hijacked aircraft. Measures of that kind, I think, are very helpful, and we need them.

Another example is the Convention on the Suppression of Terrorism that has been passed by the European Council which is of great importance. I want to take issue with the idea that the international world has done nothing against terrorism. That's not true. I don't say we did enough, but I want to say — and I draw on my experience of several years during the 1970s — that European countries have been willing to cooperate to find the best and the most effective method to fight terrorism.

You might argue that until now the number of acts of violence against civilians has not decreased, but I think you should put the question the other way around. You should ask, what advantage until now have terrorist groups taken from their actions? I think we have just begun on the right way and we should continue to prove that terrorist actions are counterproductive.

Terrorism as an Expression of
Nationalist Aspirations

Many speakers make a link between terrorist actions and Communist Soviet policies, Soviet support of terrorist groups, Soviet training and inspiration of those groups and the Soviet Union's taking advantage of terrorists to disturb democratic societies. I won't deny everything in this field, but I think we have to be very careful.

It has been stated here that Libya under Qaddafi is one of the countries supporting the South Moluccans. To the best of my knowledge, I would say that that is incorrect information. I know that the South Moluccans have tried to get some country in Africa to represent their demands in the international field. They have never proceeded very far in this scheme.

But the situation becomes even more complicated. The South Moluccans' claim to an independent state, to the Republic of South Molucca on the present territory of the state of Indonesia, has been supported for decades by right-wing parties and groups in the Netherlands. Nationalist claims to found independent states have very often been supported, in the past and in the present, by right-wing parties who could not be suspected of being Communist-influenced or Soviet-inspired.

For instance, one example that concerns us all in Europe is the growth of Basque terrorism in the northern part of Spain. You may link it to Soviet policies, but I think this is not true. The fact is that we have to do here with a nationalist tradition, and we may observe a growth of nationalist tendencies, a longing to have independent states, for groups all over Europe. We have had this phenomenon for the last few years, and mostly these groups have been inspired and supported by right-wing factions and right-wing political parties.

I think you should be very careful to link what we call the problems of the Fourth World with any type of Soviet policies. All those national minorities exist. There is no more dangerous policy for the Soviet Union than supporting those minorities that are longing to have independent states of their own. There are some hundreds of those minorities on the territory of the Soviet Union today. I question the suggestion that is generally mentioned, that we have one monolithic Soviet policy of having some hundred terrorist groups, inspiring them to the one purpose of undermining Western democracy. This is against the terrorist tradition (for terrorist action has a deep and long tradition in Europe) of anarchism. We all know that the battle between anarchism and Soviet-Communism has destroyed anarchism.

I ask the audience not to generalize easily in drawing conclusions about what we have to do, of what is really on our agenda: how to effectively combat terrorist action.

I do not agree at all with Mr. Moss on the conspiracy of silence about the role of the Soviet Union. We should, as democratic parties, peoples and governments be very alert about anything that happens in the Soviet area in regard to terrorist action. But I am speaking again of my experience. If not all we know about what has been done by Communist countries has been revealed, that may also be due to the fact that we want to keep quiet about what we are doing in the field of intelligence. Not everything can be open in democratic societies, and that is particularly true of acts and operations of our own intelligence services. I think we should be very careful in using a phrase such as "a conspiracy of silence."

I won't go into details, but I was very much irritated when the example was given of some training camp for the anarchist MIR Movement in Chile which has opposed the Pinochet regime and has spoken about actions undertaken in that period, as we all know, by the CIA and some of those intelligence services to which we are committed. Precisely for that reason I don't want to pass in silence over those actions and those operations.

I am very much aware that some remarks make for healthy debate. We have this conference as an example.

Democratic Societies Should Not Be Terrified By Terrorism

I would like to summarize what I think should be the response of democratic societies to threats of terrorism. Let me repeat. The first thing we should do is to stress again and again the cruelty of terrorist actions which hurt innocent people. Organizations which systematically conduct actions against innocent people should be strongly condemned, and their actions viewed as crimes against humanity. No doubt about it. That is the first thing to say. The second thing to say is that the real threat of terrorism is that it could upset our democratic system.

It might disrupt our societies by causing us to infringe on civil liberties or to resort to unnecessary measures of response. We should respond as democrats carrying out all the time the very difficult process of weighing, for instance, the lives of hostages against the demands of terrorists. That is an inevitable, unavoidable process we have to engage in. We should not be terrified. There was one sentence in the speech by Mr. Moss with which I agreed very much. This was when he referred to Lenin, who said that the purpose of terrorism is to terrify. He said we should not let ourselves be terrified.

There is the essence of the answer of democratic societies. What the terrorists try to do is to bring terror and fear, to disturb our order of life. They want us to doubt the very foundations of our society. If we are firm in our responsibilities and policies, and committed to carrying them out, if we don't allow ourselves to be terrified by the attempts of the terrorists, then terrorism will be shown to be counterproductive and it will decrease. That is my true conviction.

I don't say that we don't need better cooperation between police forces and that we don't need better agreements on how to deal with plane hijacking. But our fundamental answer is that the democratic societies, which are said to be most susceptible to terrorist action, have the power and the ability not to be terrified. And it is that we should stick to.

ANNIE KRIEGEL is Professor of Sociology
at the University of Paris at Nanterre. She
specializes in the history, sociology and
development of European labor movements.
Member of the editorial board of the French
newspaper *Le Figaro*, Professor Kriegel
is also the author of several books on
Socialism and Communism, including
*Les Grands Procés dans les Systemes Com-
munistes, Un Autre Communisme?* and
other works.

PUBLIC OPINION, INTELLECTUALS AND TERRORISM
IN WESTERN EUROPE

What is the public view in the democracies of Western Europe
and particularly the opinion of its intellectuals, on terrorism?
This opinion is characterized by a large degree of uncertainty,
perplexity, confusion — in short, by a wait-and-see policy, a
kind of fence-sitting. It cannot be said that it resolutely
disapproves and condemns terrorism in its various manifestations, or that it is openly satisfied with it, celebrates
it, or finds great virtue in it. There is on the whole an uneasy
silence, meaningful enough to those who know how much
these intellectuals love to give vent noisily to their opinions.

One could observe this relative silence on the part of intellectuals during two recent events which attracted the attention of French public opinion: The appearance of Corsican
terrorists before the State Court of Security, and the threats
which Basque terrorists have begun to put into practice towards
French tourists in Spain. This silence is analogous to that
which one might also have observed in the course of the terrorist incidents which have burdened or still burden France's
four great neighboring democracies, and which one designates
by the name of the terrorist organization — Baader-Meinhof
in Germany, the Red Brigades in Italy, ETA in Spain, IRA in
Ireland and England.

From what sources does this perplexity derive? Its first source is the *uncertainty about the extent of what is meant by terrorism.* Within the wide range which includes all non-institutionalized violence, from the private vendetta to guerrilla warfare, what should be admitted as relevant to terrorism — and to terrorism alone? Are openly revolutionary movements which aim explicitly at the subversion of existing regimes to be put in the same category with nationalist movements which aim at obtaining either internal autonomy or independence for a region, an ethnic group, a nationality, a people? In the first category, that of the revolutionary movements of the extreme left or right, is it necessary to condemn uniformly all groups — those who, like the Montoneros of Argentina, the Sandinistas of Nicaragua, and even the Fedayeen of Iran, fight for very doubtful objectives but who at least fight against regimes whose democratic character is dubious or nonexistent; and those who, like Baader-Meinhof, the Japanese Red Army, or the Red Brigades in Italy, attack regimes which are indisputably democratic?

Then again, can one be unaware that the autonomist and separatist movements no longer seek to establish states whose political systems would subsequently be defined by universal suffrage, but to set up Third World-style states whose "anti-imperialist" character (that is to say, "socialist" in both its internal structure and in its international posture) is proudly affirmed ahead of time? This means that in the event that they succeed in their aims, they will follow a path remote from the model of democracy.

The Varieties of Terrorism and
Its Anti-Western Character

The confused phenomena which fall under the rubric of modern terrorism are so various that all distinctions introduced to make clear the specific nature of each concrete case are legitimate. These distinctions, however, can only be made with the understanding that all manifestations of terrorism, whatever the particular aims, constitute in themselves a global system whose spearhead is directed against Western democracy. It is essential to supply a normally skeptical public with more detailed information as to the way in which this international system is articulated. It is not sufficient to bring out the technical and material links in the terrorist chain: that they have common suppliers of arms and money, that they have virtually identical infrastructures for selecting and training recruits, and so on. Nor is it sufficient simply to be *aware* of this international system. While it is not necessary to accept the hypothesis of a world-wide plot with one clandestine orchestrator, it is appropriate to pick out the means of exchange of ideas and experience, and still more, the local and regional centers of leadership which, through intermediaries, contribute to the process of unification of this terrorist system. The system itself spreads in the manner of a cancer through the human organism.

The second source of the perplexity is the *uncertainty regarding the degree of significance and seriousness of the terrorist scourge.* Uncertain as to what should properly be called terrorism, Western Europe's intellectuals are also uncertain about terrorism's capacity to destroy the social order. First, they call attention to the fact that the intrinsic capacity of terrorism varies, depending on whether we are talking about homegrown exploders of streetlamps and suchlike, or the kind of highly sophisticated terrorism, such as the future nuclear terrorists, who would undoubtedly attach themselves to the auxiliary operations of the special services of a terrorist state.

Next the intellectuals argue that one cannot take as equivalents the endemic and petty local terrorism which has become part of the folklore of so many Mediterranean societies of the client or clan type (e.g. Sicily, Sardinia, Corsica) and the quite different phenomenon of terrorism, conceived of as the primary, elementary force of a movement which will act as a detonator, leading first to guerrilla, and then to open warfare.

The intellectuals again draw attention to the fact that not all societies have the same degree of resistance to the terrorist temptation. For example, there is a category of regions in Europe which in the remote or recent past have missed their transformation from nationality to nation, and still more their transformation from nation to nation-state. These regions (such as Croatia, Slovakia, Flanders, Brittany, the Basque region, and Northern Ireland) which often share the characteristics of decentralization, ruralism, a Catholic Church which kept out other influences, and a backwardness in industrial or cultural development, are the seat of a sort of nationalist melancholy which, either through financial collapse or the Marxist mutation of the indigenous Catholic clergy, has given birth to and maintains a chronic terrorism.

Varieties of Resistance to Terrorism

Not all societies have the same degree of resistance to terrorism, nor do all of them have the same degree of tolerance for it. So it is that Italy (or rather its central government) which has never succeeded in truly subduing the lower echelons of political life and still less the diverse components of civil society, presents a remarkable capacity for resistance. On the other hand, Spain very early realized that the unity of the regions depended on the strength and authority of the central government, and is far less tolerant of, and less resistant to, terrorist assaults on it.

Nor do societies possess the same degree of resistance to or tolerance for terrorism at each moment in their histories. The deep economic crisis in which Europe now finds itself is an additional factor which can play decisively upon the effectiveness of terrorism: for Europe is in a state of least resistance or least tolerance compared to its previous period of great prosperity. In the same way, Basque terrorism has without a doubt profited from the particular historic stage of a Spain just emerged from Francoism and started on a fragile democratic path.

Thus, the importance and the seriousness of the effects of the terrorist scourge depend on a number of variables connected both to the particular society and to the historic moment in that society. It is this which explains the ambiguous position of Communist intellectuals towards terrorism.

Communist Attitudes Towards Terrorism

Leninism, it is true, condemns and repudiates the use of terrorism as an essential arm in the revolutionary struggle. This
general censure depends on circumstantial reasons peculiar to
the history of Russian Communism. There are also fundamental theoretical reasons: the ideas the Communists have developed of the necessary relationship between the Party, the
working classes, the masses and the revolution. Thus, the
Communist parties of Western Europe do not miss a chance
to recall these positions which in principle are hostile to terrorism. One may read, for example, in a recent issue of *New
Times* (put out by the Soviet Ministry of Foreign Affairs) an
authorized study in which terrorism is once again denounced
and condemned. Whatever the circumstances, the Communists
cannot forget that they must conduct a permanent struggle of
education and propaganda against the distortions and deviations of anarchists, leftists and ultra-leftists which constitute a
constant threat to Leninism.

This being said, the concrete attitude of each Communist
Party toward terrorist episodes in its own country is much less
clear, more blurred, more supple and often defined after the
fact. Thus, it was that in the affair of Aldo Moro, the Italian
Communist Party was in the lead of those demanding that the
government resist all dealings with and yielding to terrorist
blackmail. The Italian Communists discovered their "real
vocation" — that of assuming the mantle of defending the
constitutional government, after having spent the previous ten
years deliberately trying to weaken it. On the other hand, the
French Communist Party, whose Jacobin steadfastness is well-
known, tends to assume positions which are more and more
shaded and quasi-"objectivist" toward terrorists. *L'Humanité*,
for example, discussed the recent trial of a Corsican terrorist
in a neutral tone quite different from their usual preemptory
voice expressing approval or rejection.

Prerequisite for Fighting Terrorism

The third source of perplexity is the *uncertainty as to a remedy*. It is in seeking remedies that the propensity of intellectuals

to play tricks with reality is revealed. As uncertain about the nature and limits of terrorism as they are about its significance — in short, about both the diagnosis and the prognosis — they are naturally uncertain about the proper remedy against terrorism. Since they have not the slightest intention of taking real responsibility for evil, they find it comfortable to devote themselves to observation and denunciation of the possible excesses of any repression. This is a shrewd position because in the end, for these sort of people, all repression is excessive.

It is true that the proper response to indiscriminate terrorism is not indiscriminate repression. The necessary countermeasures — such as the dismantlement of terrorist cells, the arrest, trial and sentencing of terrorists — must all be carried out in such a way so that they not appear to be the unique and exclusive weapon in the arsenal of the democracies.

All such countermeasures must be accompanied by a concerted intellectual attack bearing on the totality of the issues likely to supply the terrorists with a semblance of legitimacy and rationality. But this concerted effort should be conducted not with the terrorists, but with the general public. To believe, as the French government wrongly did for some time, that the delay in the development of Corsica could be the subject of negotiation, not with the Corsicans elected by universal suffrage, but with the clandestine representatives of the separatist terrorist movement, proved itself to be counterproductive. Democracy is weakened when it is not respected, and when men who refuse to submit to the electorate (or when they do submit, receive a pitiful handful of votes) are dealt with as interlocutors. When, as in Corsica, electoral democracy is imperfect, it should be improved rather than pushed aside for the benefit of what is in essence anti-democratic.

Difficulties in Suppression of Terrorism

All anti-terrorist suppression presents particular difficulties about which one should be forewarned. The first difficulty is that to be most effective such suppression should be exercised very early, before the terrorist machinery has attained a high degree of stability. This very necessity raises the problem that such measures then appear to public opinion as excessive, because they seem to strike at offences which are still not terribly threatening. The difficulty is that the repression of terrorism arouses in young people a certain opposition. These young people, whose moral sense is obliterated by a kind of unidimensional fanaticism, do, however, appear more thoughtful and mature when discussing the great affairs of humanity. That is the reason why one must not, when facing such people, leave the terrain of facts, illegal or criminal. It is terrorism as a criminal act and not as the expression of an opinion which is the object of social repression.

The third difficulty is that the repression of terrorism implies that terrorism be denied its external sanctuaries, which entails an internationalization of and consequently a coordination among the policies of governments whose preoccupations are not always of the same nature and the same extent, as could be observed in the Basque case.

Intellectuals and the Fight Against Terrorism

Intellectuals in general have the greatest difficulty in conceiving and admitting these conditions and these limitations to effective repression. Thus French intellectuals thought they must harshly denounce the still-localized repression conducted successfully in Germany by the Social Democratic government against the leaders of the Baader-Meinhof gang. To accusations of terrorism they countered with accusations of torture. They tried to insinuate questions of human rights and rights of defendants (as with the affair of the lawyer Croissant, whose complicity with the terrorists had been conclusively established). In the same way, French intellectuals insisted (by a sort of diseased professional solidarity) on deciding in advance that the Italian Antonio Negri could not possibly have made the leap from an academic theory about the legitimacy of terrorism to its practice. Yet such a question of guilt or innocence is not to be decided *a priori*, but only by the evidence.

Nevertheless, one must note the attenuation of the allergy to repression of terrorism. To encourage this development we must clear up these three sources of confusion on which the intellectuals feed. After the Japanese example, the German example proves that terrorism is not invincible and that the struggle against terrorism, far from reinforcing the threat of a resurgence of fascism, constitutes a major element in the reinforcement of democracy.

FRANK CLUSKEY has been the leader of
Ireland's Labour Party since 1977. He began
his political career in 1954 when he was
elected an official of the Trade Union. He
later served on the Dublin City Council and
in 1965 was elected to the National Parliament. In 1968 Mr. Cluskey held the
position of Lord Mayor of his native Dublin.
Between 1973-1977 he served as Parliamentary Secretary.

THE IRISH RESPONSE

For ten years now, Ireland has suffered from the violence and
counter-violence of a situation in which terrorism has become
a terrible reality. In Northern Ireland, but also in the Republic,
those ten years have seen thousands of violent deaths, serious
injury and maiming, much destruction of property, kidnapping, intimidation, and the deflection of political attention
from constructive areas of activity into the unhappy sphere of
security and anti-terrorist legislation.

This is not the place, and I certainly do not have the time
available, to attempt an explanation of all the historical, soci-
ological, economic and political causes of the violence which
continues to afflict my country. Indeed, the widely varying
interpretation of those causes remains a major part of the Irish
problem. Suffice it to say that throughout this century violence has played a significant part in our history, from the
armed struggle against Britain in the 1916-1921 period;
through the tragic Civil War of the early 1920s; to the periodic
outbreaks of so-called republican violence of a terrorist nature
which took place in the 1930s, 1940s, 1950s, and which have
continued now for the whole decade since 1969.

The current situation had its roots in the peaceful
Northern Ireland Civil Rights campaign of the mid-1960s
which met with a repressive and violent response from the
authorities in that part of the island. Violence escalated from

sporadic clashes between police and local groups caught up in the changing political balances of Northern Ireland to a terrible pattern of concerted terrorist action and counter-action involving the Provisional I.R.A., their Protestant or Loyalist counterparts, a whole range of sectarian murder gangs and the security forces. The violence spilled over into the Republic and has been seen there over the decade in the form of illegal paramilitary activity, assassinations, kidnappings, bank robberies, jailbreaks and so on. The whole island has been affected by this unhappy experience.

The Irish People's Attitude

There are, and there remain, great political issues in Ireland which require lasting solutions. Of that there can be no doubt. Generations of injustice, neglect and bad administration in the North and of nationalist rhetoric coupled with political indifference in the South have created fertile ground for those who seek political ends by violent means. It is the task and the very serious responsibility of all democratic political forces in Ireland to continue to seek the solutions which are required. There is no place whatsoever in this process for the men of violence. I want to make it clear, at the outset, that violence for political ends is rejected by the overwhelming majority of the Irish people. The activities of the Provisional IRA and of their counterparts are regarded with horror, anger and shame by almost every Irish man and woman. Even among those of strong republican or loyalist feeling there is recognition that the evil of terrorist violence is destructive of so much that is good and essential in society.

My party, the Labour Party, is quite unequivocal in its stand on this matter. Since the foundation of the Irish Free State, Labour has stood for peaceful and democratic political action and against all use of violence or coercion. Labour took no part in the Civil War of the early 1920s and this fact has militated against the political interest of the party in the intervening fifty years. Over the years we have condemned all those who would seek political solutions by force. In the past decade, Labour politicians have given clear and unambiguous leadership against all the men of violence and against the lying myths and specious arguments which they use to justify their evil actions.

The Labour Party condemns utterly the activities of all terrorist groups in Ireland. Their campaigns of assassination and sectarian killing are incapable of justification by any argument, however twisted. The use of terror as a means to attain any political goal is repugnant and unacceptable to us. Whoever does it, and for whatever cause, we cannot and will not condone the actions of any group in any part of the world which places bombs in cinemas, shops or buses. We condemn those who kill women and children and innocent civilians. We abhor political kidnapping and hijacking. We oppose the terror of reprisal. All of these things, which are so characteristic of the modern world, are calculated to destroy rather than to build. They tend always, because they are inherently wrong, to debase the cause for which they are pursued. We will have no part of such evil.

In the context of Irish political life this stand is not necessarily politically wise. There are many who, while they dislike the actions of our particular brand of terrorist, still retain a sneaking sympathy for their causes. These people do not like the IRA or similar groups to be too harshly condemned or criticized. We have not maintained a prudent silence and we have suffered somewhat for that. But to remain silent would be to condone what is wrong and we cannot do that.

Irish Terrorism Versus the Irish State

Terrorism in Ireland has posed a direct threat to the institutions of our state. In the Republic, the men of violence have made it clear that their targets are not confined to the situation across the border. If they were, that fact would in no way alter the wrongness of what they are doing. But, as a matter of history, these people have rejected with total arrogance the very constitution of the Irish state and have set themselves up as a force quite prepared to oppose in arms the legitimate government of Ireland.

Such a situation is clearly intolerable and it has been necessary for the Irish government to take serious and, at times unpalatable, steps to deal with it. The past ten years has been a period in which the terrorist threat, and the overspill of the total Northern Ireland scene, have dominated our political and economic life to a most unhappy degree. Much political energy has been diverted to the essentially sterile area of counter-terrorism. Economic progress has been damaged, with the tourist industry above all suffering grave setbacks. Resources have been diverted to the areas of policing and security — in 1968/69 our total spending under these headings was £23 million while in the current year it will amount to £208 million.

A number of major political, legislative and administrative steps have had to be taken to deal with the existing threat of paramilitary activity. I shall refer briefly to these.

Anti-Terrorist Measures

Strong action against illegal paramilitary groups has been taken under the terms of the Offences Against the State Act of 1939 which was originally introduced at a time of internal terrorist activity and obvious external threat. Membership of certain organizations has been proscribed and many IRA activists and others who belong to illegal bodies have been arrested, tried and jailed. A special non-jury Criminal Court was established in 1972 to deal with serious offences of a paramilitary nature in connection with which a serious history of intimidation of witnesses had been experienced. This Court is presided over by three civilian judges who decide on the cases brought before them after nominal criminal court proceedings.

The Offences Against the State (Amendment) Act of 1972 extended police powers to deal with terrorist activity and, specifically, adjusted the rules of evidence to permit the introduction of police evidence as to membership of illegal bodies. Suspected persons must rebut such evidence and this move has secured many convictions in cases where the accused could not, because of the discipline of the illegal body, deny the evidence presented.

Also in 1972 the Prisons Act was passed which permitted prisoners to be held in military custody where this was considered necessary. This legislation has been extended in force by subsequent Acts of 1974 and 1977. The immediate cause of this law was a prison riot by subversive elements which necessitated the transfer of prisoners from the main civilian prison in Dublin.

In 1976 the situation reached a particularly serious stage. In both parts of the island a number of outrages occurred which caused widespread public anger and concern. In the Republic the assassination, by bomb, of the British Ambassador and the prolonged kidnapping ordeal of a prominent businessman necessitated a firm response.

Under the terms of the Criminal Law (Jurisdiction) Act of 1976 the criminal law of the Republic was extended, so far as concerns certain serious offences, to things done in Northern Ireland. The offences in question include most of the most serious against persons and property and they have become extra-territorial offences. Thus a person may stand trial in the Republic for an alleged offence committed in the North. A similar Act has been passed by the British Parliament. This approach, which has in fact been scarcely used in practice, was introduced to deal with a situation arising from the provisions of the Irish Constitution under which extradition is not possible in any case where the alleged offence is deemed to be of a political nature.

The Criminal Law Act of 1976 further extended the criminal law provisions dealing with Terrorism and the powers of enforcement and investigation. The maximum penalties for certain offences (in particular, offences under the Offences Against the State Act, 1939) were increased. Certain new offences were created in respect of recruiting for or incitement to join unlawful organizations; of aiding, facilitating or arranging escapes from lawful custody; and of giving false information (e.g., bomb hoaxes). The Garda Siochana were given new or increased powers of search, including power to search vehicles stopped during investigation of certain offences. Members of the Permanent Defence Force, when acting in connection with the investigation of similar offences in response to a specific request by the Garda Siochana for assistance, were given powers of arrest and search and powers to stop vehicles similar to the powers of the Garda Siochana.

Following the killing of the British Ambassador in July 1976, the Irish Parliament declared a State of Emergency. Within the context of that declaration the Emergency Powers Act, 1976 was passed. The Act empowered the police to arrest without warrant and hold in custody for up to seven days persons suspected in connection with offences under the Offences Against the State Act, 1939 or offences that are scheduled offences for the purposes of Part V of that Act. These powers remained in force for a year and then lapsed. The Act itself will remain in force when Parliament resolves that the state of emergency has ceased to exist.

This long history of legislation and administrative procedure underlines the gravity of the situation as viewed by the political leadership in Ireland. The threat to our democracy from the men of violence is still great and it must be resisted by all the resources of the state. This approach has the support of all the main political parties even though there may be some differences on one or other of all the detailed aspects of law or procedure. The state must be protected, the Constitution upheld, and the recourse to violence firmly rejected.

Principles that Must be Guarded

But in all of this there is a real dilemma for those who are committed to the defence and advance of freedom and democracy. Wide-ranging anti-terrorist legislation involving new and sweeping powers for the police, the army and the courts must give rise to problems within a state which deeply values the freedom and liberty of the individual and the traditional role of law. It must remain a constant preoccupation of politicians that the balance between necessary legal response to terrorism and fundamental freedoms and rights should be maintained.

In a situation of subversion and terrorism the security forces are placed in a very difficult and sensitive position, open to many forms of pressure and intimidation, under physical threat, and subject to close surveillance. We have had to deal with serious charges against members of the security forces, alleging ill treatment of suspects, and the findings of a recent Committee of Enquiry into necessary safeguards for persons held in custody are still at the center of political debate in Ireland.

Here it is only possible to state certain principles.

First, the fundamental human and civil rights guaranteed by the Constitution must be upheld whatever the provocation. Society cannot allow itself to abrogate these rights and guarantees in the belief that they can be restored at some future time. To do so is to surrender something very precious to the men of violence.

Second, where strong measures must be taken to defend the rights of the people as a whole these must be matched with corresponding — and equally visible — safeguards and review procedures. No effort — and no expense — must be spared in ensuring that the fundamental values in our society are maintained and in no way compromised.

Third, the role of a strong and independent judiciary is central to the balanced approach that is needed. In the Courts lies the basic guarantee of personal and group rights and the ultimate defense of the interests of all. In Ireland the Supreme Court has played a crucial role over the past few years in defense of the nation's true interest.

If these principles are honored, democracy and freedom can prevail. To do less would be to give the terrorist his greatest victory. The structures of democracy and justice are strong and they can demand, and hold the loyalty of, the overwhelming majority of the people. It must be the constant concern of all democratic politicians to work to strengthen those structures and to show the men of violence that they are sound against whatever they may do. I believe that we have succeeded in Ireland over the past ten years in maintaining and advancing our democratic system and I am certain that, insofar as we continue on that path, the terrorists and subversives can have no hope of success.

JACK KEMP has been a member of the
United States House of Representatives
from the 38th Congressional District of
New York since 1970. He is a leading
figure in the Republican Party, and a
spokesman on political and economic
matters. Congressman Kemp is a member
of the House Appropriations Committee
and the Subcommittees on Defense and
Foreign Operations, and has been an active
Congressional delegate to the SALT
negotiations.

THE UNSEEN HAND

I am honored and challenged to address the Jonathan Institute's Conference on International Terrorism on this, the Fourth of July.

Today marks the third anniversary of the raid on Entebbe and the rescue of innocent civilians from the hands of terrorists. At the same time we memorialize and honor the heroism of "Yoni" Netanyahu, who commanded the rescue and lost his life in doing so. For every lover of freedom in the world, Yoni and Entebbe symbolize the will to resist terrorist compulsion.

This occasion is doubly significant for me, because today also marks the 203rd anniversary of my country's independence. There will be a great show of outward celebration at home today. But in quieter moments, Americans will observe the day with the same sober reflection which we give to Yoni and Entebbe.

No American today will grab his Uzi when the firecrackers explode, nor will the rockets bursting overhead be aimed by terrorists. We in America enjoy a safety secured by the sacrifices of our ancestors who, like Yoni, often paid for freedom with a price as high as life itself. Why did they do it? Why do the sons and daughters of Israel risk the same sacrifice today? Because they know that while the price of freedom is high — it is never so high as the loss of freedom itself.

The State of Israel is to the world today what the United States may have seemed 170 or 180 years ago: a city on the hill, a place where it was important to protect, defend and display the light of freedom, even if you never made it personally to the citadel. Our anniversary at home will flicker and dim unless we who enjoy the rewards of independence and freedom can also help our friends and allies in Israel to pay its price.

This year marks the thirty-first year of the rebirth of Israel. The rallying cry of that state was "never again." Never again would the Jewish people be left without a homeland. There is, however, another anniversary. This year marks the 41st anniversary of Munich, when Hitler cried to the western world, "All I want is the Sudetenland," and the western world said "Yes."

This year, the cry is, "Just give us the West Bank." Next year, terrorists will then say, "Just give us Israel." Our rallying cry must also be "Never again."

I am encouraged to participate in a conference not only with figures directly involved in the eradication of terrorism from the international community, but also with my colleagues in Congress who have been in the forefront of formulating an American policy that may contribute to the fight against international terrorism.

I know this conference can stimulate our best efforts to take concrete steps to stop international terrorism before it consumes the democratic societies that are its natural enemies, and I would hope that next year it can be held again in the U.S.A.

The Terrorist International

Terrorism itself is not new. What is new about it is its transnational character — the internationalization of what Brian Crozier has called "motivated violence for political ends."

The internationalization of terrorism has many immediate causes. Vast improvements in transportation allow terrorists to move swiftly and anonymously from nation to nation without fear of detection. The diffusion of modern military technology has simplified the process of inflicting destruction of an unprecedented scale, and modern communication eases the international coordination of terrorist activities and the dissemination of its "message." Other factors are also important to the growth of transnational terrorism, but are incidental to explaining why terrorism has become a major threat to the security of every non-communist nation of the world.

Many views of international terrorism in the Western world have tended to be myopic, identifying only the most immediate motives for a local terrorist incident and overlooking deeper causes which usually originate outside the national jurisdiction in which the incident occurs. A more thorough examination of international terrorism can help us identify the common elements which have made it the menace it has become.

International terrorists, contrary to their image, are not usually the warped, demented individuals so often portrayed in the news media. They are highly motivated ideologically. They are almost uniformly to the far left politically, unlike strictly local terrorists who reflect every shade of ideology and opinion.

International terrorists are well-financed, able to move throughout the world with changing identities and forged documents, and they have safe places in many nations to hide from pursuers. They are well trained in organization, frequently proficient in the use of small arms and explosives, competent with modern communication equipment, and particularly well informed about the vulnerabilities of their local adversaries.

The Ultimate Source

I am pleased to see an emerging consensus as to the ultimate source of international terrorist support in an overwhelming number of cases — the Soviet Union.

I am convinced it is crucial to our discussions and to our successful common effort to combat terrorism that we recognize — at the outset — the central role that the largely unseen hand of the Soviet Union has played and continues to play in both the direct and indirect use of terrorism in many parts of the world.

The United States and allied nations in Western Europe have been engaged in a decade-long effort to improve relations with the Soviet Union. We have signed a variety of agreements with the Soviet Union in the name of diminishing tensions and reducing the possibility of violent conflict between the two nations. Lofty declarations of principle have been drafted with the Soviet leadership relating to non-interference between nations in the expectation that this would diminish international Soviet adventurism that could place American security at risk.

But an examination of the Soviet role in promoting international terrorism casts grave doubt on the assumptions about Soviet policy upon which American, and Western, policy toward the Soviet Union is based, particularly those policies which relate to SALT, Helsinki and Detente itself. The Soviet Union, in fact, has a central role in training, equipping, transporting and protecting the most important international terrorists and terrorist organizations in the world. Although the initiative for individual terrorist acts rests with the terrorists themselves, the Soviet effort has been supported and sustained for "Political Ends."

The Soviet Union promotes international terrorism because it stands to gain from terrorist success. The Brazilian theorist of terrorism, Carlos Marighela, has described the purpose of terrorism as to "make life unbearable" for ordinary people, to create a "climate of collapse" in the target regime. This favors the ends of both the terrorists and their Soviet mentors. The Soviet interest lies with disruption, disorientation, and chaos (as in Iran, for example), as often as it lies in outright takeover (as in the cases of Afghanistan, Angola, and Ethiopia). Thus, we face the prospect of continuing to seek formal improvements in relations with the Soviet Union while the Soviets continue to support a covert terrorist effort aimed ultimately at Western democracies.

Trainings, Arms and Proxies
This dangerous predicament of the West has been elaborated

upon by Professor Richard Pipes, Robert Moss, Brian Crozier, Dr. Ray Cline, Senator Henry Jackson and others. The international department of the central committee of the communist party of the Soviet Union has established two training schools for foreign terrorists. The first, the Lenin Institute, trains the hard-core Marxist-Leninist cadres, while the second, the Patrice Lumumba University in Moscow for communist-oriented students, trains terrorists primarily from the developing world. Several hundred foreign nationals are trained each year at several sites within the Soviet Union. Additional training takes place in North Korea and Cuba. In addition, terrorist training is done in Libya, PLO camps in Lebanon, East Germany, Czechoslovakia, and other East European nations. Many of the terrorists active in West Germany and Italy were trained with KGB assistance at PLO training camps in Lebanon. Terrorists in Northern Ireland have been assisted by Omnipol, an element of the Czech Intelligence Service controlled by the KGB.

The Cuban Intelligence Service, the DGI, has been under the command of a Soviet KGB major-general since 1968. Cuba is now becoming the major Soviet link with the international terrorist movement. The Cuban DGI, which has the major role in support of international terrorist activities on behalf of the Soviet government, has sent its representatives to virtually every area of the developing world. Representatives of the Cuban training establishment have been sent to PLO camps in Lebanon to assist terrorists of Popular Front for the Liberation of Palestine. In late April of this year, an agreement was made by the PFLP to have several hundred terrorists trained in Cuba, following a meeting between Habash and Cuban officials.

PLO terrorists are also being trained under KGB supervision in Hungary and Bulgaria. A vast arsenal intended for use by terrorists is being built up by the Soviet Union in Libya. Equipment sufficient for five Soviet motorized rifle divisions has been stockpiled in Libya ready to support large-scale guerrilla operations. It can be shipped to Zambia and Mozambique as well as used to support the more modest requirements of small terrorist organizations in West Europe, Africa, and the

Western hemisphere. Indeed, Qaddafi sponsored a conference in Benghazi earlier this year which included a large number of Latin American terrorist organizations with PLO elements. Among the results of the conference is an effort to support the Sandinistas in Nicaragua via Cuba and Panama, and pressuring Brazil to permit the opening of a PLO office in Brazil — moves likely to be precursors to the spread of transnational terrorism to the Western hemisphere. Nowhere is the hand of the Soviet Union directly in sight. Libya, Cuba and East European states are the only nations directly involved. The Soviet Union, the ultimate source of weapons, logistic support, intelligence collection, transportation of terrorists, and related matters, is not routinely identified, neither by Western governments and the press, nor — incredibly — by the U.S. State Department. In sixteen pages of testimony before the U.S. Congress, there was not one word of mention of the Soviet role.

The Soviet Union's extensive involvement in international terrorism is a fact few Western governments will acknowledge in public. It is also a fact that no Western government can afford to ignore. Until Western governments face the difficult problem posed by covert Soviet support for international terrorism, many well-intentioned international efforts to control terrorism will be doomed to failure.

Soviet policy has never been more deceitful than on the subject of international terrorism. Soviet propaganda criticizes PLO terrorist incidents, while the Soviet Union provides the weapons, intelligence, and training to the PLO and splinter organizations. Soviet propaganda criticizes West European terrorists, but provides a safe haven for fleeing terrorists in East Berlin and Czechoslovakia.

The Necessary Effort

From the perspective of organization and strategy, the American response to terrorism has on the whole been useful, even though it so far has failed to address the fact of Soviet participation in the support of international terrorist activities. Within the logic imposed by responding only to the symptoms of terrorist violence, the strategy has succeeded in reducing the attractiveness of directing terrorist incidents against the U.S. government. Nevertheless, in the 3,000 terrorist incidents which have taken place since 1970, at least 25 percent of the 5,000 wounded and 2,000 killed have been American nationals.

More than 30 U.S. government agencies have a role in dealing with the terrorist threat, and, organizationally, their efforts have been coordinated in a manner which effectively supports the U.S. policy of offering no concessions to terrorists. While this posture has undoubtedly led to some loss of life, it has saved far more than it lost. The wisdom of this is shown by the experience of every other nation which has adopted this posture.

There has been an unfortunate divergence between the practices of public and private American institutions in responding to terrorist assaults. Too frequently, U.S. corporations operating abroad capitulate to terrorist extortion. Naturally, this is done to save the life of a kidnapping victim or to protect property from destruction by terrorists. But it comes as no surprise to learn that U.S. corporations abroad have become prime targets for terrorism. As a consequence, tens of millions of dollars extorted from corporations have gone into the coffers of terrorist organizations, financing still further attacks on U.S. commercial interests abroad. The United States is not alone in this problem. This points to a conspicuous shortcoming in the response of most Western governments to terrorism, including the United States. Most of the attention in coping with the terrorist threat has gone into protecting governments from intimidation by terrorists — a necessary first step in meeting the threat. However, it is not sufficient simply to protect governments from terrorist threats if private citizens and property are to become easy victims of extortion, kidnapping, sabotage and other acts of violence by terrorist organizations. There is little to be gained if governments manage to free themselves of terrorist intimidation only to preside over a wasteland in which no private citizen or business firm is safe from terrorist attack.

One hopeful dimension of the American response to terrorism is the attempt to develop international controls

over terrorism. The most notable success to date has been
with the problem of aerial hijacking. Yet hijacking is only
a small part of the terrorist menace. Even if this problem
were solved by international agreement, it would not address
the most dangerous types of terrorist incidents we are likely
to see in the coming decade as a result of the profligate Soviet
policy of distributing shoulder-launched anti-aircraft missiles,
sophisticated mines and advanced high explosives. The international effort is not likely to yield the results we hope for
unless some means are identified to induce the Soviet Union
to cease its support for international terrorism. It will otherwise be possible for the Soviet Union to sign every international convention dealing with the suppression of terrorism and
yet continue to aid and abet the international terrorist movement on a worldwide basis.

A bill recently introduced into the Congress would require the U.S. government to terminate military and economic
assistance to any nation which the President determines has
demonstrated a pattern of support for acts of international
terrorism. Although this legislation might affect the behavior
of some nations, some of the worst offenders in supporting
international terrorism — Cuba, Libya, North Korea, and the
PLO — do not receive any U.S. assistance, and hence such
legislation would have little effect in diminishing terrorist
activity. But the Soviet Union receives food, technology,
credit, and is even now requesting Most Favored Nation status
for trade.

What is required is a determined effort by the nations
most affected by terrorism — the U.S., West Germany, Britain,
France, Israel, and others — to take more direct, and where
desirable, joint action against the Soviet Union and its conduits for terrorism.

Israel has shown the way in attacking terrorist organizations at their centers of operation. This reflects a great determination at the highest levels of government, combined with a
well-organized and responsible intelligence establishment, to
deal effectively with terrorist organizations.

Similar coordination is also called for from a diplomatic

perspective. Greater efforts must be made to deny known representatives of terrorist organizations the undisturbed freedom to travel in western nations. I regret to say that Western democracies, including the United States, unwittingly support international terrorism in special ways. In my country, as well as in many of the European countries represented here, some P.L.O. members and officials are allowed undeterred entry into the country and unchallenged access to the communications networks free societies cherish. Not too long ago, the U.S. State Department permitted the entry of Shafik el-Hout, the director of the P.L.O.'s Beirut office. He was granted permission to ply his trade, to travel to several campuses and to propagandize freely.

But Shafik el-Hout was not the first and only P.L.O. terrorist to pollute our atmosphere. Barely two miles from the White House sits the P.L.O.'s propaganda arm, the Palestine Information Office, allowed the legitimacy of open and full operations by the U.S. State Department.

I am persuaded that it would be in the interests of all nations affected by terrorism to make a vigorous effort to deny access to known terrorists or representatives of such organizations.

In addition, it would be useful if nations threatened by terrorism would refrain from diplomatic initiatives that lend international status and prestige to terrorist organizations. By affording organizations like the P.L.O. and other terrorist organizations which claim de facto "government" status the slightest gesture of recognition, they merely help establish the legitimacy of terrorism as a means of gaining political ends.

International terrorism must be understood in the form it has taken, namely a transnational weapon, primarily sponsored by the Soviet Union to achieve its political ends. Some years hence, the Soviet Union may be displaced by another nation as the principal sponsor of terrorist organizations. The basic issue remains: International terrorism must be made an illegitimate means of conflict and this can only be accomplished if the intended victims are prepared to take the steps necessary to deny international terrorists the objectives they seek.

PIERO LUIGI VIGNA is one of Italy's
leading jurists and is currently the District
Attorney of the Republic of Florence.
Mr. Vigna is a member of the Institute of
International Relations in Rome. His
most recent books are *Crime vs. Public
Property* (1973), *The Law on Public Order*
(1975), and *Arms, Ammunitions and
Explosives* (1977).

ITALIAN RESPONSES

Ladies and gentlemen. Allow me first of all to thank the
Jonathan Institute for the honor of being invited to this
important conference. It *is* necessary for democratic countries
to develop common guidelines and methods for meeting the
challenge of the terrorist phenomenon which threatens to
jeopardize the very foundation of their existence, namely,
democracy itself. My perspective is not that of a scholar, but
of a practicing District Attorney in Florence. I am convinced
that democracy has a right and a duty to defend itself by the
most effective means possible against the violent actions that
threaten to destroy it. I shall make here some remarks taking
the Italian situation as my point of reference.

Terror Groups in Italy

Allow me first to describe in a cursory way the situation in
Italy, where terrorism has recently met with some serious
defeats.

- In Italy there exists terrorism of the extreme right and of
  the extreme left. The latter is, at present, the most active.
- Both these groups of terrorists aim at provoking an
  authoritarian transformation of the State.
- However, while this is the final aim of the extreme right
  terrorism, the extreme left aims, instead, at provoking the

revolution through the authoritarian involution of the democratic state.

- Extreme leftist terrorists include, in addition to the Red Brigades, about another 150 groups.
- The Red Brigades have a clandestine structure, a rigid military one, inspired by Marxist-Leninist principles. The other groups are more fluid and have various ideologies based on "social needs." They have a "philosophy" that is similar to that of the American Weathermen.
- There are proven international connections among terrorist groups of the same political camp, and occasionally even of opposing camps. Here are a few examples drawn from my personal experience:

    — Judge Occorsio was killed in Rome in 1976 by a group of the extreme right, with an automatic Ingram gun, which had been sold to the Madrid police, a city where some extreme rightist activists were taking refuge.

    — The Palestinian Arab terrorist movements have established contacts with Italian groups of the extreme right.

    — Mario Tuti, an extreme right terrorist, who killed two policemen near Florence in 1975 and who had carried out sabotage operations against the railway system, wrote in his diary that he had received aid from Libya.

    — Judge Coco, Judge Palma, and the Honorable Aldo Moro, who were murdered by the extreme left terrorists of the Red Brigades, were all killed with Skorpion automatic guns of Soviet make. The Red Brigades are conclusively linked with the Rote Arme Fraktion.

    — Last year, a terrorist of the extreme left, arrested near Florence, had on him a map with directions to reach a Lebanese training camp near Baalbek, Lebanon.

All this gives some idea of the gravity and nature of the problem.

Essential Measures

I am convinced that the winning hand in the struggle against terrorism should not be — at least in Italy — judicial repression.

The struggle against terrorism will succeed, in the end, to the extent to which all of the citizens of the State understand the necessity for it and take part in it. At times, one hears voiced in Italy a mental attitude of neutrality: "Neither with the Red Brigades nor with the State." This attitude is a cowardly one. It is necessary for each citizen to participate in the life of democracy, to feel part of the state. Only thus can we overcome the present danger. One attempt in our country has involved the distribution of questionnaires among the population and talks in schools and factories about the problem of terrorism. Let me summarize some of the defensive measures that I deem appropriate:

First, preventive actions should concern, above all, communication among the states involved, and the exchange of all information useful for the prevention of terrorist crime. Data pertaining to the various terrorist organizations, their members, their *modus operandi*, and so on, should be centralized. Other speakers have referred to the necessity of good intelligence work; speaking as a practicing prosecuting attorney, I reaffirm this necessity.

Secondly, measures should be taken to insure that after crimes have taken place the criminal will remain in the territory of the state where he is active until such time as penal procedures to deal with him have been instituted in that state, or extradition procedures shall have been started. I need not specify those unfortunate examples where such criminals have *not* been held.

Thirdly, where there is no extradition, states must have the obligation to submit the case against a criminal to the appropriate authorities in that state. This is extremely important in order to force the perpetrator of a terrorist crime to submit to legal procedures even if he cannot be extradited. This is the only applicable principle until a distinction is made between political crime and terrorist crime. As to the former, the constitutions of many states contain provisions forbidding extradition for so-called "political" crimes (in Italy, this is in article 10 of the Constitution).

Fourth, the most comprehensive and rapid judicial assistance should be offered among states, with direct contact among police authorities and judicial institutions of the states involved. These should, in my opinion, be allowed to carry out directly in other states the necessary legal procedures in accordance with the laws of the states and with the possible participation of its institutions. Within this framework I include reciprocal communication of any element of evidence available to either state.

The Basis for an International Agreement

Having outlined these measures which I deem essential to international cooperation against terrorism, I should note that two basic approaches are possible in this fight. The first is to develop a single, joint instrument with which to deal on an international level with the phenomenon as a whole. A second approach is to consider a variety of possible agreements among states, each dealing with one or more terrorist criminal activities. It would appear that the latter system is most easily translated into practice, for it is far easier to reach an agreement between states concerning individual criminal activities than to reach one on the general subject of terrorism, which at once carries with it political considerations which inhibit agreement.

Reaching an agreement will be easier when it involves regional associations sharing certain ideological, political, and cultural affinities. The best example, I believe, is the European Convention for the Suppression of Terrorism, which was developed in the context of the Council of Europe, and adopted in Strasbourg on January 27, 1977 by almost all the countries of the European community. This is the first concrete attempt at carrying out an international cooperative effort in this sector. As the title and preamble make clear, while the convention aims at controlling the entire problem of terrorism, it in fact adopts the case system.

Let me refer to some specific articles of that European convention. Article 2 contains provisions against all "serious acts of violence" directed against life, personal safety, or personal freedom, as well as any other "serious acts against property" which endanger persons. One cannot, you may see, extract from this a unifying concept of a "terrorist act" and the convention lacks any reference to the aims of such criminal activities. However, the operating framework of this convention deserves some attention. Among the instruments it favors for the suppression of terrorist crimes, it gives first place to extradition. For the purposes of extradition, the states making the agreement undertake not to consider as political crimes those described in article 5. The agreement does say, however, that when extradition is requested, a state of whom it is asked *can* refuse it when it has well-founded reasons for believing that it was requested for reasons of race, religion, nationality, or political opinion (or when these reasons make the position of the accused more difficult). Article 13 establishes that the states have the right to deny extradition on the grounds of the political nature of the criminal act, provided that they have taken into account the seriousness of the crime, the extent that it creates a common danger, the degree to which its victims are extraneous to the reasons inspiring the criminal act, and the extent that cruel and evil means were used.

Article 7 specifies that barring extradition, the initiation of penal procedures must take place not only *sans retard injustifie*, but also *sans aucune exception*, so that the political character of the crime may not be an obstacle to punishment. Article 8 establishes the principle that judicial assistance must be to the fullest degree, and not refused simply because a political crime is involved.

I believe (though with some reservations, because the terrorist phenomenon has not yet been dealt with on a global level) that the Strasbourg Convention is a good first concrete instrument to fight terrorist crimes. I hope I shall be forgiven the technical details of my analysis: I am a working prosecutor, and naturally such matters assume a great importance in my daily work; I offer this by way of my own perspective.

BAYARD RUSTIN is the President of the
A. Philip Randolph Institute. A founder of
the Congress On Racial Equality (CORE),
Mr. Rustin was a political adviser to Martin
Luther King and an organizer of the 1963
March on Washington. He has worked with
independence movements in Ghana, Nigeria,
Tanzania and Kenya. Mr. Rustin writes
frequently for *Commentary* and other
American magazines.

DEMOCRACY AND TERRORISM

Ladies and gentlemen. When I was invited here I felt extremely honored to come to this gathering sponsored by the Institute named after Jonathan Netanyahu. I am certain that for years and years to come, perhaps even a thousand years from now, when people are confused and frightened and when they are dispossessed of their humanity and feel that there is no way to go except to face death and destruction, someone will remember the story of Jonathan at Entebbe. That story will be told to those despairing people and someone will move into a corner and begin to whisper, and that will be the beginning of their liberation. It is for this reason that I am extremely happy to be here.

Our search here is into what response democratic societies can make to the problem of international terrorism. We are restricting our discussion to the response of *democratic* societies because terrorism poses no problem for totalitarian societies. Whatever problems such societies have, terrorism is not one of them. If anything, they are the sponsors of terrorism, not its victims — sponsors within their own societies as well as elsewhere. Indeed, our evaluation of terrorism should begin with the understanding that it is a problem only for societies that are open or partially open.

This conclusion is supported by statistical studies of terrorism, which show that terrorist incidents are most common in democratic nations, least common in totalitarian regimes, and of intermediate frequency in countries that may be described as authoritarian or partly free (it is in the authoritarian countries, however, that official terrorism is most lethal). It would be wrong to suggest that the degree of individual and political liberty is the only variable which determines how much terrorism there is in a particular country. Many other factors contribute to terrorism, including the perception of grievance, regardless of whether such grievance is real, and foreign state support for terrorists. Still, except in a free society, it is exceedingly difficult for terrorists to function. Walter Laqueur has stated the problem well: "If the terrorist is the fish — following Mao-Tse-Tung's parable — the permissiveness and the inefficiency of liberal society is the water." Conversely, where state terror is total, terrorism cannot exist.

But, can democratic societies prevent terrorism? We democrats know that when a terrorist event occurs, our societies do have means to punish the terrorists. But often we are faced with the problem of reprisals against innocents and therefore are reluctant to follow the full course of the law; or we feel constrained to allow convicted terrorists to escape their punishment because of threats of future terrorism.

All this is sad, but it is even sadder that we see no viable means of actually preventing terrorist acts from taking place at all.

Problems of Democracies in Fighting Terrorism

How, then, are democracies to protect themselves against terrorism? For three years the Tupamaros ravaged Uruguay. In the end the terrorists were defeated because the state declared total war against them and gave the army and the police the powers they wanted to wage this war. The consequence was the destruction of one of Latin America's model democracies. The revolutionary Régis Debray cheered on the Tupamaros, but he was subsequently forced to admit that "by digging the grave of liberal Uruguay, they dug their own grave."

The problem then is how to defeat terrorism without abandoning democracy.

I would not go so far as to say that democracies cannot defend themselves against terrorism. But we should not delude ourselves by thinking that there is no price to be paid. If we are to be effective in preventing terrorism, part of the price will be an increase in the surveillance powers of government security agencies. Few societies will be willing to pay this price without realizing the dangers involved. Even then, can such powers of surveillance be circumscribed, so that democratic institutions are to be preserved?

The capacity of a society to protect itself while preserving democratic procedures depends largely on the attitude that is adopted toward both terrorism and democracy. If terrorism is seen simply as an extreme means to attain just ends, I am afraid that all efforts to defeat it will be neutralized. In effect, terrorists would be accepted as part of the civilized world, which they are not. Their grievances would be recognized as legitimate, when in fact this is entirely beside the point. The only relevant issue is terrorism, which must be branded as barbaric irrespective of motives and objectives. Otherwise terrorists will profit from the division and confusion of public opinion.

For what we must grasp, quite clearly, is that terrorism begets terrorism — that the means become the ends, that victories for terrorists do not lead to peaceful adjudication of disputes but rather to increased terrorism. For regardless of the goals the terrorists profess to seek, whether honestly or not, terrorism will become the ends as well as the means. For they will come to rely on it as their source of power. I cannot emphasize strongly enough that the accumulation of means determines the ends.

Legitimation of Terrorist Violence

Terrorism is but a symptom of a much deeper problem, which is the newly revived role of ideology as a legitimation of violence. We live in an age when the most awful crimes are committed in the name of justice. So, it simply isn't enough to condemn the crime. We must also expose the source.

The Cambodian communists murdered two million people in the name of liberation.

The Vietnamese communists are in the process of expelling onto the high seas, in unseaworthy crafts, hundreds of thousands of innocent people. Many hundreds or thousands of people may die in the next month, and this is done in the name of socialism.

The P.L.O. kills Jewish children in the name of opposing racism, while the Patriotic Front of Zimbabwe threatens to kill those who vote in a democratic election as part of its struggle for "Majority Rule."

This is all surely madness, but it has insinuated itself into the heart of political cultures of many democracies. I find it in my own country. Thus, a distinguished American linguist argues that we should not criticize the Cambodian communists, for this might help the cause of reaction. Hundreds of so-called progressive Americans openly attack an appeal for human rights in Vietnam, and one of them announces that he does not believe in publicly criticizing so-called "socialist" countries.

A top official of the P.L.O. is granted a visa to the U.S. and is allowed to tour American campuses because he is not considered by the State Department to be a terrorist. And the U.S. Ambassador to the United Nations declares that the Soviet-armed terrorists seeking to overthrow the black majority government of Zimbabwe-Rhodesia have much in common with the American Civil Rights movement, presumably including the practice of nonviolence.

The root of this evil in the modern world is not the terror committed by the individual or the terror committed by the state. It is that this terror is committed in the name of ideology, that terrorists become "freedom fighters," "liberators," "defenders of the dispossessed." Here we have the big lie, the lie that allows the justification of inhumanity, the lie that tempts some people to seek to transform society at a stroke, no matter what the cost in lives and freedom, the lie that permits the fellow travellers of revolutionary violence to pose as the friends of freedom and to sleep with a clear conscience, all at the expense of the dispossessed.

The Common Outlook of Terrorism and Totalitarianism

This is also the lie which unites terrorists with totalitarian rulers, above all with those who rule in the Soviet Union. It is rather easy to document that terrorists are trained and armed by totalitarian regimes. It is more significant, I feel, to understand the source of their common outlook. Both believe that society can be transformed through force, and that the state is the agent that will remold not only society but the individual personality as well. But a society transformed by force is inevitably totalitarian. The terrorist is the totalitarian before state power is seized.

The terrorist is not opposed to injustice. On the contrary, he is opposed to a social order in which individuals have fundamental rights which must be respected, and in which the conflicting freedoms of different individuals must be constantly negotiated and compromised. He is not impatient with democracy — he stands against the democratic process itself. He seeks to exploit the democratic process in order to destroy it, to profit from the indulgence of democracy toward its opponents and from the hunger of the press for exciting copy. He appeals to justice in order to impose injustice, and depends on the sympathy arising from his professed ends to conceal the cruelty of his means.

We can appeal time and again to democratic nations to resist terrorism, but these appeals will fall on deaf ears as long as the terrorists and their supporters are conceded any moral credibility. We must fight not just terrorism but the moral double standard according to which some acts of terrorism are condemned while others are defended. There is no progressive terrorism and reactionary terrorism. There is only terrorism. There are no left concentration camps and right concentration camps, just as there are no left tortures and right tortures. There is inhumanity, and the most dangerous form of in-

humanity is that which presumes to liberate humanity against
its wishes.

Democracy's Crisis of Spirit and its
Response to Terrorism

Does this take us far afield from the problem at hand? I don't
think so. Terrorism is a manifestation of a disease that has
gripped democratic societies. The disease is not that there is
real poverty and injustice, which terrorists use as a pretext for
their acts of violence. The disease is a crisis of spirit, a loss of
belief in democracy as the essential framework for the achievement of justice. Too many in the West no longer believe in
democracy as a political order morally superior to totalitarianism.

Let me tell you about the current response to terrorism
of my own country. I do not take the view that the leaders of
the Western world, and, above all, the leaders in Washington,
need to be educated. The fact of the matter is that they understand the problem perfectly. What we are faced with is fear, a
double standard resulting from the present economic blackmail, the threat of future terror, conflicting national interests
and the incorrect ordering of national priorities. This means
that all too often the question of terrorism is, like many other
priorities, at the bottom.

There is confusion in the United States precisely because
we are attempting to have talks with the Soviet Union. There
is confusion in the United States precisely because we are
negotiating SALT II. There is confusion because of economic
considerations and because of trade agreements and because of
oil and because of military bases. We are concerned, when we
face the problem of human rights and terror, with the political
problem of what other people are going to do. When a top
PLO official is permitted into the United States to propagandize for terror, when the Patriotic Front of Rhodesia is
considered to be worthier of American support than the democratically elected government of Bishop Muzorewa, when the
World Council of Churches donates one-and-a-half million

dollars to people who practice violence as a way of life, then of course you know there is a problem, a very grave problem.

And the problem is that in the West too many have been too ready to embrace a moral relativism which denies that there is good and evil and that freedom is the most precious thing that any human being can have. They are overcome by guilt and are willingly shamed into silence by any demagogue who happens to have read Lenin's thesis on imperialism or who invokes the authority of Mao or Che or Arafat.

Democracy Alone Offers Hope to Mankind

Given all that, still it is only democracy which offers any hope for mankind. And it is not only people who possess freedom who appreciate it and want it. On the contrary, the Vietnamese refugee has a deeper appreciation of freedom than the intellectual radical of the West who has read all of the latest works on liberation. We should heed the message of these boat people from Vietnam, which is that freedom must be cherished and defended when it is under attack. Nor is this Southeast Asian love of freedom unique. India, Spain and Portugal have given us evidence of that. As long as this fundamental principle does not inform our values, our words, and our policies, we will not be able to fight terrorism with the spirit, confidence and decisiveness that democracy needs if it is to survive. The problems presented by terrorism will not be solved by treaties, laws, courts, constitutional or technical devices. It is a fundamental threat to the spirit of mankind and will be resolved only in that arena.

In the final analysis, indeed, it is only democracy that can defeat both terrorism and totalitarianism. For if and when the people really understand and exercise their freedom and are willing to defend it for its preciousness and uniqueness, then the sea in which terrorists swim will dry up and they will no longer have the power to coerce those who refuse to be helpless. That is the way to defeat terrorism — through vibrant democracy.

GEORGE WILL is a Pulitzer Prize-winning
columnist whose articles appear in
Newsweek, The Washington Post and
more than 300 other newspapers in the
United States. His book, *The Pursuit of
Happiness and Other Sobering Thoughts,*
was published recently to great acclaim.

CALCULATING THE PUBLIC INTEREST

The hero (it says much about current distempers that we use
that word awkwardly; let us use it unselfconsciously when, as
here, it fits) whose legacy includes the Jonathan Institute per-
formed his final service to his nation at the moment when the
United States was celebrating its Bicentennial. Israel's demonstration of resoluteness was a service to all democracies. Unfortunately, Israel's resoluteness regarding terrorism is not typical
of the spirit of all democracies. The current response of
democratic societies to terrorism is characterized, to a dismay-
ing degree, by a failure of intelligence, in two senses.

Whatever else terrorism involves, it always involves the
element of surprise. Thus the principal weapon against it is
advance knowledge. Such knowledge is the business of intelligence services. They should inform not only the public safety
organizations of their societies, but also the institutions, public
and private, responsible for shaping public opinion. Certainly
in the United States, intelligence services are not performing
adequately. Indeed, in the United States the reduction of the
competence of intelligence services has become a political
objective of important factions.

Furthermore, the democracies are suffering from a failure
of intelligence in the form of moral disarmament. This is a
product of bad sociology and bad philosophy feeding on each
other. From the false idea that extreme actions must have

obvious causes in the social environment, it is but a short intellectual stagger to the equally false idea that such acts are justified. This is not an occasion for dissecting this argument. Suffice it to say that, for those interested in fighting terrorism, the salient truth is this: The direct causes of terrorism are terrorists, and the indirect causes are regimes that actively support or passively tolerate terrorism.

Clearing the Confusion

But perhaps the principal obstacle to effective action against terrorism is confusion in the minds of the democratic societies that are the targets of terrorism. In these societies, intelligence is being bewitched by language. Terrorists are *not* generally "desperate men." Many are, in fact, children of privilege. They are perhaps privileged psychopaths, but they are privileged nonetheless. Terrorism, we should not flinch from noting, can be fun. "The act of terrorism," wrote Malraux in *Man's Fate*, "is very often a potent instrument of self-expression, rather than just a means toward some political end."

Terrorist acts are not "senseless." Terrorism is (in the argot of the day) "cost-effective." Or, to borrow the language of the stock exchange, terrorism is "highly leveraged." This is in part, because of instant and mass communication. Many years ago, a Chinese thinker said, "Kill one, frighten 10,000." A modern student of terrorism has rightly said that in the television age, the axiom might be, "Kill one, frighten 10 million." It is also true that terrorism is "efficient" in the sense that sporadic terrorism can make necessary the constant deployment of enormous amounts of defensive material and energies. Furthermore, terrorism is efficient because one of its aims is to spread anxiety, and modern societies, which are especially susceptible to disruptions, are especially vulnerable to anxieties. The fact that terrorism is efficient may account for the fact that terrorism is less vigorously rationalized than it used to be. Prior to the middle of the 20th century, terrorism was heavily ideological. It needed rationalizing ideas because there was little "justifying" evidence of its practicality. Today with literate publics living in "wired nations," print and broadcast

journalism change the terrorist's environment, terrorists still
carry baggage, but their ideological efforts are perfunctory.
Terrorism is obviously "justified" by its magnified effects. The
media are the magnifiers, and the subject of the next panel.

Perhaps the primary reason for the inadequate response
of the democracies to terrorism is this: The democracies have
not cleared their minds of cant about "social reforms" to
"eliminate the social causes" of "senseless acts" by "desperate
men". This clearing will take time. But it is not enough for the
democracies (in Arthur Koestler's words) to "play for time
and pray for time." The clock is ticking; the democracies
should be acting. They know, or should know, that actions can
be effective.

An Aggressive Campaign Against Terror

There must be no ransom. No negotiations. And I reluctantly
have come to the conclusion that capital punishment for
terrorism is rational. Any judgment about capital punishment must, in the end, be grounded in evidence. It is an empi-
rical question whether capital punishment deters. And it seems
reasonable to assume that no other punishment can have a
deterrent effect on people who can always hope that, if captured, they will be ransomed by terrorist activities undertaken
by their colleagues.

Every nation needs to prepare for the option of using
force, at home and abroad. The Entebbe operation demonstrated the usefulness of a policy of "hot pursuit." And "hot
pursuit" should be used pre-emptively as Israel uses it in
southern Lebanon. Terrorists and the nations that harbor them
must be made aware that there are no sanctuaries. There may
be prudential reasons for not attacking terrorist training camps
in South Yemen; there are no moral or legal reasons for not
doing so. The potential usefulness of covert operations is, I
trust, obvious, as is their potential legitimacy.

The effective campaign against airline hijacking has involved strong security measures to complicate the hijacker's
task; strong punishments to deter him; and the threat of strong

international sanctions against nations that cooperate with hijackers. It is surely not beyond the wit of man to devise other combinations of protective and reactive measures.

The Costs of Inaction

The democracies' responses to terrorism are tentative and selective. This is, in large measure, because of the demoralizing effect of the myth of détente, which has paralyzed the will of the West. The West is not challenging the principle and power behind terrorism, the Soviet Union. For this paralysis, the United States bears primary blame. It is especially culpable for the cover-up to which Senator Jackson referred, the timid refusal to make widely known all that is knowable about Soviet complicity in terrorism. This refusal is a consequence of leadership that has a political or psychological investment in the idea that détente has tamed the Soviet Union.

The United States is the principal and often the indispensable source of financial support for various international organizations, such as the World Bank. The United States has the opportunity and duty to use the leverage it has. Specifically, it should find a way to condition its contributions to each organization on the organization's adherence to this principle: No nation that harbors, finances or otherwise abets terrorists shall enjoy rights in, or benefits from, the organizations. (This principle might put some international organizations into bankruptcy. Each of us can decide whether that should make us sad.)

Thus far, the West has been fortunate. Indeed, regarding terrorism, we may well look back upon these as the good old days. The technology of macro-terrorism — the terror of mass-disruption or mass murder — exists and will become more dreadful. Vulnerability to macro-terrorism is intrinsic to modern societies, with their huge concentrations of people and their technological dependencies. Leave aside the well publicized threat of a nuclear weapon with a surreptitious delivery system: a terrorist with a nuclear device. Consider, instead, the possibilities for chemical and biological terrorism in urban areas, given the nature of their water supplies, food handling, and energy systems. Consider the number and amount of highly toxic substances routinely produced and transported in industrial societies. Even the terrorist's ordinary weapons, conventional explosives, would have extraordinary effects if skillfully applied to, say, the World Trade Center in Manhattan, or the tunnels and power grids that serve Manhattan. We know that some terrorists have contemplated macro-terrorism. Such terrorism may produce another demonstration of the fact that democracies do not act decisively until they have been decisively acted upon.

The Journalist's Role

In conclusion, and in anticipation of the theme of the next panel, I return to the role of inadequate ideas in producing the inadequate response of the democracies to terrorism.

The idea that seems to underlie some media coverage of terrorism is this: Politics is a kind of physics, a field of forces. Journalists should maintain a physicist's detachment, a sophistication too languid for moral judgments. Terrorism is parasitic off the media, and the next panel will wrestle with that problem. But columnists are by nature givers of gratuitous advice, and I advise the next panel as follows.

It may be that one reason terrorists can so effectively use the media is the systematic, almost philosophic, proud and even militant irresponsibility of the media. Does not the journalism profession now pride itself on refusing to calculate the social consequences of what it prints or broadcasts? Journalism suffers from, among other things, a "Watergate paradigm." Too many journalists are inclined to think that the role of journalists in Watergate (or, more precisely, the central role that journalists are mistakenly supposed to have played in the Watergate drama) defines the normal and proper relationship between journalists and authorities. Journalists too often accept the idea that they are and should be, always, in an "adversary" relationship with government. So they need not calculate the consequences their coverage may have on the public interest. Calculating the public interest is, they reason, the adversary's business. Their business is to publish and broadcast without let or hindrance. Like all simple dogmas, this one has the charm of sparing those who accept it the unpleasant burden of thinking, of weighing difficult cases. But surely it is time that journalists think long and hard about the relationship that must exist between "the public's right to know" and the public's need to know. As regards terrorism, the crucial question is: Does the public need to know everything, immediately? The task is to make journalism less useful to terrorists. After all, terrorism is a tactic adopted by people too weak to resort to invasion, or rebellion, or even guerrilla warfare. Surely journalism need not invariably magnify the impact of individual terrorist acts. Now I shall subside, having behaved as columnists generally do: I have posed for others a problem I am thankful I am not responsible for solving.

QUESTIONS AND ANSWERS

Chairman (Ambassador Ben-Natan): Because we are short of time, we may have to give the floor to the participants only.

Brian Crozier: I would like to take up two points made by Joop den Uyl. He gave some interesting examples of the brilliant handling of terrorist situations by his government, but he omitted an example which I find of particular importance, but which did not at the time reach the headlines.

In September 1975 two Syrians were arrested in a brilliant police action in the Netherlands. They had been plotting to hijack a train coming from the Soviet Union, one carriage of which was packed with Soviet Jews. And of course this action was prevented. Under interrogation they revealed that scores of Arabs were being trained in terrorism and terrorist tactics in a village outside Moscow. And this seems to me to prove something other than the proposition Mr. Joop den Uyl put forward.

And if one can take the matter further, I simply want to say that in the friendliest possible way I challenge Mr. Joop den Uyl, Mr. Cluskey and Mr. Barrett to disprove or deny any of the facts in my paper about the Soviet participation in terrorism. Thank you.

Joop den Uyl: I'd like to answer immediately on the two points made. First, the question of two Syrians who were captured by Dutch police in 1975 . . . I know the case.

What you say is right with one exception. I have to confess and be quite frank about that. You say that they were trained in a small village near Moscow. I found it in your paper, one of the papers prepared for this Conference. It's quite new for me. I don't exclude it, but it is quite new as was for me that one incident I mentioned, that reference to some connection between Libya and the South Moluccans. About that I may be more certain; I think I know the facts fairly well about the actions of the South Moluccans, and I have not found anything pointing to a Libyan involvement.

Now your other point about the involvement of the Soviet Union in training and supporting terrorists. I want to repeat what I said about that and add something.

I said that I don't exclude that there are training centers in the Soviet Union of certain groups of terrorists. I simply am not very sure about that. If I look at your paper and what you said about that, I am inclined to think that there is some practical involvement of Soviet authorities in the training facilities.

What I'd like to add to that is that the Soviet Union has acted so far in condemning terrorist actions and in refusing to be involved in any deals made by Western democracies. For instance, some governments have tried to send off some terrorists by plane to Eastern bloc countries, the Soviet Union included. This has always been refused.

The question I would like to present is this. I have pointed out that in my view there is a very great risk for the Soviet Union in having training facilities for terrorists or in supporting terrorist actions as we are discussing in this conference. Why?

We all take it as fact that totalitarian societies are invulnerable and may exclude terrorist activities. It is true that a totalitarian society is entirely under command. But if you look at the history of some decades of uprisings and upheavals in Eastern bloc countries, Poland for example, if you look at what goes on in those countries, it must be quite evident that terrorist activities, terrorist resistance actions, perhaps resistance actions to be admired by you and me, may not be excluded for the future to come. Perhaps earlier than many of us think. And it is for that reason that my concept of Soviet behavior is that I can't exclude certain supporting actions, but that there is a great interest for the Soviet Union itself to get rid of many people who try to exploit terrorism for their side. It is a great interest of the Soviet Union not to be mixed into those affairs.

You should, if you are of another opinion, point out what is the interest of the Soviet Union in such activities.

Robert Moss: I'm afraid that I didn't have the pleasure of hearing the former Dutch Prime Minister's remarks this morning because of other commitments, but I would like to mention a few more of what George Will called "inconvenient facts" of Soviet involvement in this matter.

We can debate the motives for the Russians to do these things, but I would like to know whether any of us are seriously prepared to dispute established facts confirmed by many Western intelligence sources and sources inside the Palestinian movement.

The first fact I wish to cite is on the systematic training of PLO and other Palestinian Arabs in Russia. I did not have time to go through this in detail in presenting my paper yesterday although some details are in my prepared text.

The military academy in the Crimea is regularly the scene for training groups of 50 to 60 Palestinian Arabs in special terrorist techniques, sabotage, river crossings, things of that kind, directly relevant not only to the security of the State of Israel but to the security of West European countries.

Before embarking on these courses — in which, by the way, supposedly rival Palestinian groups such as Fatah, Saiqa, and the PLFP are all represented together — they receive political indoctrination courses in their camps in Lebanon. These classes are usually conducted by members of Fatah's political department, not Russians. The specific Fatah man involved in this indoctrination, by the way, is Abu Khalid Hussein. Before they begin, he conducts political indoctrination courses on the glories of the Soviet system and the Bolshevik Revolution. This is going on, ladies and gentlemen, every year.

Those PLO, PLFP and Saiqa people who have been trained in the Soviet Union do not only come here to try to kill Israeli men, women and children; they also go to Western Europe. And when we ask how they go to Western Europe it is extremely interesting to note that one of the main conduits for their operations in Europe has been East Berlin. There are many cases of Palestinian operations in Europe for which East Berlin has been the jumping-off point, just as East Berlin was where the kidnappers of Peter Lorenz, the Christian Democratic politician, found sanctuary for a while.

Now these, as I say, are inconvenient facts. We can cling to our hopes or fears or delusions. I may have some, we all may have some in different ways, about what we may think the motivation of the Soviet leadership is. But let's postpone our debate about motivation until we've considered these inconvenient facts. That is the only basis, I suggest, upon which we must found any informed and realistic discussion of the problem.

Unidentified Speaker: (Addressing Joop den Uyl) You made a great deal of the fact that the Soviet Union officially denies support of terrorists. Does it occur to you, sir, that this is done deliberately so that people of good will and decency and honesty like yourself can be confounded?

Professor Mordechai Abir: Mr. den Uyl, I had the pleasure of disagreeing with you two weeks ago in the Hague and I disagree with you once again. We can be very good Socialists but at the same time we can disagree with the Soviet Union's policies.

Now, you have asked what is the motivation? The motivation is power politics, and power politics are centered today in the Middle East and in oil. The oil problem is crucial and that is why the Middle East is crucial. And both lead to

the PLO, because the PLO has remained one of the bastions of
the USSR's influence today in the Middle East. The PLO has
become the agent for other international organizations with
the knowledge of its Soviet mentors.

Joop den Uyl: Once again Mr. Moss produces some intelligence
facts about training facilities in the Soviet Union or East Bloc
countries for Palestinians or other terrorists. I don't contest
him. I can't even discuss intelligence facts. The points that I
have made are: What is the interest of the Soviet Union? And
that getting involved in terrorist activities of this kind may
include great risks for the Soviet Union itself.

There is the political question again. Is there a conspiracy
of silence, is there a non-willingness to view the facts and
refute them? My answer is no.

My first remark is that of course there are certain facts
about Eastern bloc countries, of activities which are not
publicized, which are not exposed, by governments. I have said
this morning, I am aware of *that*, as I am aware, having been
responsible for intelligence services, that we dispose of facts
which we do not publicize and which we do not expose.

And there are very good reasons for that. I am not able to
judge if the administration of the United States is part of a
conspiracy of silence when it doesn't publicize certain facts
that it knows about the activities of East Bloc countries in
training terrorists.

I would say that I can find a very good argument in
knowing which type of operations of Western intelligence
services are going on. I simply ask you to think about that.

Now my last remark to this question is this. I said this
morning and I repeat it now: We should be very alert to any
activities of the Soviet Union or other totalitarian states in the
area of terrorism. But it would be a great danger, in my opinion, to focus on a conspiracy by the Soviet Union, of supporting or inspiring or managing terrorist actions of hundreds in
the world. It makes it impossible for us to think about some
other backgrounds, roots, aspects of terrorist action.

And I would say it is much more common to our spirit, with our democratic responsibility, not to generalize but to try to get the facts as they are. And they are very different, as Frank Cluskey pointed out this morning, as I tried to point out as to the South Moluccans and the Basques. I think we do not live up to our responsibility if we do not produce the facts to the world as they are. We can't generalize them into one central conspiracy of the Soviet Union.

It would be rather easy if it were the case, but unfortunately it is not so simple as that.

Chairman (Ambassador Ben-Natan): I am sure that on this subject we will certainly not be able to make a neat summary. And the discussion will continue.

I would like to summarize our discussion today on the response of democratic society by saying three things:
1. Stop terrorism now.
2. Don't compromise with terrorism.
3. Terrorism is much more dangerous to democratic society than the measures taken to combat it.

Fifth Session
Subject:
THE ROLE OF THE MEDIA IN THE
STRUGGLE AGAINST TERRORISM
Morning, July 5, 1979
Chairman: Paul Johnson

PREFACE

Without the collaboration, unwitting or not, of the mass media, terrorism would be impotent. By dramatizing the terrorist's threats and demands and by refusing to condemn them outright, the media often contribute to the moral confusion which tends to romanticize the terrorist and leave his victim forgotten. This was one of the melancholy conclusions of the participants in the session on the media and terrorism.

For the most part, speakers felt that the free press has displayed a dangerous lack of understanding of terrorism and its aims. The press sensationalizes terrorist incidents while still in progress. Bombings and guns and the taking of hostages, with the attendant excruciating tension, are considered good copy. To "cover" the story in this way is already to accord terrorists the millions of dollars of free publicity they covet.

How should we set about drying up the sea of publicity in which the terrorist swims? Some speakers suggested that governments could impose on *publicly* owned stations a code for the treatment of terrorism and specific terrorist acts. This code, striking a balance between the public's "right to know" and the public's "need to know," could also serve as the basis for voluntary adherence by responsible journalists of the private press and television. For example, it could provide for the laconic, non-sensational treatment of terrorist events. Such a "brownout" would severely limit the publicity value of terrorist acts.

An underlying problem, speakers noted, is the constant confusion of terms in the reporting of terrorist acts. Are they "terrorists" or are they "urban guerillas," "commandos" or "freedom fighters"? Should the media simply accept the terrorist's self-description, or examine their deeds and name them accordingly? Examples of irresponsibility on the part of the press in reporting about terrorism were given from several countries.

The notion that is so widespread in the media that extreme violence must necessarily be rooted in extreme "social evils" (and therefore indirectly justified) was seen as a major excuse for this irresponsibility. The first victims of this perverted "objectivity" are the language and the truth. Can the journalists of the press and television come to understand that their putative "objectivity" in fact leads directly to moral obfuscation and falsehood?

All of these matters were discussed by the participants, who dwelt as well on the spirit of the age, a spirit that encouraged specious moral symmetries and an unthinking identification with any movement expressing itself in the cliché-ridden lexicon of "liberation."

GERHARD LÖWENTHAL is a well-known
German writer and journalist. Since 1969 he
has been the manager and moderator of the
German Television's Second Channel.
Mr. Löwenthal has written many articles,
and his book, *We Will Live Through the
Atom*, has received the European Award
for Literature.

THE CASE OF WEST GERMANY

Many things said during this Jerusalem Conference have given
me great satisfaction, because so many speakers did not skirt
around the facts, and reported on the devil in the devil's language. The participants revealed that an international network
has launched a war against our free, liberal and tolerant social
democracies. It is enlightening to be part of this dedicated
international group and to be rid of the sense of isolation you
experience when you come from a country in which large
parts of the mass media collaborate, however unwittingly, with
terrorism. I shall quote these sentences of Mr. Paul Johnson:

> "The wrong approach is to see terrorism as one of many
> symptoms of a deep-seated malaise in our society, part of
> a pattern of violence which includes juvenile delinquency,
> rising crime rates, student riots, vandalism and football
> hooliganism, which is blamed on the shadow of the H-
> bomb, western materialism, TV and cinema violence, ris-
> ing divorce rates, inadequate welfare services and poverty,
> and which usually ends in the meaningless and defeatist
> conclusion that society itself is to blame and — to quote
> the caricature psychiatrist, 'We are All Guilty.' I believe
> that one central reason why it is such a formidable threat
> is that very few people in the civilized world — govern-
> ments and parliaments, TV and newspapers, and the pub-
> lic generally — take terrorism seriously enough."

I have repeated these remarkable sentences because they lead directly to my remarks on German mass media and terrorism. In West Germany we have also experienced what Robert Moss calls the "Conspiracy of Silence." Very few in Germany would dare call the New Left a *reactionary, dark movement*. For years the members of the Baader-Meinhof Gang have been pictured as misled young people who were obsessed by their strong feelings for social justice, desperate, frustrated and lonely young men and women who could express their impotence and despair in no other way than in applying violence. And this in a country which gives everybody the utmost freedom to express himself and to work for the betterment of social and political conditions in the framework of the most liberal constitution in German history! In this country the internationally known writer Heinrich Böll could write an article in January 1972 in which he compared the criminal members of the Baader-Meinhof gang to those persecuted under the Nazi regime. Böll wrote about a "merciless society" that hunted down those poor people at a time when leaders of that very society, far from being "merciless", had irresponsibly begun to renounce the vigorous defense of our democratic system. The article by Böll stirred up a heated controversy which even produced a book in which those who, like myself, had dared to criticize him were themselves bitterly attacked and dismissed as "fascists."

At the same time the head of the German Federal Office of Criminal Investigation stated in a meeting of the Ministers of the Interior that "the climate in the mass media had considerably deteriorated." He mentioned explicitly television, radio, *Der Spiegel, Die Zeit, Vorwärts, Süddeutsche Zeitung* and *Frankfurter Rundschau* as those media "that had adopted a distinctly negative attitude." The highest ranking police officer of the Federal Republic quoted a public opinion poll which revealed that the sympathy for the Baader-Meinhof gang had grown within the youth, and that the field of sympathizers had broadened in university circles and in the press.

Explaining Away Terrorism

I have a long list of concrete examples demonstrating how terrorism has been played down, minimized, explained away in a so-called "objective" fashion. I shall for a moment concentrate on one publication. In 1975 I sponsored an investigation of its articles which were not simply journalistic reports or commentaries on terrorism but often sympathetic transmissions, at times verbatim, of terrorist demands, declarations and manifestos. My investigation revealed nine such articles between 1968 and 1975. Some came from wanted terrorists in hiding — one was even smuggled out of the famous Stammheim jail, for which this magazine paid DM 15,000 fee (the intermediaries were the lawyers of the gang). Most of the terrorist pamphlets were published by this magazine without any commentary or dissociating footnote. One striking example: On April 1972 that magazine published the famous pamphlet of Ulrike Meinhof "Serve the People — Red Army Faction: Town Guerrilla and Class Struggle."

Well-known German magazines have in numerous articles dealt with the deplorable situation of misled young people, of terrorists who have become terrorists only because of their social "commitment." Most of these articles are uncritical or contain a barely hidden sympathy common to so many of these publications. If it is correct that the success of a terrorist action depends to a large degree on the extent of publicity it enjoys, then the German media have contributed a great deal to this success. Mahler, one of the early activists who received his terrorist training in a Fatah training camp, had the privilege of a 90 minute "portrait" on television — a mostly uncritical portrayal. It was only one of several devoted to him because he claimed to have left the camp of the terrorists. Many programs have been devoted to other terrorists under the pretext of a "search for their motives" and "discovering the roots of terrorism" — but most of these exude sympathy for their subjects.

Reviewing a TV program about the terrible events at the Olympic games in Munich, the press service of the Protestant

Church chose to say: "Terrorism was neither invented by the Palestinians nor has been applied by them in the beginning of the conflict. Would the State of Israel have been achieved without terror? Would the victims of Munich subsequently dissociate themselves from the terror commandos of the Zionist Liberation Movement?" Thus the murders at Munich are conveniently "explained" by this spurious analogy.

Disparagement of Democratic Institutions

The terror propaganda and agitation have been accompanied in the German mass media with a permanent disparagement of the Federal Republic of Germany, of its free democratic system, of its institutions, and especially of those whose task it is to guarantee the security of all citizens — that is the police, the Office for the Protection of the Constitution,* the intelligence community and the judicial establishment.

Part and parcel of this disparagement is the campaign of the defense counsels of terrorists against the so-called 'isolation detention" which culminated in the use of the term "isolation torture" to describe their prison conditions. Although the prisoners enjoyed unprecedented privileges such as radio, TV, record players and separate cells for the many books and publications they were allowed — privileges that enraged the "normal" prisoners — their lawyers initiated an international campaign of protest which was taken up by the mass media, not only in Germany but even more in France, the Netherlands and Scandinavia. The famous visit of Sartre to Andreas Baader and the incredible publicity it received is yet another example.

After the murder of the State Attorney General Siegfried Buback, an anonymous pamphlet appeared entitled "Obituary to Buback" in a student paper. Although the pamphlet was nothing but cynical political pornography, many professors identified themselves with this anonymous author. Thus it received widespread publicity in the media. Moreover, the publisher of one liberal weekly revealed that she had barely man-

---

* The West German government agency charged with fighting terrorism.

aged to prevent the publication of an article which absurdly equated Ulrike Meinhof and Jeanne d'Arc.

Still another example was a sequence on Panorama, a TV program well known for its tradition of glorifying terrorists. During this program a journalist, whose close contacts with terrorist circles are also well known, created the impression that a terrorist who had defected from the scene and was killed by his former comrades, was supposedly murdered by and under the eyes of the Office for the Protection of the Constitution. He documented his story by showing a so-called "Observation Report," and had to admit in court a few days later that he had fabricated the "original" document himself.

Avoiding Inconvenient Facts

In reporting about terrorism, the German press has displayed a regrettable tendency to avoid inconvenient facts. One of the PLO contacts of the Munich murderers who lived near Frankfurt at the time and with whom the terrorists spoke by telephone several times during the attack on the Israeli athletes, was identified by the German authorities and subsequently expelled. He later returned to the country with a diplomatic passport from an Arab country to work in the office of the Arab League in Bonn. Although there is no accredited PLO representation in Bonn, this man Franghi now works openly as the official representative of the PLO and is often interviewed on television where he emphasizes again and again that the PLO has nothing to do with terrorism. None of the interviewers has ever revealed his true background, or related the fact that he secretly organizes Al Fatah groups in the Federal Republic of Germany.

Only seldom do you find hints in the German mass media about the large scale involvement of the KGB and its subdepartments in satellite countries in international terrorism. This might disturb "détente," so appeasement and the conspiracy of silence are at work. There is widespread sympathy with those who pretend to change unjust social conditions, even when they apply violence. And in large parts of the published opinion — which, by the way, often differs from *public* opinion, at least in my country — these ideas find sympathetic distribution.

The free press ought to be one of the main instruments in alerting the public to the imminent danger of terrorism. Unfortunately, it is almost the reverse. There is an undeniable tendency in the Western mass media to take terrorists at their own valuation. It is unbearable that the PLO is referred to in its verbal translation as the "Palestine Liberation Organization" instead of as a terrorist group. The same is true for some of the terrorist groups in Africa and elsewhere in the world.

Responsible Self-Restraint

Ways must be found to "instill a sense of responsibility in journalists themselves so that the same kind of self-restraint that is exercised, for example, in reporting certain kinds of violent crimes of a completely non-political nature would be extended to terrorist acts."* That this is possible has been demonstrated in my country during the kidnapping of Hans Martin Schleyer. The terrorists who held Schleyer supplied the television networks video recordings of their victim showing him in his terrible condition. The networks simply refused to broadcast these recordings. Although this refusal created additional dangers to the victim, the decision was certainly right.

In the Schleyer case the German mass media cooperated with the authorities and exercised the sort of self-restraint one wishes would become a rule internationally. Instead of reporting excessively on terrorist acts, the aim should be to deprive terrorists of their gains in publicity. "A systematic and relentless campaign of exposure, showing precisely the baseness and cowardice of the terrorists so that they are exposed to contempt, ridicule and the opposition of an aroused public, will do more than anything else to curb such acts. To this end it is essential to enunciate, over and over again, that these are not 'spontaneous explosions' or 'senseless acts' of killings, but calculated actions of groups committed to the destruction of

* See "International Terrorism: The Darkening Horizon" (The Jonathan Institute Publication Series on Terrorism).

parliamentary democracy and systematically supported by totalitarian regimes. An aroused and dedicated group of citizens could build up public pressure on timid or reluctant governments to ensure that necessary measures are taken."*

* Ibid.

MICHAEL ELKINS is the BBC correspondent in Israel and has been a consultant for
Newsweek magazine since 1966. He has also
worked for CBS (1956-1967). He is the
author of *Forged in Fury*, a much acclaimed
historical study of Jewish resistance in
World War II. Mr. Elkins is Vice-Chairman
of the Foreign Press Association in Israel.

CAGING THE BEASTS

I have been reporting from Israel for twenty three years. I have
been deafened by the bomb and splattered by the blood, and
believe me — I am not interested in political theologies or
intellectual explorations.

The point is that the killers are loose in the world, and
the first priority is to cage them. The esoterics can come later.
What we need now is not more intellectual light on the subject, but more heat. We need to generate in the world passionate revulsion to terror and terrorists; and we need always
and everywhere to deny them acceptance, to deny them
dignity, and to deny them victory.

In this effort, in what ought to be this common cause,
the media — press, radio, television — have in large measure
abdicated their responsibilities, and have done so for reasons
ranging from mistaken judgment to moral bankruptcy.

They have adapted and adopted the sour and sterile
aphorism, "He is a terrorist, you are a guerrilla, I am a freedom
fighter," as though there were no criteria other than those
reflecting personal predilection and political bias by which a
terrorist may reasonably be identified and labelled as such,
and by that label seen to be abhorrent.

I am not prepared *automatically* to define all liberation
movements as "terrorist." I reject the concept that because
terrorists call themselves "freedom fighters," *we* must call all

freedom fighters terrorists. I cannot in simple decency condemn all use of violence as terrorist. One may not deny to
oppressed people the weapon available when the ballot box is
stolen and the democratic process does not exist. If we
espouse such blanket denial, this Pavlovian reaction will separate us inevitably from oppressed peoples and will compel
them to find their allies among the terrorists and only there.
This cannot be useful to the struggle against terror.

Criteria for Identifying Terrorism

But there are such criteria which, if not perfect, are at least
reasonable and useful. The old adage, "by their actions you
shall know them," still has a compelling logic. Those who take
civilian hostages and kill them, or threaten to do so, are not
guerrillas, or commandos or freedom-fighters. Within any
reasonable judgment enabling democracy or even civilization
to survive — they are terrorists. Those who put bombs in mar-
ketplaces — are terrorists. Those who batter children to death
— are terrorists.

Within this context, it does not matter what their ultimate political purpose is — if such purpose they have. What
matters is what they *do*, and if what they do is beyond the
pale — well then, so are they.

I must mention the appalling truth that organized societies have engaged, and are still engaged and with increasing
violence, upon the slaughter of the innocents and that this is
not called terrorism, but war. It is true. It is appalling. And it
is irrelevant to my argument. Because we are not able, or are
not yet able, to banish all evil cannot mean that we must condone every evil.

The difficulty that the media have in identifying terrorist
acts as such, and in holding their perpetrators up to public
contempt, arises for the most part out of assumptions of
"objectivity," and in some cases out of its opposite — an ac-
knowledged "non-objectivity" that has gone askew.

I do not believe that "objectivity" requires the journalist
to become a moral eunuch impotent to embrace, and within

his profession to espouse, at least those basic values without which no civilization can endure.

The same argument curiously prevails against those media of the Left which either endorse, or will not condemn, the use of indiscriminate violence as a weapon of political action. Someone said that "the Left is in danger of allowing events to force it into a totally anti-humanist posture. Once the justification of the terrorist to kill is conceded, there is no logical point at which the Left can make a stand for human life."

This issue of identifying terrorists as such reveals a peculiar kind of chauvinist hypocrisy among people, and within the media, what might be called the "whose ox is gored" syndrome. For example, when a bomb explodes in a market-place in Israel, the British media (including the BBC for which I work) will often describe this terrorist action as "another guerrilla attack." But to the British a bomb in London is "terroristic."

It also works the other way. Israelis, who to my frequent discomfiture listen to the BBC, fire off indignant complaints to the local newspaper about the BBC's use of the term "guerrilla" when the dirty word "terrorist" is clearly called for. These complaints often appear in the same issue of the *Jerusalem Post* which describes the slaughter of some farmer's family in Rhodesia as done by "guerrillas." I have never seen any complaints about that. Obviously, it depends on whose ox is gored.

The Crucial Need: Self-Restraint

It is reprehensible when, as has happened, radio or television journalists in their "on-scene" reporting describe in specific detail the preparations and movements of counter-terror forces engaged *at that moment* in an action against terrorists holding hostages. It is reprehensible when, as has happened, news media in the United States report that the President wears an armored vest which can be pierced only by a rifle bullet — a Springfield 303, in the case of President Ford. What public purpose is served by telling a would-be assassin that if he wants to kill the President, he should get a rifle, not a pistol?

It seems to me that we of the news media need to re-examine our priorities and responsibilities. We have, I submit, no special mandate to endanger human lives for the sake of a news story.

And that brings me to a final point: There is ample evidence, incontrovertible, unarguable, from the mouths of terrorists themselves, that terrorist actions are often explicitly designed to achieve the greatest possible publicity.

But there is a corollary: If a cardinal purpose of the terrorist is to attract attention, the *public* purpose must be to deny it or at least to minimize it.

I am not suggesting that terrorist actions shall not be reported. I am suggesting that the reportage should be accurate, spare, and meticulously unsensational. It should, I am suggesting, be consciously and carefully pruned to convey the essential information; no more than that. If civilized countries and democratic societies should — as they should! — deny haven and sanctuary to terrorists, so the media have the responsibility to deny aid, comfort and advantage to terrorists.

The key word in all this is "responsibility." In my view, *all* freedoms — including, perhaps first of all, freedom of the press — must be exercised responsibly. The greater the freedom, the greater and the more urgent the responsibility. In *this* sense, I do not believe that freedom of the press ought to be unlimited. The right and necessity to convey and receive information and opinion are not, and should not, be designed to open the gates without limit, to create and expand, and then pander to, the anarchic attractions of violence. The "right to know" and the "need to know" are not consonant with the right and the need to know everything, immediately.

One final caution — I am not for the application of censorship to the media. I am not for legislation or legal constraints to impose responsibility upon the media in this field. What I am arguing for is a sustained and careful effort *by the media* to establish guidelines in the media-coverage of terrorist organizations and activities. I acknowledge that self-censorship is a hazardous enterprise and must be carefully explored; but it is surely better than government bans. And I would point out that self-censorship — "self-discipline" or "editorial judgment" — is in fact exercised in all media every day as editors and producers excise prurient material, or details affecting the welfare of a minor child or material overstepping the bounds of journalism into the shadowland of espionage.

These self-limitations are imposed by the dictates of responsibility, public policy and public welfare. Surely, in the case of terrorism these imperatives are also critically involved.

NORMAN PODHORETZ is the editor of
Commentary, one of America's most
influential intellectual monthlies. He is the
author of *Making It, Doings and Undoings*
and *Breaking Ranks: A Political Memoir*.
He contributes articles and reviews to major
American magazines and appears frequently
on radio and television.

THE SUBTLE COLLUSION

The theme of my remarks is the subtle collusion between the media and terrorism which has resulted in the immense success of terrorism in the past few years. Before we touch on this subject, however, it is important that we recognize that terrorism pays.

One has only to examine the history of the reputation of the PLO to be impressed with the degree to which terrorist tactics have contributed to the political success of these movements. The PLO today is far more respectable, the object of far greater deference (and in some quarters reverence), than it was a few years ago, even after repeated episodes of murder, kidnapping and hijacking. Every time a terrorist episode occurs one has come to expect a certain degree of pious deploring by the editorialists in the American press. But the pious deploring is always or invariably accompanied by an undercurrent of *de facto* justification.

It used to be said that the terrorist tactics of the PLO were necessary to call the world's attention to its allegedly ignored grievances. This can no longer be said in justification of the PLO. A brilliant letter to the *New York Times* recently pointed out that at a time when Yasser Arafat gives more interviews on television than Henry Kissinger it can hardly be claimed that the PLO is in need of calling attention to itself. So the disappearance of that classical, as one might call it, justification for terrorism has not even hurt the PLO. All that has happened is that new justifications have been developed. The latest justification offered this time on an American television network was that the step-up in PLO violence and terrorism in recent months is an expression of rage and frustration at the Egyptian-Israeli peace treaty.

Now, it seems to me entirely clear that terrorism has paid off for the PLO, and one could outline a similar course of progress in the case of other terrorist organizations. It is also clear that one of the main reasons, and possibly the most important reason, for the use of these terrorist tactics in advancing the political aims of the organizations involved is treatment by the media.

The Instrument of Publicity
First of all, as has often been pointed out, the sheer publicity the terroristic act attracts is itself the object of many of these actions and is itself a mark of success, beyond any further consequence publicity may have.

Let me say a word or two to try to explain why this is so. What the publicity does is not merely call everyone's attention to these organizations. One's attention might be called in a way destructive to those organizations. That is, it is conceivable that attention might be called with a consequent abhorrence or repulsion. In fact, however, the publicity that has been accorded the terrorist groups has had the effect of habituating the public mind to the kind of action — the murders, the kidnappings, the hijackings — that once seemed so horrible as to be virtually unthinkable, so outrageous as to be almost beyond condemnation, so as to leave people literally speechless in response.

This habituation to these tactics has had an immensely important effect. It has helped to undermine what Paul Johnson has rightly called the natural moral response to acts of random brutality, cruelty and violence. It has had the effect of making it harder and harder for people to trust those responses and to act on the basis of their natural repugnance. We become habituated, we lose the sharpness of our sense of outrage, we lose the clarity of our moral judgment. This is the first way in which the publicity that terrorism has received helps to further the aims of the terrorist.

The various discussions of terrorism in the media have similarly undermined the natural response to terrorist acts. The programs on television called "The Mind of a Terrorist," or articles called "Portrait of a Terrorist", even if they appear to be balanced and critical, lend a kind of status and dignity to the terrorist and his rationalization that would otherwise be denied him. The discussion itself turns into an overturning of moral values. It even sometimes leads to a kind of titillation of the audience, a kind of a *frisson* with which it reacts to any extreme statement or action.

Social Apologetics

The second way in which the media have subtly colluded in the success of terrorism is through the regnant assumption behind both the publicity and the discussion of the phenomenon. The regnant assumption in the American press concerning the rise of terrorism is that it is rooted in what may be called "social causes." Now, it is possible to discuss any form of human behavior in those terms; and while it is not necessarily true that *tout comprendre* is to forgive everything, it is invariably psychologically the case that explanations of anything in terms of social causes tend to exculpate the thing being explained.

To stray a minute from the subject of terrorism proper: In the United States we have had sporadic outbreaks of terrorism, but they have been minor compared to those suffered by other countries. We did, however, have our share of much lesser, and certainly not terrorist, forms of violence in the universities in the late 1960s. Everyone wanted to know what these students "were trying to tell us." That was the great cant question at the time. You might have thought that the student leaders and the student radicals were either inarticulate or shy or tongue-tied. On the contrary: at the drop of a hat, or let us say a camera, they were ready to expatiate at endless and tedious length on what they were trying to tell us. But this rarely satisfied commentators in the media who wanted always to tell us what they thought they were trying to tell us. And of course what they were trying to tell us was invariably whatever the commentator himself had been trying, usually unsuccessfully, to tell us about American society.

This was, oddly enough, a way of not taking the radicals seriously, or at face value. On the one hand, it tended to undercut the full effect of the radical message; on the other, it tended also to make this message more respectable and to spread its influence. It was, if I can be forgiven the use of a term with this kind of resonance, a dialectical result.

This "what are the terrorists trying to tell us" syndrome tends to underlie a good deal of the discussion of terrorism in the American and the Western media generally. It blunts the normal or instinctive response of horror to the concrete actions of the terrorists.

Can Publicity be Curbed?

If it is the case, as I have been arguing, that the media have been in collusion with terrorism and have helped to make it a successful political weapon in our time, the question naturally arises, what is to be done? I believe that there is nothing that can effectively be done about the problem of publicity accorded by the media to terrorist activity. I do not believe that in the United States, for example, it would be possible to legislate successfully against coverage of terrorist activities, even if that were deemed desirable. It would certainly be deemed unconstitutional. I myself would also deem it undesirable as indeed would most people who know anything about these matters.

Nor do I place much faith in self-restraint on the part of the media as some others seem to do. The media have not been notable for self-restraint in our time. On the contrary, the tendency has been to decry the self-restraint exercised in the past as a betrayal of the true function of the media. I simply do not believe that self-restraint, voluntary self-restraint, can be depended upon. It is possible that some editors and some producers might exercise it in a given situation, but I don't believe that the media are capable of policing themselves effectively any more than are the corporations, whose freedom to police themselves the media are the first to denounce.

I would not say that the situation is entirely hopeless, however, because it is possible that the very same degree of publicity that leads to the habituation of the public mind to the horrors of terrorism might also lead to boredom with terrorism — boredom both on the part of reporters and editors and on the part of the reading public. The American sociologist Robert Nisbet once said that boredom is the most underrated force in human history. This seems to me a profound observation. Many things happen because people are bored, and many other things cease happening because people are bored, and for no nobler or baser reason than that. It is entirely possible that terrorism will get less publicity and the kind of chaste coverage that has been recommended here, because everyone may — incredible as it seems — grow bored with the details. After the 900th hijacking or the 1,000th kidnapping, the *ennui* may begin to show, even among the editors and producers. Of course, there is the more dismal possibility that out of such boredom the tactics of terrorists might be forced to escalate to capture the attention of a saturated media, and we would be off again on another round, only this time on a higher — or lower — level of the spiral.

A War of Ideas

What about the problem of the governing assumptions which underlie the publicity and which help to dignify and in some sense justify the actions of the terrorists? Here too I see nothing that can be done in the way of legislation, just as I do not see anything that can be done in an organized fashion to promote or encourage self-restraint. Yet, there is something that could be effective. We are dealing here with an issue related to ideas and ideologies. It is bad ideas which have helped terrorism to succeed, and it is good ideas which will defeat terrorism.

This means that constant arguments are necessary, and more than necessary, essential — but not random arguments, nor merely hortatory denunciations of the evils of terrorism to which all pious people can agree and nod, and at which they can begin to doze off. There are points to be made that wake people up rather than put them to sleep. In fact, several people have been more than awakened by at least one of these points at this conference. They have been prodded into something resembling political fury by the assertion made several times, and documented rather impressively within the limits of short conference papers, that the Soviet Union is deeply involved in the training, inspiration and financing of terrorist activities throughout the world, including, and perhaps especially, the PLO.

The impulse to deny or blunt this fact is one of the major problems in the fight against terrorism. We have seen that impulse at work in what has been rightly called the conspiracy of silence of governments. We see it at work in the media as well.

The only way that we can effectively counter this kind of cooperation or collusion given in the media and by the media to terrorism, is to continue insisting on the facts of the case, including the facts of Soviet involvement and the implications of that involvement, because these are far from being part of an academic or a theological exercise. They have immensely practical consequences, which need not be spelled out. One of the reasons that everyone wishes to deny the facts is that they do not wish to be held to the consequences, to the implications and actions which flow from a clear recognition of those facts. This is well known, not only in the field of terrorism, but in the field of politics generally.

The second point that has to be addressed, and addressed vigorously, is the notion that terrorism can be understood or explained or dealt with in terms of its social causes. I shall say once again that the cause of terrorism is terrorists. The ability of terrorists to operate effectively depends on financial support and sanctuary by states. Terrorists may indeed have particular grievances, but they only become an effective force if they get the kind of support that terrorists such as the PLO have gotten in our day from the Soviet Union, its agents and Arab allies — financial support, training and sanctuary.

If we wish to look into the cause of terrorism in a way that would be fruitful — that is, in a way that would indeed lead to the caging of these beasts — we could do no better than to focus on the factors related to the support offered by terrorist states. These factors are not the kind of causes whose investigation leads almost inexorably to the exculpation of terrorists and their brutal actions.

MIDGE DECTER is a well-known writer
and journalist in the United States whose
articles appear frequently in *Commentary*
and elsewhere. She is the author of three
books: *The Liberated Woman and Other
Americans, The New Chastity,* and *Liberal
Parents, Radical Children.*

THE NEED FOR CLARITY

In discussing the problem of the media and terrorism, what
we need above all is *clarity*. It's a wonderful, precise and
perfect word to define our primary need, from which all acts
of political wisdom and courage follow.

This brings me to the American journalists, by whom I
mean the editors and writers of the dozen most influential
newspapers and magazines, the vocal members of the literary-
intellectual establishment, the leading television news commentators, and so on. Like the famous anecdote about recognizing an elephant, the community of influential journalists is
rather difficult to describe in every particular, but absolutely
and instantaneously recognizable.

With rare and notable exceptions, the role of this community in the struggle against terrorism has not been to bring
clarity, but to serve as an outright impediment to it. I will not
say that America's journalists are the only impediment, but I
will say that they are among the most important.

The main obstacle they offer to the achievement of
clarity can be found in a simple idea which lies at the center of
their thinking on terrorists — that terrorism is a response to
some form of injustice, real or imagined. I do not mean to
imply that the American press sympathizes with terrorism; of
course it does not. The American press stands second to none
in its love of virtue and hatred of evil. But it is given to what

has been called the "I don't hold with their methods, but . . ." school of analysis.

According to this analysis, terrorists are young men and women who either as a result of quirks of personality or genuine suffering have been driven to impermissible extremes. Thus, for instance, the Weathermen were, we were told, responding to those three conditions long understood to have reached a more intolerable level in the United States than anywhere else on earth, namely, war, racism and poverty. Thus the FALN are patriots driven by the colonialist depredations against their island homeland of Puerto Rico to deeds of darkness on the shores of Manhattan. Some journalists view hijacking and terror as a "now-they've-gone too far" version of the trashing of Harvard. About the PLO it hardly pays to speak: The PLO no longer even qualifies for the category "terrorist." I need not bore you with further examples.

Facing Today's Terrorists

The question raised here, however, is not funny at all. Why does the American press seem incapable of understanding such a direct and immediate threat to us all? They are not stupid people. They are not evil people. And if a bit sanctimonious and hypocritical, they cannot really be called pathological. Yet they give evidence of a condition that, carried to extremes, might merit some clinical name or other. For our purposes here, let us just call this condition the inability to distinguish the moral nature of one kind of act from the moral nature of another, the lumping together of things questionable or unpleasant with things horrific; this confusion is achieved by the kind of escalation of language which calls the slightest unpleasantness or difficulty, for example, by the name of genocide, or equates the expression of a determination to defend Western democracy and Western values with a plea for the sanctity of ill-gotten capitalist gains.

The other side of this escalation of language is, of course, the kind of de-escalation by which none but the mildest of epithets is applied, say, to a hijacking, especially a hijacking in which no one gets "hurt." Nowadays, people interviewed after returning safely from a trip on a hijacked plane are all but invited to advise us about the quality of the food in the Havana airport.

The real nature of this condition is, to be sure, neither mental nor psychological but political. The American journalist community, with a few notable exceptions, suffers from an inability to recognize any threat from, to understand any dangerous implications of, or to admit any damning evidence in the case of, those movements it perceives to be on the Left. It perceives the terror to be coming from the Left (hence, for instance, the comic-opera confusion over Khomeini), and thus feels powerless to mobilize against it. It does not condone terror, but does the next best thing, which perhaps from the point of view of sowing the kind of confusion which breeds resignation to terror, is even more harmful than condonation. Faced with a terrorist act it asks, what did those *other* bad people — be they the Americans, the English, the Israelis, the Italians or the Dutch — what did these *other* bad people do to drive terrorists into such "tragic" misconduct?

Had the main actors in terror been neo-Nazis, neo-fascists, people pledged to the spread of apartheid throughout the world, there would have been not one moment's confusion or hesitation in the American press, neither about the threat posed nor about the country's clear-cut duty to take every stern measure to stamp it out, not *up to* capital punishment but *beginning with* capital punishment and going on from there. But terror from the Left is something the American press cannot face.

The American press will not be enrolled in the war against terror unless and until there is a general change of climate in the American body politic in the direction of mounting a larger resistance to attacks on the free world. Such a change cannot take place in the media; it will, in fact, be resisted by the media. It can only come from a realignment and strengthening of those forces in the political community who know that it is time for the United States and for Europe to shoulder the burden of responsibility that comes with great power.

BEN J. WATTENBERG is a Senior Fellow
at the American Enterprise Institute in
Washington, D.C., and co-editor of the
magazine *Public Opinion*. He was an aide
and speech writer to President Lyndon B.
Johnson at the White House from 1966 to
1968. Mr. Wattenberg is the author of
several books, including *Against All Enemies,
The Real Majority,* and *This U.S.A.*

A POLITICS OF FREEDOM IS THE ANSWER

I want to make two short and simple points this morning. They relate *indirectly* to the topic of this session, and *directly* to the topic of this conference.

First, one reason that terrorists are able to present themselves effectively as freedom fighters, is that freedom fighters have not presented themselves effectively as freedom fighters.

Second, never has the time been so ripe as now to reverse this situation and to develop a strategy for the ascendancy of what Senator Daniel P. Moynihan has called the *Liberal Party*.

To the first point — A question: How important to the purposes of this Conference is it that the democracies of the West have not instilled in their citizens the passion and the primacy of the cause of freedom? How important is it that the western nations face what is generally referred to as "a crisis of the spirit"? It is very important. Many remedies to the terrorist plague have been suggested in this conference. If we can operate in a climate of public opinion that understands the current threats to freedom, many of the proposed remedies are politically plausible. But if we must operate in a climate of public opinion that yawns and takes democratic values for granted, a climate of opinion that measures gasoline by the tankful and ideology by the thimbleful, *any* of the proposed remedies will be very difficult to realize.

The task before us then seems quite simple: To change the climate of opinion — or more precisely, to change it in order to change our policies and our politics. Just as a New Politics emerged in the 1960's predicated upon the guilt of the West, so must we set about in the 1980's to build a newer politics based upon the pride of the West. That, I suggest, is the pre-condition to dealing not only with the problems of terrorism but the pre-condition to dealing with several other related major problems that afflict the democracies — most notably the rise of Soviet power and the rise of petro-power.

This task to create the newer politics of the Eighties may be less difficult than it seems. It is important to note that too many battles have been lost because generals in the field thought they were too weak to attack. Let me explain.

All of us who operate in the arena of politics and public policy are unhappily familiar with the Law of Unintended Effects. A well-intended social welfare designed to help poor people may yield bureaucracy and inflation which hurts poor people. Military action designed in part to demonstrate global credibility and constancy may end up yielding not only neither, but the reverse of both — as witness American activity in Vietnam.

Asserting the Cause of Freedom

But the Law of Unintended Effects does not always work against us. I believe we are at a moment when the Law of Unintended Effects is about to cast its pall upon our adversaries for a change. Consider our global situation. It is one where weak powers assail strong powers. A technologically primitive society challenges the armed might of powers that are technologically sophisticated. How strange. Backward countries that are dependent upon the machinery and markets of advanced societies threaten that they will withhold the fluid that keeps those markets and machines alive. How very strange. Terrorist groups that are so weak that they can mount neither war nor guerrilla action, seek to bend to their will states that are militarily potent. Very strange indeed. We are witnessing the weak pushing around the strong.

I believe there are tipping points in the affairs of men. Mercifully, I believe the Western nations may be about to tip, and not a moment too soon. This approach toward a tipping point has been described wrongly as "a move to the right." In the realm of international affairs, I believe that to be a misnomer. We ought not to be talking about the right and the left, about social democracy or conservatism. The issue is how far the strong and the free will be pushed by the weak and the un-free. That is, or ought to be, an issue beyond conventional Western right versus left ideology. Indeed, it would be a political tragedy if this struggle becomes identified with one wing or the other.

The issue is this: How do we rally our nations to say, finally, *we have been shoved around long enough*? How do we construct a rhetoric and a politics that will get our nations to consider acting, if only occasionally, not as *shovees*, but as *shovers*? When that happens, and it may be soon, the military strategists in the Kremlin, the economic strategists in OPEC, the terrorist strategists in the cabarets of Beirut, may face the Law of Unintended Effects — and they may be sorry they decided to confront the West.

Now, let me make a tactical point. I cannot speak about all the democracies, but I can tell you that in the United States the politics of asserting the cause of freedom has been successful in the past, and will be still more successful in the future. It has been successful, moreover, at many spots on the political spectrum.

American Responses to the Call of Freedom
In 1975, Pat Moynihan stood up for this cause in the United Nations and became, overnight, an authentic American hero.

In 1976, Dr. Kissinger thought it would be unwise if Alexander Solzhenitsyn was welcomed at the White House. By the time that little drama played itself out, Solzhenitsyn had in effect written the Republican platform on foreign policy, and through the odd vehicle of Ronald Reagan almost unseated Dr. Kissinger's candidate, Gerald Ford, who happened to be President.

Later that year, when Governor Carter was sinking rapidly in the polls and due to face President Ford in a foreign policy debate, he called to Plains for advice none other than the former Secretary of Defence, sacked for being *too* tough — James R. Schlesinger. When the debate took place, Carter attacked on human rights, Ford obligingly "freed" Poland. The result is history.

In the aftermath of that election, held in a peaceful moment, at a time of general tranquillity, pollsters for both Carter and Ford stated that while foreign policy was not the number one *issue*, it was the number one *way* in which voters attempted to determine the essential character of the candidates — and the tougher the better.

Among our own number at this Conference consider the case of Henry Jackson. It is true, alas, that he never quite made it to the White House — at least not yet. But he has become a global symbol of the fight for freedom. He is admired by an American constituency running into the tens of millions. He may right now be as influential in the shaping of big-power arms agreements as is the American President. In bad years he wins his elections in his home state of Washington with a vote in the high seventies percentile.

The Politics of Pride in the Eighties

I stress the tactical political bonus of active membership in the Liberty Party for a reason. The reason is not a cynical one. I do not believe that most elected office-holders are craven beasts who will say anything or do anything for a vote. Quite to the contrary, most politicians I know are honorable men with strongly held views. They will not say what they do not believe.

But neither are they fools. Like many of you here I have had occasion to work on the campaign trail of more than one election. Unlike many of you here, I have never held elective office, but I have worked for elected office-holders, including a President and a Vice-President. I have never met a politician who likes advice on how to be unpopular, or how to throw himself on his sword for the greater glory of policy A or policy B. So, it is only because I believe in the *substance* of the newer politics of the Eighties, I commend them to you on *tactical* grounds.

Finally, a word about the media.

I believe that a resurrection of the politics of pride in our system may also deal, perhaps only in a small way, with one of the problems of the mass media discussed here. We have complained, properly so, that the press tends to glorify terrorism, to label terrorists as freedom-fighters. To some measure, terrorists have been glorified because we have been unsuccessful in glorifying our own cause. The democracies stand for more than dreary material suburban pleasures. They are decent, free, fair, prosperous societies — even in moments of recession, inflation and energy shortages. They remain heirs to an heroic tradition building upon human rights from one generation to the next. When we again make our own heroes from our own situation, it will be harder for our adversaries to make heroes out of thugs.

JACQUES SOUSTELLE is a French statesman and scholar. He was a leader of the
Resistance in occupied Europe during World
War II and later served in a number of posts
in several French cabinets, including that of
Minister of Information. M. Soustelle is a
member of the French National Assembly.

LIBERTY OR LICENSE?

The most accurate definition of terrorism is: to kill innocent
people as blatantly, as spectacularly as possible, in order to
intimidate other people, to undermine democratic states, to
provoke a collapse of law and order. From the beginning of
the Algerian conflict in 1955 to the terroristic activities in
several African countries today, from the PLO's attacks
against Israeli schoolboys or athletes to the random bombing
of pubs and hotels in Northern Ireland, the victims of the
terrorists have been mainly children, civilians and tourists.

It should be emphasized, therefore, that the targets of the
terrorists are not to be compared with those of the resistance
fighters in France, for instance, under Nazi occupation. They
are not military targets. The aim of the terroristic attacks is
not to physically weaken an army. It is to create a state of
psychological weakness. Terrorism is a variety of psychological
warfare.

From these remarks stems the primary importance of the
reaction of the media to terrorism. When PLO or "Patriotic
Front" killers slaughter some unfortunate children in Israel or
some poor Black farmer in Zimbabwe, what they want to
achieve through those deaths is to force themselves upon the
attention of the public in the country affected or abroad.
They kill to deliver a message. But who actually broadcasts

that message? The news agencies, the press, the media: radio and television. Hence their tremendous responsibility.

When one considers the lengths to which the terrorists are ready to go (e.g., by kidnapping diplomats and threatening to kill them) only to get long-winded and fanatical statements broadcast or printed, one realizes that what they seek is publicity, what they fear more than anything else is silence.

Is silence possible? In democratic states, the answer, obviously, is no. A Soviet Government can give orders to its *Pravda* or *Izvestia*; no Western government can gag the Paris or London newspapers. The press in a democracy is supposed to publish "all the news that's fit to print." To "cover" the news is the duty of the papers and the media.

On the other hand, should the news coverage deteriorate into more or less blatant, even if involuntary, propaganda for the murderers? After all, practically all the Western countries have laws which impose limits upon the publication of squalid, obscene texts. Under French law, the very fact of "praising an act qualified as a crime" is itself punishable. Such a rule could be applied to extreme, openly favorable coverage of terroristic actions.

This however, does not solve the most frequent dilemma of democracy: either to tolerate criminal behavior, or to impose excessive restraint upon the freedom of the press. In many cases (leaving aside the openly pro-terrorist comments of the Communist papers, for example) the psychological gain sought by the killers is provided by the press or the media, not as an act of conscious assent, but by thoughtless sensational-ism, a taste for dramatization, a lack of understanding of the real issues.

Corruption of Language
Either spontaneously or through insidious influences from certain circles (e.g., false "liberals" who sympathize with the PLO terrorists, or Soviet agents masquerading as leftist demo-crats, or even some misguided, "ecumenic" Christians), an alteration of the vocabulary takes place. The murderers are called "patriots", "freedom fighters", "guerrillas". No hint is

given of their brutish cruelty and their cowardly attacks aimed
at unarmed civilians, peasants and schoolchildren. The very
words used to name them provide the terrorists with an aura
of heroism. To hide a time bomb in a basket or a bag so that
it explodes and kills or maims twenty or fifty innocent passers-
by is nothing but one of the lowest forms of wholesale murder. Calling it an act of resistance, or an "operation against the
Zionist enemy" gives it a pseudo-military tinge. When a group
of killers murder a hostage, nine times out of ten the newspapers announce that the victim has been "executed", as if it
were the result of a sentence under the law, which would be
"respectable."

Obviously, no government can order the press to use or
not to use this or that vocabulary. Neither is it possible for any
democratic state to regulate by decree the length of the
articles, the size of the headlines, the more or less sensational
tone of the descriptions. That would amount to censorship,
which no Parliament would countenance in any circumstance,
short of an actual state of war.

The only way to a solution, therefore, appears to be a
careful action aimed at provoking self-restraint on the part of
the newsmen and media. Such an action could take place at
different levels, at the level of the managers of newspapers or
broadcasting stations or at the level of the newsmen themselves. Meetings and conferences should be organized to show
the responsible press or media people the danger of the paramilitary or pseudo-revolutionary vocabulary, or the advisabil-
ity of covering the terrorists' actions in a sober, matter-of-fact
way, excluding all kinds of dramatization. Special attention
should be given to the fake "ideological" pretexts the terrorists like to invoke, in order to show the emptiness of their
pretenses. To sum up, the main effort to make is to open the
eyes of those who, in good faith, contribute to the success of
international terrorism's psychological warfare.

QUESTIONS AND ANSWERS

Chairman (Paul Johnson): Now, ladies and gentlemen, I am going to throw the discussion open. May I remind you that what we are discussing — so as not to stray too far outside it — is the role of the media in the struggle against terrorism, and that the working definition of terrorism we have for the purposes of this Jerusalem Conference is, "the deliberate systematic murder, maiming and menacing of the innocent to inspire fear in order to gain political ends."

Professor Richard Pipes: As I was listening to the speakers the following thoughts occurred to me. Why is it that the media so often give favorable treatment to terrorists' activity? Setting aside other ulterior factors — self-seeking, political commitments and so on — it seems to me that one can find two causes, one which I call historiographical, the other philosophical. By historiographical I mean our historical textbooks (not historical monographs written for specialists) which are dedicated almost overwhelmingly to what may be called the progressive outlook. I don't mean that the people who write history books (and I have myself written textbooks) are people of the Left, but that there is in the writing of history a kind of professional commitment to the view that change is what matters, and change is by its very nature progressive. Therefore, there is in historical writings, being taught in

schools and pervading our popular culture, the notion that any
movement which is for change represents a positive force and
must be treated favorably. In that sense, historians and people
who are influenced by historical writings are predisposed to
view a movement such as terrorism as something good, even if
somewhat deviant.

The other has to do with a philosophical outlook. I find
from experience that whenever honorable and decent people
disagree on political matters, as has been expressed here by our
socialist friends and those who have been labeled "cold
warriors," the difference boils down to different perceptions
of human nature. People who profess socialist outlooks, or
what in my country are called liberal outlooks, essentially
believe that man is by nature good, and therefore that if he
behaves in a manner which is evil it is because he has just cause
to do so. Those people, including some journalists, who justify
acts of violence and who assume that these people "are trying
to tell us something" operate in most cases subconsciously
from an assumption that if people behave in such an outrageous manner, in a manner which is so contrary to what they
perceive to be human nature, they must have a genuine
grievance. Therefore, they believe, what we must do is look for
the grievance. I think this outlook is fundamentally wrong,
that one must get rid of what is an improper legacy of the
Enlightenment. The Enlightenment has left us a valuable
legacy, but it has also given us a very superficial conception of
human nature. We should recognize that there *is* evil, that
there are people who *are* evil, people who enjoy killing and
maiming, who derive distinct satisfaction from persecuting and
harming others; that the causes which they espouse are
nothing more than pretexts and justifications for what they
wish to do in any event. If we understand that, then I think
we will do away with the notion which has been expressed
occasionally during this Conference: the idea that where there
is terrorism there must be some kind of justifiable grievance,
and that, therefore, the way to get rid of terror is to get rid of
the grievance, which is to me faulty thinking.

Now, I don't deny that there may be occasions where this is true, but it isn't necessarily true. In order to cope with the problem of terrorism, I think it absolutely vital to recognize the existence of evil as a fact of history and to permit ourselves to prevent evil from disrupting our lives.

Manford Christensen, Denmark: I would like to ask the panel's opinion on how to deal with journalists who deliberately mislead people — I mean, when they do this not subconsciously, but intentionally. In my country the local news agencies' director has been called by the Syrian newspapers the Arabs' best friend in Scandinavia. When he visits Arab countries his visits are paid for by Libya. The secretary of the news agency is a member of the Danish Communist Party and his attitudes towards these problems are also clearly known. Other journalists on TV are paid by Arab countries; when they visit Arab countries their expenses are paid, and public protests against their false reports are kept down. It is simply not possible to get through.

How do you suggest to deal with journalistic colleagues who deliberately fight *for* terrorism? (Applause).

Dr. Edmond Bezalel Rose, Israel: As regards your very fine distinction between freedom fighters, guerrillas and terrorists, I do not sympathize with the "freedom fighters" of an imperialist empire of 12 million square kilometers extending from southern Turkey to Agadir, or maybe to Senegal (if you count Mauritania), an empire which possesses 60% of the world's petroleum reserves, and is in the process of strangling the free world. I cannot sympathize with the "freedom fighters" of the IRA, or the Provisional IRA, who kill innocent British children all over England, not only in Ulster; at the same time, if I am not mistaken, there are 3 or 4 million Irishmen living and making their livelihood in Great Britain.

I also do not like the "objectivity" of the British press. The majority of the British press, including the BBC, reports matters pertaining to the Israeli-Arab conflict in a very scandalous manner. It amounts to an international scandal. And do you know what they and other parts of the press of the free world are driving at when they report about Israel's response to terrorism? They want to deny Israel the benefit of Article 51/61 of the Charter of the United Nations, the right of legitimate self-defense. I am not exaggerating the case. The facts are well known here (applause).

Ken Anderson, USA: I'm a student here at the university, and one of the reasons we are here is because three years ago yesterday Israel decided to do something no one else would do, and you are here because, I assume, you want to continue this. I am just wondering, what is being done? When I was in the United States last, I noticed a change in journalism. It was decidedly against this nation specifically. Is there anybody who is lifting up his voice in protest? And are you men willing to literally commit your lives to what we hear you saying here today? In other words, are you willing to devote your lives to changing this situation? We know that if we won't, as we've heard over and over again, we're going to be overcome.

Norman Podhoretz: I think the tenor of the discussion about the role of the media and journalists was that censorship ought to be avoided but that the press ought to use self-restraint, be responsible. The trouble is there are too many journalists from whom it is unreasonable to expect any self-restraint at all. I don't see the *New York Times* or the *Washington Post,* for example, becoming responsible overnight. Nor do I want the government censoring their stories or forcing them to insert accurate stories about terror. So I make a modest suggestion that there should be Truth Squads. Now, as it happens in the United States, there is a man named Reed Irvine who sends out about twice a month a pamphlet called "Accuracy in Media" (AIM) and he makes it his business to pick up and criticize the failure of the press to report news which the editors of the *Times* and the *Post* don't think ought to be reported, or the distortion by the media of such news as they do report. For example, it took the *Washington Post* about two years to find out what was going on in Cambodia. They

systematically suppressed the story. Their reporter in
Cambodia was pro-Cambodian. She was admitted of course by
that vile government because they knew they could count on
her to soft-pedal the horror. Irvine spent a lot of time on that,
and I think that it might be a good thing if a similar publication, similar to Accuracy in Media, existed in other western
countries.

*Jay Bushinsky, Correspondent in Israel of the Chicago Sun-
Times and the Westinghouse Broadcasting Company:* As a
former correspondent with the Chicago *Daily News* I covered
many of the events of the category that we have been discussing here at the conference. I think that a few observations
are in order. What some of the speakers may not realize is that
a code of conduct has to be devised for the authorities in the
respective countries that are afflicted by terrorist problems. In
Israel, in the Sudan, in Cyprus and other places where we have
witnessed such situations, there has often been a tendency on
the part of the authorities to be nervous and somewhat embar-
rassed over the fact that their security had been penetrated.
We have therefore witnessed a practice of suppressing, withholding and denying information from the correspondents
who are out there to gather the necessary information. In
some cases information is distorted or twisted, resulting in correspondents finding it necessary to figure out what really happened and who may have been to blame, if something that
should have been told isn't being told. Then, of course, in Israel
you get into the problem of censorship which at times doesn't
seem to worry merely about the nation's security but about
the defense establishment and its status in the eyes of the
general public. In brief, if the authorities would give the journalists the proper access to the scene of the crime, journalists
might concentrate more on the nature of the crime and less
about the possibility that something went wrong or someone
wasn't telling the truth.

I would also like to comment on the attitude of the
world public in general, the public that in 1972 was not exactly favorably disposed to the idea of closing down the Munich

Olympics because of the massacre of the Israeli team. That refusal to close down the Olympics was not the fault of the journalistic community.

And finally, when we consider the performance of the press over these years, perhaps we should bear in mind that, at least in the United States, the press, because it is by and large a commercial operation, has tended to cater to the desires and the preferences of the American public. Whenever the publishers and others poll the public as to what they are looking for in their newspapers and other media, it is anything but foreign coverage. Yet I've heard no reference here to the need perhaps to explain to the public that a larger investment of funds and energy towards covering the world with the proper kind of personnel and budget might enable the public to get a better and more accurate understanding of what is happening in foreign countries where terrorism does occur.

Mr. Michael Comay, Former Israeli Ambassador to Britain: Mr. Chairman, I'll first say how indebted we all are, or should be, for the brief but admirably lucid statement we heard from Mr. Soustelle this morning. I agree heartily with him on one point, that it is no use expecting the press and the media to refrain from publishing news about terrorist activities. The press will reply that it is its job to publish the news.

Now, the press should be willing to take a position, and if I were charged, as I'm not likely to be, with the job of drawing up a manual of guidelines for editors, I would include in it at least 3 points. The first point is that to which Mr. Soustelle has already referred and rightly so, and that is the semantic aspect. When I was in London, I had a running battle with the *BBC*, the *London Times* and the *Guardian* over one specific point which irritated me a great deal. When an Irishman planted a bomb in a public place in London, he was invariably a "terrorist." When an Arab planted a bomb in a public place in Jerusalem, he was *never* a terrorist (applause).

I think that the press should be vigilant against this kind of double standards in its reporting.

The second point is that the press, including the most responsible and serious press media and magazines, is too much obsessed with the question of root causes, of grievances, of what is behind terrorism. That, in my opinion, is the domain of psychiatrists and social scientists. It is of no concern whatsoever to governments. Governments must make up their minds that certain types of behavior cannot be tolerated in the civilized society and act against them. And all this discussion about the grievances of the terrorists does not promote, but inhibits, effective action.

The third point I would like to make is that the press in a vague and general way keeps on calling upon the international community to act. There is no such thing in this context as an international community. There have been over many years efforts of the United Nations, particularly after Munich and other spectacular acts of terrorism, to produce some consensus, some common ground for international action against terrorism. It is a hopeless cause. There is not the slightest prospect of the Western world, the Communist world, and the Third World getting together even on a definition of terrorism, much less on the possibility of united action against it. For the Western countries the lesson is perfectly plain. Either they make up their minds to go it alone, to get together among themselves (as in the last two or three years they have to some extent succeeded in doing), to bypass the United Nations and the international community and act as a group against terrorism, or nothing will be done (applause).

In this rather bleak view of the capacity of the international community, I would like to make one exception: The protection of civil aviation against hijacking and attack. There I think some effective collective steps are being taken for the simple reason that all countries of all blocs recognize the common vulnerability of their aircraft. But having said that much, I think that is the beginning and the end of looking for deliverance to that quarter. Thank you.

Eric Silver, Correspondent in Israel for the Guardian and Observer of London: I would like to begin with a general observa-

tion, which is that just as there are no entirely objective newspapers and news media of every kind, just as we and our editors
have our prejudices, sometimes conscious, sometimes unconscious, so — and I think it's been proved, particularly by the
contribution from the floor to this discussion — there are no
objective and non-prejudiced newspaper readers either. I hope
that will be accepted in the spirit in which it was intended,
which was actually rather aggressive.

Let me take up a point made earlier. It is true that there
are psychopaths, men of violence and madmen in probably all
of the terrorist organizations, just, incidentally, as there are
psychopaths, men of violence and madmen in pretty well
every army in the world, certainly including the Israeli army,
as anyone who had actually lived in Israel knows perfectly well.
I'm not talking about the majority. I'm not talking about predominance, but there are people who succeed in armies, in
combat units, precisely because they have these qualities, and
there are times in war when these are very useful for their
commanders and for their governments and to their people.
But let me nonetheless take up the argument about the objec-
tivism of the British press. What I would like to say is that
simply because there are psychopaths and madmen and men of
violence in all these organizations, it doesn't mean that there
are no grievances and it doesn't mean there are no causes. It
doesn't mean there are no genuine conflicts. I happen not to
like the way in which the terrorist organizations decide to
wage their conflicts, but that doesn't mean that the conflicts
do not exist, and I would say that what explains the objec-
tivism, if that's the word, of the British and the American and
most of the free world's news media in covering this particular
conflict, the Arab-Israeli, the Palestinian-Israeli conflict, is
precisely that they do recognize that there is a grievance, there
is a cause and that indeed a war, a continuous war, is being
waged. It is the duty then of the press to report what is happening and to report from the outside, not from the inside.
Not to say these are the good guys, these are the bad guys, full
stop. It's not that simple, and I must add that I am not in
favor of the Palestinian terrorists. I live here. I and my wife

and children are prospective targets. I have had friends killed in bomb explosions. I am not defending it. All I am saying is that it is a war and that the media cannot dictate to the participants in the war how they should fight it. The job of the media, certainly those of us who are essentially reporters, is to report what happens.

Professor Zvi Eyal: I am a surgeon, I am not a politician. I am a victim of the Holocaust and I am very much surprised that until now I have not heard a word about antisemitism. The Mufti of Jerusalem was the first who started the ideas that eventually led to the establishment of the PLO. He was in fact looking in at Auschwitz when people were being burned. The export of the Middle East is oil, terror and antisemitism, and antisemitism aims ultimately not only at the Jews. If you think that terror endangers civilization, then I think that anti-semitism also not only endangers the Jews but all civilization (applause). Until this has been understood and publicized and responded to, I am afraid civilization will not know how to defend itself against this new Arabic empire which is exporting antisemitism in the most vicious way all over Europe and America.

Chairman (Paul Johnson): I am afraid those are all the questions we can take from the floor. I would like Michael Elkins to have a few moments reply because he was challenged by name from the floor.

Michael Elkins: My colleagues will address themselves to other speakers, but I must address myself to the man who spoke to me directly. I admire his passion, but his hearing leaves something to be desired. The gentleman said that he does not like the objectivity of the media treatment of terrorists. What I said about objectivity, and I have the pleasure to quote myself, is, "I do not believe that 'objectivity' requires the journalist to become a moral eunuch, impotent to embrace those basic values without which no civilization can endure." It seems to me that ought to have been plain.

The gentleman also said that he does not like these "freedom fighters," named any number of repulsive organizations, and addressed this to me. Sir, I don't like them either, and if you had listened, you would have heard me say, "I reject the concept that because the terrorists call themselves freedom fighters, *we* must call them freedom fighters. In other words, we must call them terrorists."

Finally, the gentleman said, again with his admirable passion, that he does not like the BBC coverage of terrorism. I would point out that my only reference to the BBC was in that same context, that I did not like it. And with regard to my friend, Michael Comay: Michael, you are no longer a politician, but if ever you were, you would know you must never use the word "never." You said, "when an Irishman plants a bomb in London he is a terrorist to the BBC; when a Palestinian Arab plants a bomb in Jerusalem, he is never a terrorist." Michael, from Jerusalem I speak for the BBC, and I *always* call them terrorists, and the BBC always carries what I say. Unfortunately, I'm not responsible for whatever else they carry (applause).

Chairman (Paul Johnson): Ladies and gentlemen, I am not going to attempt to sum up this morning's session because a great many and very complex matters were raised, but I would like to say that I think any conflicts between the media and the public *can* be resolved. So long as the *facts* are given in the press we have nothing to fear. As our great-British poet John Milton said, "Whoever knew truth vanquished in a fair and equal combat." I think if this Conference on International Terrorism has succeeded in placing a number of facts before the public and the media, then we have accomplished some of our purpose.

Sixth Session
Subject:
PROPOSED COUNTERMEASURES FOR
THE DEMOCRATIC WORLD
Afternoon, July 5, 1979
Chairman: Justice Meir Shamgar

PREFACE

What sorts of measures can be taken to counter the threat of terrorism? What can be done to prevent such acts, or minimize their effectiveness? Once a terrorist act has taken place, how can its *political* effect be minimized, or even turned against the terrorists? What is not only desirable, but realistic, given the kinds of forces at work in international forums?

These and other questions were discussed at the session on Countermeasures.

As a practical matter, participants noted that the restoration and strengthening of the weakened intelligence systems of the West were essential steps. Terrorist acts depend largely on the element of surprise for their success, and only superior intelligence can deter or preempt an attack before it begins, or help to quell it after its inception.

It was suggested that governments undertake common measures to punish terrorists or extradite them for punishment. The melancholy history of the attempts at the United Nations to pass anti-terrorist agreements, con-

stantly stymied by the objections of the
Soviet and Arab blocs, was also noted. Speakers observed that some progress had been
made through agreements between states that
shared a common faith in democracy and its
survival, and suggested that this was the most
fruitful path to follow. What is needed, they
emphasized, is in effect to create an *anti-
terrorist alliance.*

Such an alliance could, among other
measures, impose economic and political sanctions on those states, such as the Soviet Union,
Cuba, Iraq, and Libya, that offer support to
terrorism. These and other proposals were
probed at the session.

Finally, considerable attention was given
to the problem of safeguarding civil liberties
while fighting terrorism on the national level.
Citing the examples of Ireland, Italy, and
Holland, speakers noted that it was possible
to introduce effective anti-terrorist measures
without jeopardizing fundamental civil liberties.

MEIR SHAMGAR is a Justice of the
Supreme Court of Israel. From 1961 to
1968 he served as Military Advocate General.
As Legal Adviser to the Ministry of Defense
in 1968, he was instrumental in creating the
legal framework of the Israeli Military
Government in the administered territories.
In that year, he became the Attorney
General of Israel, and remained in this office
until his appointment to the Supreme Court
in 1975. Justice Shamgar is a member of the
Executive Board of the Jonathan Institute.

CHAIRMAN'S OPENING REMARKS

Ladies and Gentlemen, it is both my privilege and my pleasant
duty to act as moderator of this distinguished panel, which
will present its views on the *Proposed Countermeasures for the
Democratic World*, and to sum up the main notions and proposals voiced in this panel and in the previous ones.

Incessant efforts to find ways and means in order to free
the civilized world of terrorism, or at least of support of terrorism, have been and are being made by member states of the
international community, especially since 1972. These are
mainly attempts to further the adoption of a treaty prohibit-
ing terrorism in general or of treaties banning certain specific
types of international terrorism (e.g., terrorism against the
civilian population, against diplomats and against educational
institutions). But not only is there a basic difference, as there
always has been in international reality, between treaty provisions on the one hand and their implementation or further-
ance on the other hand, but there is, so far, no basic agreement
among the majority of states on the definitional framework
and the basic principles of such a treaty. Although much lip-
service has been paid in international institutions to the need
for the better protection of mankind from terrorism and its
inherent dangers to the human race, there is, as yet, no accord
on essentials.

Terrorism Justified

In 1972 the General Assembly of the U.N. established a 35-member *ad hoc* committee on International Terrorism. Its first and second sessions were held in New York in July/August 1973 and March 1977, respectively. Just recently, in April 1979, it terminated its third session, which, like the previous ones, was mainly a continuous general debate in which the different states expressed their views on how to react to international terrorism. But it appears that even the term "international terrorism" does not have an agreed and uniform meaning in the eyes of the different states. On the contrary, entirely contradictory interpretations and definitions were offered. As a result, no formulation of *practical* and *specific* measures to stop or decrease terrorism has been arrived at. One of the main reasons for the futility of the efforts to arrive at any agreement on such measures lies in the recurring attempt by certain states to focus the attention of the U.N. Committee only on the theme of what is called "the underlying causes of terrorism" (paragraph 7 of resolution 32/147) which is the "nom de plume" or "nom de guerre" of the attempt to justify and excuse existing terrorism in its various expressions by referring to the "misery, frustration, grievance and despair. . . which cause some people to sacrifice human lives, including their own, in an attempt to effect radical changes". [23.9.72 the sixteen power draft allocated by the General Assembly to the Sixth Committee, Doc. A/C 6/2 880/Rev. 1]

This is as if we could postpone the inclusion of the crime of larceny or robbery in the penal code of a given country as long as there has not been found a solution for the economic, social or psychological causes underlying such deviation from the legal norms of behavior.

The Italian author Mario Bettati has pointed out that this resolution includes 68 words, but only 21 deal with terror from the point of view of the victim. In other words, in addition to the contradictory basic approaches which are dividing the free democratic nations on the one hand and the extremist states who are themselves supporting terror in its well-known expressions on the other hand, there is a persistent effort to destigmatize terrorism and the intentional sacrifice of the lives of children, women and innocent civilians generally, by elevating it to the status of necessity, which according to the well-known expression knows no law. The so-called "grievances" are regarded as sanctifying each and every means, including murder of children. This paganism, which reminds us of the dark ages of human sacrifices is a new myth, like the "mysticism of the race" one generation ago.

Here and now we have the mysticism of the "frustrations and grievances", which again knows no bounds and no boundaries and regards the lives of children and other innocent civilians as expendable. We are forced to the melancholic conclusion that these deliberations at the U.N. are extremely unlikely to give birth to a binding convention.

Partial Solutions

The alternative attempt to try and solve only one segment of the problem at a time has also progressed very slowly: the 35-nation U.N. Committee dealing with a draft convention against the taking of hostages has submitted the text elaborated by it in February this year to the General Assembly.

It has been working on that very draft in annual sessions since the Committee was created by the Assembly in 1976, using a draft submitted by the Federal Republic of Germany as the basic working document.

Agreement was reached resolving disputes which had blocked agreement in earlier sessions — on application of the convention to national liberation movements and on infringement of national sovereignty (relating to foreign intervention to free hostages), but these so-called "agreements" were actually material retreats on vital points, namely deep breaches in the original version relating to the right to free hostages if need be by force, and prepared the ground for the actual vindication of present day practices of terrorism.

The points remaining to be settled, probably in the Sixth (Legal) Committee of the General Assembly later this year, concern the right of asylum and a proposal for exemption from extradition in certain cases. Since the Committee is a subsidiary group of the Assembly, the draft could be reopened for negotiation when the text is taken up by that body.

The Committee expressed the hope that the gains achieved "will receive a favorable response from the Members of the General Assembly and will lead to the adoption of the international convention", but the practical outcome of the deliberations on the draft is very doubtful.

Further treaties worthy of mention are the Tokyo convention of 1963, The Hague convention of 1970 and the Montreal convention of 1971, all of them dealing with air transportation and hijacking; and the New York convention of 1973 [Convention on the Prevention and Repression of Offences against Persons having Special Protection (Diplomats)] and some regional treaties of the OAS and the Council of Europe. But all of these treaties are unsatisfactory from the point of view of adherences and ratification and most of all because of the insufficiencies of their provisions, especially in relation to jurisdiction and extradition.

Terrorism and the Rules of Warfare

During the last decade there have been constant efforts to amend the existing rules of warfare in order to improve the protection accorded to civilians and civilian objectives in time of war. These efforts reached their apex when the protocol added to the Geneva conventions of August 1949 was signed in July 1977.

Terrorism is calculated to destroy all vestiges of the international rules of warfare.

As defined by one well-known legal authority, in international relations war is the alternative tactic to negotiations and its function is to impose the will of one group upon another, by force. International law purports to control the *modalities* of warfare, legal and illegal alike.

Rules of warfare are the result of a pull between two major formative forces — the necessities of war, on the one hand, and the requirements of the standards of civilization, on the other hand. These standards are applied in order to put restraint on the unbridled exercise of wartime sovereignty and in order to try to eliminate unnecessary brutality and dehumanization.

As has been very aptly stated (by Professor Greenspan), War and Law are, at first sight, a contradiction in terms. War means unrestrained use of physical force in order to achieve victory over the enemy, whereas Law expresses rules and norms of behavior according to which sheer physical force has been superseded by submission of disputes to adjudication, arbitration or other juridical process. But this apparent abyss between Law and War has been narrowed, and bridges have been built in order to define and govern *even war* with norms of law, so as to decrease unnecessary savagery and replace the laws of the jungle, as far as possible and practical, by human behavior even in times of war. Warfare is always destructive and deadly, but efforts have been made to restrain wanton brutality. These efforts, translated into the customs of war, international conventions and declarations, have led, *inter alia*, to the "outlawing" of the use of certain means, weapons or ammunition, and to the exclusion of civilian sites not used for military purposes from the category of military objectives, especially so as to protect the civilian population, women and children, from military attack.

In war the enemy's power of resistance may be weakened and destroyed, but the means that may be employed are not boundless. Rule 22 of The Hague Convention of 1907 lays down, e.g., that belligerents do not possess an *unlimited* right as to the choice of means for injuring the enemy. As mentioned, they are restricted and held in check by international conventions and declarations and by the customary rules of warfare, relative to certain kinds of arms, e.g., projectiles below a certain weight, asphyxiating gases and other weapons which cause unnecessary suffering. Intentional killing of noncombatants, killing of combatants after their surrender, assassination of selected individuals, all these are war crimes and punishable as such.

Those who conducted wars saw a definite practical advantage in observing restraints and controls, namely the advantage

derived from mutuality. Pragmatism means that every country
knew that inhumanity by its own soldiers would be met by
that of its adversaries. Religion, civilization and humanism are
also believed to have contributed — aside from the main pragmatic reasons — to the development of mitigating and humanizing influences. All this reached its peak when after the Second
World War, when crimes of war and crimes against humanity
were punished by international and national tribunals.

In the Hague Conventions of 1907, which are rightly regarded as failing to cover all possible situations, the following
general clause was added to the preamble:

"Until a more complete code of laws of war can be drawn
up, the High Contracting Parties deem it expedient to declare that, in cases *not covered* by the rules adopted by
them, the inhabitants and belligerents remain under the
protection and governance of the principles of the law of
nations, derived from the usages established among
civilized peoples, from the laws of humanity, and from
the dictates of the public conscience."

To this view the International Military Tribunal which tried
the major German War Criminals at Nuremberg, 1945-1946,
has added its massive weight. In its judgment that court declared that the law of war was to be found not only in treaties,
but in the customs and practices of states which gradually obtained universal recognition, and from the general principles
of justice applied by jurists and practiced by military courts.
This law is not static but by continual adaptation follows the
needs of a changing world. Indeed, in many cases treaties do
no more than express and define, for more accurate reference,
the principles of law already exisitng.

Another source of international law lies in those general
principles which are common to the legal systems of the
nations of the world. If murder is a crime condemned and
punished by the laws of each separate state, then it would be
curious indeed if it were not so regarded and treated in the law
governing the international community. The Nuremberg Tribunal affirmed the proposition that murder is murder in all
languages, including the language used between nations.

Killing of Civilians: Incidental and Wanton

It happens and has happened that civilians are killed and wounded during house-to-house fighting in a battle-area or during bombardment of military targets or air raids on such objectives, because of the close proximity of non-combatants to legitimate military targets or combat operations. Generally, such close proximity of civilians to military targets does not render an area immune from aerial or ground attack, and unintentional suffering resulting from a proportionate engagement of the target is not a violation of the laws of war. If military stores, headquarters or gun sites are set up in places inhabited by civilians, direct danger to the civilians is created because these stores, headquarters or gun sites turn into legitimate military targets and have no claim to immunity. Incidental to fighting, to bombardment or to air raids on military objectives, regrettable losses of human life are often inevitable and therefore not unlawful nowadays, according to the rules of warfare now in force. It goes without saying that they should be prevented as much as possible, but if there is no possibility to tackle military objectives otherwise, because the military character of the place is tightly interwoven with its civilian character, these attacks are tragic but not illegal.

The conciliation of the necessities of war with the laws of humanity is necessarily a compromise between conflicting aims. Such compromises are based on the *consensus of all participating parties*, on traditional and customary behavior and on the principle of reciprocity. If international society were to absolve or condone wanton and intentional murder of civilians in the course of ordinary traditional warfare or in the course of terrorist acts, one could by the same logic go on to acquiesce in the legalization of murder as such. In other words, if you accept only the rules of necessity and relinquish the present norms on account of their occasional failings (e.g., by stating that because civilians are killed in air-raids on military targets you can kill every civilian everywhere and always) you are left without any norms at all. Pragmatism of this kind is likely to lead the civilized world into an abyss of murder. What would in future be the realistic prospect of persuading soldiers and non-soldiers alike to obey rules of warfare, e.g., to respect those rules that prohibit mindless murder of women and children, if such acts are practiced openly and declaredly by terrorist groups which later on are welcomed with standing ovations by the General Assembly of the U.N. and participate in the deliberations of the Security Council?

All the achievements of the Hague and Geneva Conferences are at present in danger of being swept aside. The progress towards humanization is in jeopardy of utter disregard and nullification because of the modern revival of barbarous terrorism and the tacit acquiescence by States and international organizations in inhuman behavior and even their *de facto* acceptance of it.

An International Convention

The first and foremost conclusion is that an *international* threat has to be countered by effective *international* means and mainly by international cooperation.

International cooperation has to be based on a set of precise and agreed principles and find expression in practical arrangements; such orderly regulation which defines objects and ways and means can find its expression only in an *international convention*.

Naturally, at first such a convention would be binding and engender powers and rights only in relation to states *inter partes*, the states which have ratified it or acceded to it, but the participation of the nations of the free world, especially if headed by the U.S., will ensure its effectiveness and its pervasiveness and advance the cause of further adherence.

The efforts to arrive at a comprehensive and effective international agreement have so far been successfully foiled by those elements who figure among the beneficiaries or instigators of terrorism. Other neutral elements have adopted a passive attitude which also prevents the adoption of effective steps against the further transmission of the disease. In other words, the attempt to draft a convention within the framework of the U.N. is futile. It seems therefore that the free nations, taking note of the blind alley into which the deliberations in the *ad hoc* committee lead, should try *independent* action by calling a conference of the free democratic states ready to participate (most ideally, with the U.S. taking the lead), in order to negotiate a convention. The Gordian Knot can be cut only by the independent framing of norms, by the democracies themselves. This is the first and most important countermeasure. Such norms should include a definition of terrorism as the deliberate and intentional killing and maiming of innocent civilians, children, women and men, so as to inspire fear in order to gain political ends. This would include intentional attack on civilian targets, the hijacking of civilian aircrafts and vessels and the taking of hostages, in order to spread panic and terror. All these have to be declared *Crimes Against Humanity*.

What Should be the Other Specific Provisions?

a)   Such a convention shall declare terrorism an *international crime*, like piracy *iure gentium* (according to the Law of Nations) and accord to every signatory the right to arrest a terrorist and to bring him to trial before its courts, wherever he has committed his crime.

b)   The only alternative to the prosecution shall be the extradition of the offender to another state, in order to be tried there for his terrorist acts: The maxim *aut dedere aut judicare* shall be adopted and applied. Terrorism shall be recognized as an extraditable offense. The offense shall be treated for the purpose of extradition as if it has been committed not only in the place in which it occurred, but also within the jurisdiction of all the states party to the convention. The convention shall establish an extradition regime between the parties, whether any previous bilateral or multilateral extradition treaty between the parties exists or not.

c)   Offences of terrorism shall be *denied* the status of political offences, of offences connected with a political offence, or of an offence inspired by political motive, like war crimes and genocide.

d)   According to the provision of such proposed conventions, each state should undertake to include in its national law additional penal provisions against terrorism, as far as necessary, conforming with a proposed uniform code which could be included as an annex to the convention: such provisions will establish the jurisdiction of the national courts and define the offences, including the maximum punishments they entail. Because of the heinous character of the offence there should be no statutory limitation of actions.

e) States shall afford one another the greatest measure of assistance in connection with such criminal proceedings, including the supply of all evidence at their disposal.

f) According to such a convention, the democratic nations should undertake to abstain from any negotiations with terrorists, not to succumb to extortions, and not to pay any bribe, protection-money or ransom-money to terrorists.

g) Moreover, such a Convention should include effective sanctions against states actively supporting terrorists, permitting their open propaganda activities, harboring them or according them asylum; including, *inter alia*, the countermeasures of denial of military and political aid, rights of overflight and rights of landing. A state *failing* to act according to its obligations will be committing thereby a tortious act and shall be liable to pay damages to all victims of a terrorist act, public or private, and this, without detracting from its obligation according to the convention.

Other Measures

The second main countermeasure which could be applied immediately: The democratic states can and should take all practicable measures to prevent preparations, in their respective territories, for the commission of terrorist offences within or outside their territories, including the establishment of mobilization and information centers of terrorist organizations.

Moreover, the free nations should cooperate with one another closely and permanently in the adoption of concrete and effective steps against terrorism, including exchange of information and coordination of actions and other measures for the prevention of these offences and the apprehension of offenders.

For this purpose a conference of Government Agencies of the Free World could be convened in order to arrive at co-ordinating procedures and to prepare ground for strategic and tactical cooperation.

Last but not least: Leadership in the democratic nations could enlighten public opinion in the free world about the morally, socially and politically disruptive and corruptive effects of terrorism, and foster and strengthen, on the other hand, the confidence and belief in the concepts and values of free democratic society.

In order to strengthen these concepts we must preserve the rule of law and the judicial safeguards which are an essential and vital precondition for its enforcement, because this can be the only appropriate criterion, even in situations of distress and panic.

The more the comprehensive scheme of terrorist aggression unfolds itself, the more vigorous the answer to this inhumane phenomenon has to be. The conception of war crimes seemed to cover the acts of indescribable barbarity committed by the aggressors of World War II; but now it has become evident that indiscriminate violations of the laws of humanity committed by terrorists — spreading explosive buttons in schoolyards, blowing up aircraft in midair, turning school buses into targets, or killing children with the butt of their gun — are facets of a developing phenomenon, and are a representative selection from the multitude of nefarious techniques used by the new generation of offenders against the Law of Nations. If, therefore, International Law is not to remain completely helpless and impotent in such an emergency, its defences and remedies must fit the magnitude of the challenge. Only a generation ago humanity paid a very costly price, because it underrated at first the dangers inherent in a new epidemic.

As George Santayana said — Those who do not remember the past are condemned to repeat it.

MERLYN REES served as Britain's Secretary of State for the Home Department from
1976 to 1979. He has been MP for South
Leeds since 1963. Mr. Rees was Labour's
front bench spokesman for Northern Ireland
Affairs in 1972-74, and in 1974-76 was
Secretary of State for Northern Ireland.
In this office he dealt with the problems
posed by Irish terrorism.

TERROR IN IRELAND —
AND BRITAIN'S RESPONSE

I have been asked to speak about anti-terrorist measures in the
United Kingdom. But as I am sure you are all aware, terrorism
in the United Kingdom has been mainly concentrated in
Northern Ireland and I will therefore begin with the measures
which successive British Governments have regrettably had to
introduce in that province. There are measures which cover the
rest of the United Kingdom, but I will deal with them later on.

Emergency Provisions in Northern Ireland
The use of violence for political ends has been a feature of
Irish history for over two hundred years. Since the establishment of Northern Ireland itself in 1920 there have been four
distinct terrorist campaigns; in the 1920's, during the 1939-45
world war, between 1956 and 1962 and the present campaign
which began in 1969. In 1972, following the prorogation of
the Northern Ireland Parliament and the imposition of direct
rule from Westminster, the United Kingdom Government
appointed a Committee under the chairmanship of Lord Diplock, the eminent jurist, to consider "what arrangements for
the administration of justice in Northern Ireland could be
made in order to deal more efficiently with terrorist organizations. . . . " Diplock found that the main obstacle to dealing
with terrorists in the ordinary courts was the intimidation of

jurors and witnesses by terrorist organizations, and the principal recommendations in his report were embodied in the Northern Ireland (Emergency Provisions) Act 1973. This provided for:

- all terrorist-type offences to be categorized as "scheduled" offences;
- trials of scheduled offences to be by a senior judge, sitting alone, but with more than the usual rights of appeal;
- bail in scheduled cases to be given only by the High Court (rather than by a magistrate) and then only if stringent precautions were made;
- the arrest without warrant and detention by the police for up to 72 hours of any person suspected of being a terrorist (the normal requirement in Northern Ireland is that arrested persons must be brought before a court within 48 hours of arrest);
- the arrest and detention of a suspect for up to 4 hours by members of the Army;
- wide powers of search and seizure by members of the security forces;
- reversal of the normal onus of proof in relation to offences of possession of arms and explosives;
- a fresh system of detention by the executive. (Detention orders could be made by the Secretary of State on the basis of information which the security forces believed to be valid, whereas conviction for offences under the normal criminal law is of course on the basis of evidence tested in court. I should add that, although the emergency legislation in Northern Ireland still provides for a system of detention, this power has not been used since 1975; all persons in custody in Northern Ireland have thus been convicted of criminal offences or are awaiting trial for criminal offences.)

For the first time in United Kingdom statute law, terrorism was defined as the use of violence for political ends, including any use of violence for the purpose of putting the public in fear. This 1973 Act was itself subject to review in 1974 by a

Committee headed by Lord Gardiner, another eminent jurist, whose task was to consider the anti-terrorist measures in the context of civil liberties and human rights. The main changes which were made as a result of their report were in regard to the procedures for detention which, as I have said, is no longer in use.

Any legislation of this kind clearly necessitates some loss of liberty and human freedom. The powers which have evolved nevertheless represent a determination by successive British Governments that such legislation will depart as little as possible from internationally agreed principles and from the traditions of British justice. The aim is to ensure both that the security forces have every assistance in their task of bringing terrorists before the courts and that the integrity of the legal system is maintained.

Moving on from the legislation itself, security policy in Northern Ireland has been and continues to be based on the fair and effective enforcement of the law. At the heart of the policy is a determination to develop the effectiveness and acceptance of the police to the point where a military involvement in the maintenance of law and order is no longer required. Much progress has been made; the strength of the Royal Ulster Constabulary now stands at more than 6,000 compared with 3,800 in 1970, and there have also been significant organizational changes in the force. Fundamental to this security policy is the belief that terrorists are criminals under the law; they are prosecuted for criminal offences and not for the political beliefs that they may hold.

Terrorism in Great Britain

I now turn to the position in the rest of the United Kingdom. Here, although the incidence of terrorism has not been as extensive as in Northern Ireland, it has been bad enough. In the past 7 years there have been approximately 300 terrorist incidents in Great Britain (that is England, Wales and Scotland) which have resulted in the deaths of 75 people and over ten times as many injured. The overwhelming majority of these incidents have been connected with the situation in Northern Ireland. It was after a particularly horrific example — an attack on two public houses in Birmingham in 1974 which killed 21 people — that the Government introduced the Prevention of Terrorism (Temporary Provisions) Act.

The Act (and its subordinant legislation) is intended to prevent acts of terrorism connected with Northern Irish affairs. To this end it provides two important powers. The first is the power given to the Home Secretary to exclude a person from Great Britain or from the United Kingdom as a whole. (The Secretary of State for Northern Ireland is also given similar power to exclude a person from Northern Ireland or the United Kingdom.) The Home Secretary or his Northern Ireland counterpart may exercise this power only if he is satisfied that the person is, or has been, concerned in the commission, preparation or instigation of acts of terrorism, or is attempting, or may attempt, to enter the country for that purpose. This is an executive power which does not involve court procedures, and could not because the information on which the Home Secretary takes his decision is usually intelligence information which could not be revealed in open court. There is provision in the legislation for a person to make representations against exclusion which are considered by independent advisers appointed under the Act. But the final responsibility for deciding whether to exclude rests with the Home Secretary.

The second important power provided is the power to detain a person for up to a maximum of seven days without bringing him before a court. The police are empowered to arrest a person without a warrant if they reasonably suspect that he has committed an offence under the Act or is involved in acts of terrorism; and they may detain such a person on their own authority for up to 48 hours. The Home Secretary may extend the period of detention to a maximum of seven days in all. The purpose of this power of detention is to give the police time to make enquiries about the person detained in order to decide whether to apply to the Home Secretary for an exclusion order or to charge the person and bring him before the courts.

These are the most important parts of the legislation. It also provides for the proscription in Great Britain of organizations which the Home Secretary considers are concerned in terrorism in the United Kingdom connected with Northern Irish affairs. (A similar power to proscribe organizations in Northern Ireland is contained in other legislation). At present, only the IRA is proscribed in Great Britain because it is that organization which has been responsible for most of the acts of terrorism which have taken place in Great Britain. In Northern Ireland 7 organizations are proscribed. It is an offence to further the aims of a proscribed organization. It is also an offence under the Prevention of Terrorism Act to raise money for acts of terrorism connected with Northern Ireland but unrelated to proscribed organizations, and to fail to disclose to the police information about terrorism connected with Northern Irish affiars. Finally, I should mention that regulations made under the Act lay down a framework of controls at ports. These controls give the police power to examine, search and detain people at ports for the purpose of determining whether they are involved in terrorism or have committed an offence under the Act.

How to Preserve Civil Liberties?

It will be apparent from what I have said that in responding to the threat from terrorism we have been compelled to make some inroads into our civil liberties.

This brings me to the most important question which this conference is concerned with, namely, the conflict between the preservation of civil liberties and the protection of lives and property from terrorist attack. I use the word "conflict" deliberately. There is no way in which we can take powers to deal with terrorism without at the same time diminishing the ordinary, innocent citizen's own freedom. The terrorist knows this and rejoices at every such measure introduced. For in a democratic society the terrorist's aim (whatever his political coloration) is to discredit the Government. He tries to do this first by sowing seeds of doubt about the Government's capacity to defend its citizens and then, more insidiously, by trying to bring about the steady erosion of civil liberties to a point where the Government and society's commitment to democratic values is fatally weakened.

This means that those of us who are caught in this "conflict" have to keep a steady nerve. We must be especially alive to the addictive effect of anti-terrorist measures — once introduced into the body politic it is difficult to contemplate giving them up. It is specifically in order to prevent what I might call entrenchment by stealth that the Northern Ireland Emergency Provisions legisltion has to be approved by both Houses of Parliament every 6 months. The Prevention of Terrorism Act has similarly to be approved, every 12 months, if it is to continue in force. By this means we hope that we can keep alive the realization that these measures are emergency ones only and should be temporary.

The problems of Northern Ireland are unique and I have no doubt that there have to be political as well as security solutions to them. Many other countries in the West are increasingly finding that their democratic institutions are under attack by terrorist groups of one complexion or another. The motivation of terrorists may differ from country to country, but their ultimate aim is the same: to overthrow by violence the democratically elected government and to impose their own views upon the public.

European Convention on Suppression of Terrorism

Such methods must not be allowed to prevail, and if they are not to do so it is clearly necessary for democratic governments to cooperate in measures to ensure that those who commit terrorist acts are brought to justice. An example of such cooperation is the European Convention on the Suppression of Terrorism, drawn up by the Council of Europe, and concluded in 1977. The United Kingdom has ratified that Convention without reservation by means of the Suppression of Terrorism Act 1978. Briefly, the Convention provides that certain terrorist-type offences are not to be regarded as political offences for the purpose of extradition between contracting states. The Convention also embodies the requirement to consider prosecution in cases where extradition is refused. It is designed to ensure so far as possible that terrorists cannot escape justice by taking refuge outside the country where they committed their offences and pleading that those offences were politically motivated as a defence against extradition. I should say that neither the Convention nor our own Act is a threat to genuine political refugees, whose interests are properly safeguarded. A recent development has been the drawing up of an agreement among the member states of the EEC concerning the operation of the Convention among themselves until such time as all of them should have ratified it without reservation. As well as their practical value, agreements of this kind demonstrate the determination of democratic governments not to capitulate to terrorism. I hope that this conference, by focusing attention on the problem, may in some small measure contribute towards finding a solution.

HARRY VAN DEN BERGH has been a
Socialist member of the Dutch Parliament
since 1977, where he serves on the Foreign
Affairs and Defense Committees. He has
also been an active participant in the
Political Affairs Committee of the Council
of Europe. Mr. Van den Bergh writes
regularly for several Dutch newspapers and
magazines on foreign affairs.

MAINTAINING THE BALANCE

Ladies and gentlemen, Mr. Chairman, I would like to say that
as a Democratic Socialist I've been rather disappointed, to say
the least, with some of the remarks I've heard in the previous
days. Many speakers spoke implicitly or explicitly against
Social Democrats, or Democratic Socialists, alleging that our
movement, which I am proud to belong to, has taken a soft
stand on terrorism. To begin with, I may remind you that those
were governments of Democratic Socialists in many European
countries, as well as in Israel, which took very firm stands in
the past few years against terrorism. I can speak on behalf of
the whole Democratic Socialist movement and say that our
starting point regarding terrorism is and will be that no political
objective may be achieved through the murder of innocents.
Those who have suggested here in the last few days that our
socialist movement has taken a different stand are unjustified,
and they make the dialogue among different political movements, in democratic societies outside as well as within Europe,
quite difficult.

Mr. Chairman, I would like to warn against the illusion
that terrorism is invincible. Our experience in the last few years
in European countries has proved that an effective solution
against terrorism can only be found against a background of
comprehensive social and economic policies. It doesn't mean
that we should go back even one millimeter on the fight against

terrorism, but that we should have a more comprehensive policy. We need an anti-terrorist strategy which will preserve our liberties, national as well as international.

I may remind you that the democratic societies have been rather successful in fighting terrorism, and I say beforehand that of course any person killed by terrorism is one too many. If we compare simply what we have done so far, I might say that since 1965, about a thousand people, a thousand too many — I repeat that with all emphasis — have been killed by international terrorism in our democratic societies (with the exclusion of Northern Ireland and Israel), and I may say just as a matter of comparing, that about 600,000 people in those same years have been killed by road accidents. The democratic societies in general have been rather successful in their fight against terrorism and we should not forget it.

A Strategy Against Terrorism

The strategy I mentioned should be conducted on two levels: First, the national level, and second, the international one. On the national level, I would make the following points which were also discussed within the framework of the Council of Europe:

First, we must strengthen national police forces. The fight against terrorism should be basically a task of police forces and not of military forces, although it may include preventive action by intelligence services. Secondly, with regard to air transport, I feel very much that we need standardization of procedures in airports. This is absolutely essential. I remember an instance when I boarded a Dutch airliner in Madrid, where it would have been easy to load a whole tank into the aircraft. So what is very important is that within the democratic countries, within all the member states of the Council of Europe, those procedures should be standardized. It doesn't make sense if at the airport of London or Amsterdam or Paris there are strict security measures and at others there are none.

Finally, on the national level a number of deterrent measures should be taken. The most important thing is that after terrorists have been captured, say at airports, we must, as democratic countries, stick effectively to our legal procedures. I think nothing is worse than what has happened in the past few years when governments have captured or arrested terrorists and then released them just a few days later. Psychologically and politically, it is absolutely unacceptable that democratic societies act in this way. If we fail, this would be psychologically devastating for our societies, and it would diminish our political will to resist terrorism.

With regard to further measures in the struggle against terrorism, I should like to make one remark, because there is a disturbing question. New repressive legislation which might improve security could dismantle the freedoms of society, and once we adopt such laws it would be very difficult to regain liberty. If we accept the idea that a certain strategy is vital for the preservation of our democratic institutions, how can we make sure that it is also compatible with the structure of our democratic society? As a guiding principle we can take Chancellor Schmidt's own words in his address to the European Parliamentary Assembly in April, 1978 on the flexibility of democracy in cases of terrorist blackmail. He said, "No terrorist can, no terrorist shall, force us to sacrifice constitutionality and democracy." In other words, the democratic state must certainly defend itself and take appropriate legal action against terrorism, but such action must always be subject to the rule of law. This is an essential point of our democratic society, and we should stick to it.

International Cooperation Against Terrorism

Now, I come to the problem of international cooperation. We know that we have enormous problems in the international community in the struggle against terrorism, and we know that the international community is ideologically divided on this issue. The international community, then, doesn't have a set of common values in the fight against terrorism. Still, though I have the same doubts others have expressed, we should continue the discussions within the United Nations. If we don't, we would lose a chance of persuading other countries.

We should emphasize, more than we have done before, the cooperation within the Council of Europe, in which the State of Israel is an observer. We need an improvement of the Tokyo Convention of 1963. I will not elaborate, but I'll just mention it. I think we need also to improve the Hague Convention of 1970 and the 1971 Montreal Convention. I know that sharp criticism of those conventions is fully justified, but from the point of view of international law there is no other basis. I feel that even when those conventions are not fully workable, more states should be asked to sign them.

Another point is the badly felt need for a separate convention that would backstop the three above-mentioned conventions with effective enforcement measures, such as ending air services to the countries refusing to comply with the three conventions. I feel that the agreement reached at the Bonn Summit in July, 1978 is a positive step forward. We have suggested that concerned states, mainly the democratic states, should consider the unilateral invocation of economic and other sanctions against states encouraging and condoning terrorist acts. The Federal Republic of Germany, for example, did so when it cancelled all its flights to Algeria until that country agreed to allow unarmed West German flight attendants to check passengers boarding Lufthansa flights. This is an example of the kind of measures we should take.

There is one other problem. We should consider very carefully the problem of the diplomatic bag. We have proved that arms are sometimes smuggled through abuse of diplomatic immunity. I think there is a strong case for taking greater advantage of certain safeguards because we have them already in the 1961 Vienna Convention of Diplomatic Relations. I do not say that we should renounce that convention, but it would be quite reasonable to take advantage of its provisions to investigate from time to time the baggage of embassy officials where intelligence reports lead to the suspicion that arms are being brought in. It might be wise to consider whether all forms of immunity of baggage of individual diplomats still retain their original value.

Last but not least on the international level, the member states of the Council of Europe should rapidly implement the European Convention on the Suppression of Terrorism which was signed on 27 January, 1978. It should also be considered whether this convention which was, and still is, an important step forward should be expanded to non-member states of the Council of Europe.

Support of Freedom in the Third World

Mr. Chairman, after those specific remarks, I want to finish with a few general political remarks, which reflect a bit on the points we have heard from previous speakers, because I very much feel that our discussions and our dialogues could have been more useful than they have been so far. I doubt whether it is useful that so many speakers have been speaking in terms of communism as a conspiracy behind almost everything in the world and, on the other side, talked of the free world. I doubt whether this is a useful approach and I doubt whether it is a justified approach. Indeed, the Soviet Union and other states supported by Moscow help and aid terror and oppression, and I do not have the slightest sympathy for those countries and for those people. But if we want to look at a more general view, a more general approach to why movements sometimes commit terrorist acts, I think also we should look at our own responsibility in Western countries. I ask the question: How far are Western countries themselves — or in particular, their intelligence services — responsible for lack of freedom and repression in parts of the world that belong to the so-called Western commercial interests?

If we look at one side, it is incumbent upon us also to look at the other side of the world, where Western countries and Western intelligence services are until today responsible for repression and a lack of freedom. I refuse, as a Social Democrat, to look at one side and to say nothing about the other side.

Another remark in this general framework. If liberation movements (and a few of us have talked about that), for instance in Africa, turn to Moscow, and I know it has happened many times and I regret that, it is because in many cases the free world chose to support its own commerical and economic interests, instead of showing an understanding of the wish for national freedom and liberty. We Dutch have learned a hard lesson from our Indonesian experience in our former colonies. But the same has happened in Africa and elsewhere and today in Latin America, because it seems that freedom in the view of quite a few people can only exist in the Western world, and not in other parts of the world. We should not choose too late against the many Somozas we still have today in Latin America and elsewhere in the world. If the people there — I say this regretfully — turn to Moscow, we should ask ourselves whether we have not fulfilled our responsibility to freedom and liberty in a very selective way.

One last remark, Mr. Chairman, if you allow me, with regard to the furious attack we have heard on détente policies. I have heard attacks on détente policies which in my view are totally unjustified and have more to do with American domestic policies than with responsible political analysis. However incomplete détente might be, it has preserved, and I hope it will preserve, peace in Europe.

MORDECAI BEN-ARI served as Executive
Chairman of El Al Israel Airlines from 1967
to 1979. In this capacity he supervised the
development of El Al's unique anti-terrorist
security system, and was a leading proponent
in IATA for the adoption of effective anti-
terrorist measures.

PROTECTING THE AIRWAYS

Scheduled Air Transportation is one of the main targets of
national and international terrorist organizations. Since safety
and security are the bases of the very existence of scheduled
aviation as a worldwide international air transport system, it
is only natural that IATA, the association of scheduled airlines, has been and is presently in the forefront of initiating,
coordinating and executing actions on an international basis in
the field of airline security, with a view to safeguarding the
very existence of its members — individually as well as a group

El Al Israel Airlines, after the hijacking of one of its aircraft in July 1968 by Arab terrorists, has developed — with the
assistance and under the guidance of the Government of Israel
and the cooperation of the governments of the countries in
which it operates — a comprehensive security system, which is
designed to counteract all possible facets of armed perpetration
against its passengers, its aircraft, its personnel and its installations at airports and cities.

Due to this system, which is continuously being improved and dynamically adapted to new developments, the
airline has been successful in securing the continued existence
and development of a safe and regular airlink between Israel
and the outside world, despite several terrorist attacks against
its operations.

In September 1976, following the hijacking of the Air
France aircraft to Entebbe and the liberation of the hostages
by the heroic and brilliant action of the Israel Defense Forces,
led by the late Lt. Col. Yonatan Netanyahu, El Al submitted
a memorandum to IATA, a copy of which is attached here,
proposing far-reaching changes in the policy of scheduled
airlines related to security. In submitting its proposals, El Al
has acted as a member of the international scheduled airline
community, for the benefit of this community — and for no
other reason.

We are pleased that part of our proposals have already
been accepted — while other elements are under active study
and discussion. There is no doubt in our minds that airline
security will be greatly enhanced by the implementation of
our new security program by all scheduled airlines.

*

EXCERPTS FROM A MEMORANDUM

submitted by
Mr. Mordecai Ben-Ari, Executive Chairman,
El-Al Israel Airlines, to Mr. Knut Hammerskjold,
Director General, International Air Transport Association,
September 7, 1976

Subject: Security of International Scheduled Civil
Aviation

1.   **General**
The hijacking of the Air France aircraft by Arab terrorists,
assisted by members of international anarchist groups,
and the ensuing events which culminated in the freeing of
the hostages, who were held prisoners at Entebbe, by the
swift and unilateral action of the Israel Defence Forces,
as well as other similar events, demonstrate two points:

a. That air piracy in its latest manifestations is international in scope and organization and as such endangers the very existence of scheduled civil aviation; and

b. That determined and coordinated action against the pirates of the air taken by all concerned, including governments, is the only effective course to combat the evil.

Since safety and security are the basis of the very possibility of the existence of scheduled aviation as a worldwide international air transport system, it is only natural that IATA, the International Association of Scheduled Airlines, has been and must be in the forefront of initiating, coordinating and executing actions on an international basis, with a view to safeguard the very existence of its members, individually as well as a group.

The regrettable fact is [that despite IATA's efforts] air terrorism continues to develop both in scope, viciousness and intensity. Furthermore, it is increasing its technical sophistication through cooperation between various terrorist and anarchistic organizations on an international scale.

Based on a thorough analysis of recent developments in this field, I feel that IATA and its members should review their policy and actions with a view towards evolving a new, more comprehensive plan, encompassing every facet of the problem.

2. A New Policy: Active Defence

Hitherto the security actions taken by governments and airlines have been mainly passive in their nature. Accordingly, airlines, aircraft and their passengers have had to absorb the first shock of the terrorist attack. In order to diminish the risks involved, it is suggested, that a new policy, a policy of active defence, be adopted by the governments, IATA, and the airlines. The main elements of the [proposed] policy of active defence are:

a.   Active intelligence;

b.   Active pre-emptive measures against all forms of armed attack, based on information obtained in advance;

c.   Active opposition and offensive action in cases where the two first elements have been successful in preventing armed attacks.

3.   **A New Security Program for IATA**

In order to implement the policy outlined above, the following line of action is recommended to IATA:

a.   *Establishment of a Central Security Committee* consisting of a number of airline presidents, having the task of formulating a unified policy for all members regarding the measures to be taken for actively defending their installations, aircraft, personnel and passengers against armed attackers.

As has been confirmed by developments in the field of air piracy since 1968, the only effective method of combating terror in the air is the policy of active defence by governments and airlines.

A unified and coordinated policy of all airlines worked out by the Security Committee will greatly improve the chances of more secure airline operations in the future, and may even lead to the cessation of terrorist activities against airlines.

b.   *Establishment of an Airline Security Intelligence Center at IATA Headquarters*

The tasks of this center will be collection and dissemination of information and data related to activities of various terrorist groups engaged in air piracy with a view towards enabling preventive action by governments.

The intelligence center will cooperate with the Security Authorities of all countries and with Interpol.

c.   *Establishment of an IATA Security Enforcement Authority*

The tasks of this Authority would be as follows:

a)   Supervision of the security measures taken by the authorities;

b)   Supervision of the security measures taken by the airlines;

c)   Establishment of a security rating for each airport and airline, thus enabling constant and unified improvements in the field of security measures by all concerned.

d.   *Mobilization of all Airline Presidents for the following activities:*

a)   Representation of IATA's security policy to their governments;

b)   Active assistance [by the President of each airline] to other airlines in all fields connected with security and defence against air piracy in all its forms;

c)   Personal supervision of the implementation of security measures taken by each airline.

JOSEPH W. BISHOP, JR. has been Professor of Law at Yale University Law School
since 1957, and has held positions in the
faculties of several European universities
including Cambridge and Münster. Among
Professor Bishop's recent publications are
Justice Under Fire: A Study of Military Law
(1974), and *Obiter Dicta* (1971). He also
contributes reviews and articles to leading
law journals and magazines.

LEGAL MEASURES TO CONTROL TERRORISM
IN DEMOCRACIES

No democratic country is today immune from the problem of
terrorism. In some countries, of course, the murderous zealots
are more of a problem than in others. It is difficult to generalize about terrorists, but I think they can roughly be divided
into two categories. The first, exemplified by the Irish Republican Army, are those who have fairly well defined political
goals and a substantial basis of support in the population. The
other kind, exemplified by the Baader-Meinhof gang in
Germany and by the Italian Red Brigades, may be described as
homicidal maniacs. Their political goals are fantastic, and they
have virtually no popular support. They seem to destroy and
kill for the sheer pleasure of it.

What they all have in common is a murderous hatred of
their own government and its allies and a readiness to stop at
absolutely nothing, no atrocity, however brutal, in order to
achieve their notion of the millennium. Unlike common criminals they do not make Benthamite calculations about benefit and risk, nor are they greatly concerned for their own
hides. They may be able to intimidate witnesses and jurors.
They may be able to seize hostages in order to extort the
release of those of their colleagues who have been imprisoned.
Some, such as the IRA and the PLO, may receive substantial
aid, in the form of weapons and money, from abroad. There

seems to be some degree of contact among the various terrorist groups, although I suspect that it is generally fairly loose. For example, German and Italian terrorists, and a number of Palestinian terrorist groups, seem to have received both help and sanctuary from such lawless countries as Libya. Obviously they present the authorities responsible for maintaining law and order with problems much more difficult than those presented by ordinary criminals.

It is not my intention to try to analyze the philosophy of terrorism. My humbler and more pragmatic purpose is to consider the legal measures which may be taken to control violence which is too much for ordinary methods of law enforcement and ordinary criminal process. A goal of most of the terrorists is to provoke oppressive countermeasures, to deprive the government of popular support by turning it into a police state. The dilemma was best stated by Abraham Lincoln in 1864: "It has long been a grave question whether any government, not too strong for the liberties of its people, can be strong enough to maintain its existence in great emergencies."

Of course, Lincoln's question is relevant only in democracies under whose constitutions or traditions the citizens have substantial liberties. Despotisms like Soviet Russia, with a ruthless and omnipotent secret police, have little to fear from dissidents, violent or peaceful. Democratic countries which are now suffering from terrorism include, among others, Israel, West Germany, Italy, and the United Kingdom. The United States is certainly not immune from terrorism, although it does not at present suffer from violence which cannot be kept within bounds by the ordinary processes of law enforcement.

The Relevance of the British Example

The United Kingdom, the oldest and one of the most stable of the world's democracies, has for ten years been struggling with a campaign of violence amounting almost to armed insurrection. I propose to examine briefly the extraordinary measures which the British have taken to deal with terrorism in Northern Ireland and to ask which of them would be constitutional in the United States, if we were faced with a similar emergency. England, of course, has no written constitution and no higher authority than Parliament. In dealing with an emergency, Parliament is restrained only by tradition and its sense of what the British public will tolerate. But the other democracies I have mentioned do have written constitutions, and those constitutions are to some extent influenced by that of the United States. Therefore what I have to say about the measures which would be permitted by the American Constitution may throw some light on the problems of other constitutional democracies.

Let us examine briefly the options which were available to the British government when large scale violence erupted in Ulster in 1969. One, which was never seriously considered, was full-fledged martial law — that is, turning over the government of the province to the military and giving it carte blanche to do whatever it thought necessary to control the violence. England has seen no rule by soldiers since Cromwell's time. What Parliament did do was pass legislation dealing with the particular problems posed by the particular situation, notably the Emergency Provisions Act of 1973, applicable only in Northern Ireland.

Arrest, Search and Seizure

One problem was that ordinary powers of arrest, search and seizure were woefully inadequate. For example, a person effecting an arrest was required to inform the person arrested of the precise legal authority. That was not unreasonable where arrest by an experienced police constable in normal circumstances was concerned, but it was practically impossible for a young soldier, not versed in criminal law, who might be making the arrest under a hail of rocks and bottles or even sniper fire. Now the soldier need do no more than explain to the suspect that he is effecting the arrest as a member of Her Majesty's Forces, and the person arrested may be detained up to four hours without a warrant. They may arrest merely to check identity, even if there is no particular reason to suspect that the person arrested is a terrorist. (The Supreme Court of the United States has just held that a state statute authorizing such arrests is unconstitutional, at least in normal circumstances.) Similarly, the Act allows warrantless search for and seizure of arms and explosives by both police and soldiers. In brief, there are few technical restraints on the power of the security forces to arrest and detain for a limited period, permitting further investigation and, if appropriate, the issuance of a warrant or the filing of charges.

Proof and Admissible Evidence

Likewise, there was a relaxation of the more technical rules of proof and evidence. For example, under the ordinary rules, if arms or similar contraband were found in premises or in a car occupied by two or more people, the government had the burden of proving that one or more of them was in possession of the weapons, that is, that he knew that they were on the premises. In one case, in which a pistol and ammunition were found in a drawer of a bureau in a room occupied by three brothers, an appellate court reversed the conviction of all three, on the ground that the evidence did not support a finding that they were in possession of any particular one of the brothers, let alone all three. The 1973 Act provides that in such circumstances the burden is on each occupant of the premises or vehicle to satisfy the court that he neither knew nor had reason to believe that the contraband was there. This is, of course, a radical departure from the usual role that the government has the burden of proving all the elements of an offence beyond a reasonable doubt.

Another section of the Act considerably modified the restrictions on the admission of incriminating statements made while a suspect was in police custody. Such a statement can be admitted unless "it is proved by a balance of probabilities that it was obtained by subjecting the accused to torture or to inhuman or degrading treatment." There have of course been many allegations, whose truth I am not in a position to judge, that the police and, to a lesser extent, the Army have used rough methods to coerce confessions. The trouble is that those who make such charges are exactly the ones the security forces would be tempted to mistreat, and also exactly the ones who would claim they had been abused even if they had not.

Terrorist Intimidation in the Legal Process

By far the most serious problem was the intimidation of witnesses and jurors. Not much can be done about the witnesses, since it was practically impossible to give them adequate protection. The problem of biased or intimidated jurors, however, was dealt with by a provision permitting terrorist offences to be tried by judges, sitting alone and without a jury. Although the use of these juryless courts has very substantially increased the number of convictions for serious terrorist crimes, it is still difficult to get a conviction unless the offender was caught in the act, so that the principal witnesses against him are members of the security forces, or in cases in which there is strong circumstantial evidence, such as finger prints or ballistic evidence, or where there is a confession of self-incriminating statement. I may note, in passing, that of the appellate decisions I have read there are very few in which the conviction appeared to rest only on the admissions of the accused.

Pre-Emptive Internment

For approximately four years, beginning in 1971, the British resorted to internment — that is, locking up suspected terrorists without trial or even the filing of criminal charges. Many of the people interned, especially at first, were probably innocent, judging from the fact that about half of the 650 people arrested in the initial sweep were released within a few weeks. At the very least, internment should not be resorted to except upon strong and reliable evidence, and after review of that evidence by experienced administrators, preferably lawyers. Although a Royal Commission found that internment had probably prevented a good deal of violence, it was naturally very unpopular in the Catholic community, and also in the Protestant community when its militants began to join the IRA in the Maze prison. Largely as a consequence of the increasing number of criminal convictions obtained under the Emergency Provisions Act, the British felt able to end intern- ment in December 1975, and although it is still permitted under the law, there is no immediate prospect that it will be reinstated.

The Crime of Membership

Almost the only new crime created by the Emergency Provi- sions Act was that of membership in a terrorist organization. The fact of membership was somewhat easier to prove than the crime of conspiracy, and thus it was possible to reach the command and staff of the IRA, who might plan terrorist operations and recruit young fanatics to carry them out, with- out themselves participating in the actual bombings or assas- sinations. (Actually "membership" was not a new offence, since it had been made punishable by the old Special Powers Act of the former government of the province, which was in effect from 1922 until the British government assumed direct control of Ulster in 1972.) Incidentally, the Federal Republic of Germany similarly prohibits active membership in and sup- port of terrorist organisations. Otherwise, the criminal acts of terrorists are denounced by existing law, and the problem is simply to establish that they have been committed by the par- ticular accused.

I must return briefly to the extraordinarily difficult prob- lem of restrictions on the use of coerced confessions. The Emergency Provisions Act, as I have already noted, bars state- ments obtained by torture or inhuman or degrading treatment. In practice, the judges in Northern Ireland have been extremely reluctant to admit any self-incriminating statement obtained in circumstances which suggested that it was not completely voluntary. I think this is right. In the first place, there can be no guarantee that a coerced statement is true. In the second place, the use of such statements tarnishes the image of justice and furnishes propaganda to the terrorists. I would be reluctant to say that the use of force to extract information is *never* justified. Indeed, Jeremy Bentham came to the conclusion that in limited circumstances and for limited purposes the use of torture might be permissible. If, for example, the police apprehended a man who had planted a nuclear bomb in the center of a city, designed to go off in a few hours, it would be expecting too much of human nature to insist that the police use no force. But in real life such situations are probably going to be few and far between.

Capital Punishment and Censorship

Is there need for severer punishments, including death? Although British public opinion strongly supports the death penalty for terrorist murderers, Parliament does not. The Emergency Provisions Act starts off by providing that no one shall suffer death. My own view, for what it is worth, is that the death penalty is unlikely to deter the kind of zealot who becomes a terrorist, although it is possible that it might deter some potential murderers and bombers. I believe that the main argument for it is that imprisonment is not a very satisfactory method of dealing with more hardened terrorists. In the first place, most of them believe that their cause must prevail and that, when it does, they will leave the prison on a red carpet, to the accompaniment of drums and trumpets. In the second place, an imprisoned terrorist is an invitation to his fellows to hijack airplanes or to seize hostages for the purpose of extorting his release. I agree with the policy, initiated by Israel and now followed by some other governments, that one should never yield to a terrorist demand. But perhaps it is better to remove the temptation in the first place.

One other remedial measure which needs to be considered is censorship. In all countries afflicted with terrorists there have been complaints that the media, especially television, give them and their propaganda far too much attention. But the British have not provided for censorship, and again I think that they are right. Some limitations on the freedom of the press, which perhaps do not deserve the name of censorship, I do regard as legitimate. For example, I see no objection to penalizing the preparation and distributions of manuals on the making of cheap, simple and efficient bombs, or terrorist tactics.

Application of the British Experience to the US

Now this is a very brief and doubtless inadequate and over-simplified description of what one very civilized and humane democracy had done to control organized, large scale terrorist violence. There are, of course, people here who are more familiar with the United Kingdom's legal measures than I am. I have had to omit many details, some of them important. But I hope the general outline is reasonably clear — relaxation of many of the rules of law which in normal circumstances make it difficult to obtain convictions. Has it worked? I think that, on the whole, it has. It is probably impossible to eliminate terrorism altogether in Northern Ireland, in Israel, or anywhere else except in a totalitarian state in which there are no legal restrictions whatever on the power of the secret police. Personally, I prefer the chance of being blown up to the KGB. But without really serious derogations of normal civil liberties, the annual death toll in Ulster (whose population is only 1.5 million) has been reduced from 640 a year to about 100. So far in 1979, there have been, I believe, 38 killings. This is pretty bad, but it can be tolerated. Some American cities have a higher murder rate than Ulster.

Now let us look to see which of these measures might be held constitutional in the United States, or in countries whose constitutions more or less resemble that of the United States, if a similar emergency existed. On its face, the Constitution of the United States and particularly the Bill of Rights would seem to bar some of the measures to which the British have resorted in Ulster. For example, the 5th Amendment provides that no person shall be compelled in any criminal case to be a witness against himself. That would seem to bar a coerced self-incriminating statement, even if the coercion did not amount to torture or inhuman or degrading treatment. The Fifth also provides that no one shall be deprived of liberty without due process of law. Internment is certainly a deprivation of liberty, and it usually involves no more legal process than an administrative determination that the internee might be dangerous. The Sixth Amendment provides that in all criminal prosecutions the accused shall enjoy the right to trial by an impartial jury. How could a trial before a judge alone, without a jury, be squared with that requirement? At a conference on terrorism which I attended in England last fall, a group of distinguished British judges and lawyers took it for granted that these provisions of the Emergency Provisions Act would be impossible in the United States, under the Bill of Rights. They were unaware of the famous dictum of Charles Evans Hughes, a great Chief Justice of the United States, that "We are under a Constitution, but the Constitution is what the judges say it is." (Hughes made that observation at a time when he was not on the Court.)

The Supreme Court's Flexibility

The fact is that the Court has never treated the commands and prohibitions of the Bill of Rights as categorical, and has usually been slow to invalidate the actions of the President and/or Congress in a real emergency, particularly when the two branches of government acted together. In a nutshell, the willingness of the court to interfere with the President and Congress in an emergency varies in inverse ratio to the nearness and size of the emergency. The court never interfered with Lincoln, although he suspended the writ of habeas corpus, tried civilians by military commissions which operated without either juries or the usual rules of proof and evidence, and interned in military prisons many people who were or were suspected of being Confederate sympathizers. In the last and most famous of the trials by a military commission, a number of the people who had conspired to assassinate Lincoln were condemned and executed, without objection by the Supreme Court or any other court of the United States. But after the last army of the Confederacy had surrendered, the Supreme Court held in 1866 that a military tribunal could not constitutionally try a civilian when the civilian courts were "open". Despite this case, *ExParte Milligan*, the Supreme Court held in the midst of another great national emergency, in 1942, that a military commission could constitutionally try eight Nazi saboteurs, all of them civilians and one of them an American citizen. In that case, *ExParte Quirin*, it managed to distinguish the Milligan case. After World War II had been won, however, the Court in *Duncan v. Kahanamoku*, returned to the doctrine of *Milligan*, and held that military courts could not constitutionally try civilians during the state of martial law which was declared in Hawaii after Pearl Harbor.

Internment has been held constitutional in a number of contexts. Probably the most extreme example is the World War II internment of American citizens of Japanese descent. In ordinary circumstances few acts of government would be more clearly unconstitutional than locking up citizens solely on the basis of race. But in *ExParte Korematsu*, decided in 1944, the Supreme Court upheld exactly that. Few commentators have ever had a good word for the decision, for in the light of hindsight we know that virtually all Japanese-Americans were loyal. But at the time, with the war in full swing, the Supreme Court was not about to interfere with the judgment of the Congress and the President. I may add that even in the two ringing affirmations that the liberties of citizens survive in even the greatest emergencies, the *Milligan* and *Duncan* cases, the Court emphasized that these holdings did not affect what the latter case called "the power of the military to arrest and detain civilians interfering with a necessary military function at a time of turbulence and danger from insurrection or war."

The Supreme Court has said more than once that the power of the President is at its zenith when Congress has authorized whatever it is that he is doing. Congress has given the President the broadest imaginable authority to do what he thinks necessary in domestic crises. The most sweeping of these statutes, the so-called Klu Klux Klan Act of 1871, empowers him "by using the militia or the armed forces, or both, *or by any other means*, to take such measures as he considers necessary to suppress . . . any insurrection, domestic violence . . . or conspiracy" if it so hinders the execution of law that people are being deprived of their legal and constitutional rights (as by being murdered), and the civilian authorities are unable or unwilling to enforce the law. If that statute is constitutional, and it has never been tested in the courts, it would seem to authorize every step taken by the British in Northern Ireland, and maybe more.

The Dangers in Emergency Powers

The obvious danger in broad emergency powers is that they will be abused. The legislature may overreact and attempt virtually to suspend normal freedoms. The executive may overreact and go beyond what the legislature has authorized. Under the American constitution, at least, in the last analysis only the courts can guard against such abuses of power. What I regard as the true rule in such circumstances was laid down by Chief Justice Hughes nearly half a century ago in a case whose facts would be laughable if they had not generated such important law. The Governor of Texas had declared martial law and ordered the state militia to block the enforcement of an order of a federal court. He was trying to restrict oil production in order to keep up the price, which was ten cents a barrel. In reality there had been no violence and no threat of violence. The Supreme Court struck down the declaration of martial law and the steps taken pursuant to it, saying "What are the allowable limits of military discretion, and whether they have been overstepped in a particular case, are judicial questions." The principle seems quite as applicable to the question of civilian discretion. It means, in a nutshell, that the Court must be satisfied that there really is an emergency, that it cannot be dealt with by the ordinary process of law enforcement, and that the derogations from normal civil rights are the minimum necessary to maintain law and order.

If the Court does not wish to raise a constitutional issue, it can always or usually do what the British courts have on rare occasions done: construe the statute in such a way as to find unauthorized (or, as the British say, *ultra vires*) the measures which the government has taken pursuant to that statute. If a court finds abusive measures taken by the government under a very broadly worded statute and holds them ultra vires, the legislature may well be unwilling to authorize such practices in explicit, unmistakable language.

Of course abuses can occur far below the governmental level. A real problem is the tendency of ordinary soldiers and policemen to use more force than is necessary, to shoot to kill when the suspect might be apprehended by other means. I do not know an easy answer to this one. Of course, if the case comes to court in a civil or criminal proceeding, the court can decide whether the soldier or policeman used more force than was necessary. There have been a number of such cases in Northern Ireland. I do not know of any in which a soldier or policeman has been convicted, although I believe that the judges of Northern Ireland are generally honest and impartial. The trouble is that typically all the civilian witnesses will swear that the circumstances were such as not to justify the use of force, and all the soldiers will swear that the use of force was essential to protect their own lives. Somebody is lying, but it is not easy to tell who. And many such cases are never prosecuted at all. The problem is that the authorities are naturally reluctant to prosecute the security forces in such circumstances. Perhaps there should be appointed a body of distinguished civilians whose task it would be to examine the facts and allegations and decide whether the case should be prosecuted. Such a body should, of course, be completely independent of the security forces.

Principle of Self-Defense
The object of the whole exercise, I repeat, is to restrict ordinary civil freedom only to the minimum extent necessary to deal adequately with the emergency. But I do not think there should be any absolute, categorical prohibitions. As Abraham Lincoln argued long ago, defending his suspension of habeas corpus, no government, however democratic and liberal, can be expected to stand by and see itself destroyed by people who know no law and no restrictions on their violence. I expect that, to the extent that the courts of particular democracies have power to review the discretion of the legislature and executive, they would follow this broad, basic principle, as the Supreme Court of the United States has done. It is my opinion that, if in some part of the United States we had a

terrorist crisis comparable to that which now exists in
Northern Ireland, the Supreme Court would hold constitutional everything the British parliament has done.

Perhaps I should add a few words on another extremely
important aspect of the control of terrorists, that is, international agreement on the subject. I know that I am much less
well informed than many other people at this conference.
Obviously, it ought to be possible to extradite terrorists who
commit acts of violence. I do not think that murder, though it
may be politically motivated, entitles the murderer to claim
political asylum. There will of course be countries, such as
Libya and North Korea, who will give aid and comfort to
terrorists from other countries, who will offer them sanctuary,
who will supply them with arms and money. Perhaps it is possible to devise sanctions to discourage such international lawlessness. But I fear that the principal difficulty is that little or
no cooperation can be expected from the Communist world,
except to the extent that those countries fear that they may
themselves be the objects of certain kinds of terrorism, such as
airplane hijacking.

HANS JOSEF HORCHEM is the head of the
Office for the Protection of the Constitution
in Hamburg. He is widely recognized as one
of Europe's leading anti-terrorism experts,
and in 1978 served as a special adviser to
the Spanish government in anti-terrorist
countermeasures. Earlier in his carrer
Dr. Horchem was a judge in the Rheinland.
Among his publications are *West Germany's
Red Army Anarchists* (1975) and *Right
Wing Extremism in Germany* (1974).

PRE-EMPTING TERROR

Mr. Chairman, ladies and gentlemen, most of the topics I
wanted to speak about have already been touched on by the
former speakers. This is the advantage of being at the end of
the line. Let me make a few general remarks about the topics
I wanted to speak about.

During the Conference a great deal was said about Soviet
influence on terrorism. Other speakers have told us that the
Soviet Union doesn't support terrorism because it says so. Of
course it is true that Lenin, in his book *Left Wing Radicalism:
The Infantile Disease of Communism,* warned against terrorism. He described it as *petit bourgeois.* But this was meant
only for the Communist party. It didn't mean that Communism shouldn't take advantage of terrorism by other organizations. The strategy of the Soviet Union, therefore, is twofold.
The Moscow-linked Communist Parties are operating as a fifth
column of Soviet imperialism in the free Western world. They
look for fellow travellers and try to create a political alliance
with some of the trade unions. They openly condemn terrorism. The Italian Communist Party today even gives information about terrorist activities to the Italian police, but it is
they who will harvest the seeds of terrorism if we are not able
to uproot terrorism now.

On the other hand, the KGB both engineers international
terrorism and exploits already existing terrorism. The exam-

ples given by Jack Kemp, Robert Moss, and Brian Crozier are almost all correct, can be proven and documented, and are well known in the international Western community.

What is to be done?

The importance of Intelligence

First of all, improve intelligence, which means strengthen the effectiveness of the intelligence services. A few speakers were afraid of this, raising the spectre of the overwhelming power of the intelligence services. I thank Mr. Brosio for confirming the indispensability of intelligence services.

Well, is it really so dangerous? Let us have a look at a few intelligence services. The CIA, for a long time the leading intelligence power in the Western world, is now almost paralyzed. Do you know why? Four years ago the CIA still had 4,800 case officers abroad. Today, it has only 1,200. The FBI is emasculated too. It is not allowed to place agents in organizations which are only *planning* violence but not yet employing it. The result is that they don't have agents now either within the Socialist Workers Party of Puerto Rico, within the Communist Party of the United States, within the Klu Klux Klan, or within the Nazi movement in the United States.

Let us have a look at Italy. The Italian intelligence service, and to some extent also the police force, experienced the effects of a 25-year long campaign engineered by the Communist Party and by the New Left. The Socialist politicians, the liberals, and the majority of the Christian Democrats stood apart and didn't defend the intelligence service. This led to a few attempts at reorganization with new names: in fact, a few weeks before Aldo Moro was kidnapped, the Secret Service got a shiny new name, the Service for Information and Democratic Security. In the meantime, most of the veteran intelligence officers had left the organization and had returned to the police or into the administration.

When Aldo Moro was murdered, the Service had only seven experienced intelligence officers able to conduct the case. You can imagine how difficult it is to fight under those conditions against 200 Red Brigade activists and thousands of supporters in Italy.

Now as to Germany. During the last six months, there has not been one week in which there has not been published, in at least one leading magazine or newspaper or television program, an attack against the police, against the Office for the Protection of the Constitution[1] and against the Attorney General. Ten days ago, on a German television program, a journalist broadcast a program in which he accused the Office of having had a hand in the murder of an agent (who in fact was not really an agent). This TV journalist also claimed the murder was observed by a surveillance group from the Office. A day later, the journalist had to admit in court that the sheet of paper which he showed on the television program was a falsification. But this man is still on television in Germany, and no politicians stood up to defend the intelligence service or the police. This indicates the kind of atmosphere we must work in. It also means that we have a difficult task in a few countries in gaining enough intelligence of terrorist activities.

An Alliance against Terrorism

A precondition for effective inter-state cooperation is the efficiency of countermeasures on a national level. Each country within this framework should have a good intelligence network, a police force ready for operation (including a special task force), and a decision-making board which regards international terrorism exactly as it is — a threat to democracy and liberal society. The possibility and the willingness to learn from each other and to benefit from the experience of other countries is a first step towards inter-state cooperation. This will succeed only if the policy-makers of each country will agree to common procedures in exchanging information, in extradition or punishment of arrested terrorists, and in mutual security measures.

I can only emphasize again that to wait for an international convention means wasting time, especially waiting for

---

[1] The government agency established in West Germany to fight terrorism.

one from the United Nations. There are many reasons for this:
Only a small percentage of the members of the UN are liberal
democracies. The majority are not as vulnerable to terrorism
as Western democracies are. A rather large number of the
members of the UN got their independence from "colonialism"
through terrorist and guerrilla warfare. A few support terrorism and use it as a means of politics in their own interests.
Some governments are so weak that they have to tolerate
terrorists using their countries as havens and training grounds.
Others hope to protect themselves against terrorism by paying
tribute to terrorist organizations.

The democratic states, therefore, will succeed in combating international terrorism only if they rely on themselves. If
they do achieve a convention among themselves, they have at
their disposal police forces which have the capacity in man-
power, in skill and in technical facilities to cooperate on an
inter-state level. They further have the economic strength to
inflict sanctions on countries which provide weapons, money
or refuge to terrorists.

It may be that there is no formal international alliance of
terrorism, but there is at least a kind of brotherhood of these
criminals, and we should establish a counter-alliance against
this kind of terrorism. Inter-state cooperation should start with
the pooling of information about all terrorist organizations
available to each member of this "Alliance Against Terrorism",
within the following categories: Organization, *modus operandi*,
ideology, links between terrorist organizations, responses of
governments to terrorist attacks, and personal data about
individual members of terrorist organizations and their
supporters.

I should note that the current discussion about data-
collecting and privacy in Germany, in the United Kingdom,
in the United States, and in France jeopardizes the effective
pooling of information.

The security measures in passport control and checking
of passengers at the airports and the borders should be similar
in each country of this Alliance. One act of negligence in this
framework will render vulnerable the whole net. To agree

either to extradition or to the same punishment of terrorists in each country is a political question. The answer will be crucial for success or failure in the fight against terrorism. A decisive attitude on the part of the governments toward the terrorists, especially during and after the terrorist attack, is essential.

A successful action by terrorists is usually followed by fresh violent crimes. Nothing succeeds like success. The occupation of the German Embassy in Stockholm and the murder of two German diplomats, in an attempt to release terrorists from German prisons, resulted *inter alia* in the government's giving in to the demands of the terrorists over the kidnapping of the CDU politician Peter Lorenz. The resolute attitude by the government during the attack on the Stockholm embassy contributed to the fact that there were no further serious attacks for the next year and a half.

Denying Publicity

A firm attitude by the Government is made more difficult by the publicity given to terrorist actions in the mass media which to a certain extent is a part of the terrorist action itself. During the Stockholm Embassy attack in 1975, Swedish Television had a camera focused on the Embassy for several hours. After the kidnapping of Hans-Martin Schleyer in 1977 the first ultimatum of the terrorists contained two demands to the media: At 10:00 a.m. one of the prisoners was to issue a proclamation on television about the departure of the prisoners who were to have been set free, and the announcement was to have been broadcast on the main news at 8:00 p.m. In a subsequent message the kidnappers demanded that a video tape of Schleyer reading a letter be broadcast. Copies of video tapes, polaroid photos, and ultimatums and announcements were constantly sent to the domestic and foreign press.

At the Government's request, the German press conducted itself in its treatment of information during the Schleyer case with remarkable restraint. The terrorists lost thereby the publicity which they had calculated would be forthcoming.

The Need for Unexpected Responses

When Palestinian Arab terrorists, in an attempt to exploit the situation during the Schleyer kidnapping, hijacked the Lufthansa plane and thereby put pressure on the German government, the Government reacted offensively. They ordered the GSG 9 special unit to try to release the hostages. This succeeded in Mogadishu after discussions with the Government in Somalia. This action led to the suicide of Andreas Baader, Gudrun Ensslin and Jan Karl Raspe in prison in Stuttgart-Stammheim. Hans-Martin Schleyer was murdered.

Each single terrorist attack requires a special defense and reaction determined by the situation. Experience to date has shown that reactions must be determined by one rule during an attack — the responsible organs of state must not react in the way the terrorists expect. Such a reaction would produce the success which would breed repeated attacks. Nations must always show that they will not give in to blackmail and that violence will not be tolerated. Otherwise a problem which is basically a problem of security could well become a question of the future existence of free societies and states. Perhaps we are not at war, but we are being attacked by criminals, and we have the right and the duty to defend ourselves, our freedom, our society.

Let me conclude with a sentence from the Talmud which I was told about: *Hakam le-horgekha, Hashkem le-horgo.* For those in the audience who do not understand Hebrew I will translate it: "If someone comes to kill you, rise and kill him first."

MANLIO BROSIO is a renowned Italian
lawyer and diplomat. From 1964 to 1971
he was Secretary General of the North
Atlantic Treaty Organization (NATO).
He has served as Italy's ambassador to
the Soviet Union (1947-1952), to Great
Britain (1952-1954), to the United States
(1951-1961) and to France (1961-1964).
Mr. Brosio is currently the chairman of the
Italian Atlantic Committee.

FIGHTING TERROR
WITHIN THE INTERNATIONAL FRAMEWORK

*Mr. Chairman, distinguished colleagues, the panel and fellow
delegates, ladies and gentlemen.* I will try to stick to the subject
of our discussion which is terrorism in general and more
specifically for this panel, countermeasures to terrorism. A
speaker, however, always finds a good reason — more or less
good — for allowing himself a digression even if he wants to
stay within his bounds. In the very interesting previous meetings of this Conference we have heard many remarkable and
correct judgments about the state of the world in general, including *détente*, peaceful competition, the defense of and
threat to liberal democracy, and even war. Some here, I think
Mr. George Will and Mr. Norman Podhoretz in particular, have
rightly remarked that this is an arguable extension of the
theme of our discussion. Be that as it may in general, the
existence of a state of war has been also mentioned here,
meaning mainly a limited war with the organizations and men
who promote and implement terrorist plans. May I suggest
respectfully — and this is my digression — that we be wary in
using such expressions.

First of all, we would be doing too much honor to the
terrorists, raising them more or less to the level of our free
democracies, with the consequence that we should, strictly
speaking, grant them the status of war fighters, something

which we have denied them and rightly so. They would thus be considered as waging war against our societies, but we do not really recognize either their qualifications or their ability to do so. Even in Italy where in the past few years terrorism had reached a high level of activity, daring and impact, it has recently been more effectively checked. The large majority of people in my country, while scared at times, do not consider terrorists as enemies, but simply as criminals. After all, they feel more fear of kidnappers who take away their husbands than of so-called political terrorists who blow up party offices or public buildings or occasionally shoot political leaders.

As for the states which encourage, support and protect them, these are the same states which want to maintain normal diplomatic and economic relations with our free democracies — in order to enjoy our credit, our technology, our superior initiative and organization, our better way of life. I fully agree with those who feel that *détente* has always been an ambiguous and deceptive word, whose credibility has been fading away more and more in recent times. But still we live in a state which vacillates between peace and cold war, between competition and confrontation, and we should refrain from too easy a use of the word "war," which has in itself a dangerous and explosive potential of expansion.

Indeed, in an unforeseen future development, a sudden aggressor might reply to our complaints: "Didn't you say it yourselves that we were already at war and we were your enemies?" Certainly in our times we have to stand a lot of double talk and double standards, of which I recognize without hesitation that the Soviet Union has always been and remains the great master, but what would be the advantage of denouncing it without being prepared to follow up with practical measures? Now, I think it is time for me to drop my digression and to come back to our theme, about which my suggestions can be simple and short, because they coincide with most of those which have been already indicated here by several remarkable speakers.

Measures Against Terrorism

May I repeat and list the countermeasures we should take.

First, steadily continue effective and stern national police and judicial measures, both to prevent and to suppress terrorism.

Second, work to intensify intelligent coordination of efforts between the national police forces of the free democracies with full and timely exchange of information about individual terrorists, their groupings and their movements.

Third, improve cooperation among the intelligence services. May I add here that I do not entirely share the misgivings of those who mistrust (perhaps not without good reason) their own intelligence services, who fear that an internationally coordinated intelligence would allow such services a dangerous range of uncontrolled action and arbitrary initiative. I am convinced that the governments should and can control their intelligence services at the national level, and could even exercise greater control in close association over their coordinated activities. We should not blame our intelligence services for the lack of authority and energy of our governments.

Fourth, mass media should stop dramatizing and advertising the sordid terrorist action and provide instead, as one perceptive newspaperman has written, if not a blackout at least a brownout. Many of our colleagues here have forcefully developed this point, and we should add it to our action list. This should be voluntary self-discipline, and might become a coercive rule of law only in case of strict necessity. Here too we should not cry too early about lost press freedom. The seriousness of the terrorist danger has already forced us to accept quite willingly many limitations on our usual liberties. Think only of the severe checks at all entrances to public offices, of the frequent road blocks, of the uncomfortable search of luggage and persons at the airports, and so on. A line of austerity in reporting terrorist misdeeds would not limit so much our right to information as deny to the terrorists one of the main goals of their activity, that of impressing and scaring a maximum number of people with the most sensational quantity and quality of news and details.

Fifth, the reintroduction of the death penalty proposed by Hugh Fraser should be very seriously considered in my opinion — at least for a limited time of 3-5 years, and only against the most cruel forms of kidnapping and murder. The principle of the sanctity of human life has entirely lost its meaning in face of the cynical indifference by which the terrorists dispose of it, with a light heart and often with a sinister sense of joy of fulfillment. The real problem, as somebody rightfully said yesterday, lies in a serious evaluation of the effect of the death penalty as a deterrent. I believe that, in present circumstances, this deterrent would work, at least to a considerable extent. I would of course readily yield to rational, realistic and really convincing arguments to the contrary.

Sixth and the last of my points, international agreement about the treatment of terrorism should be urgently discussed, extended and improved. My young friend, Piero Luigi Vigna, yesterday quite appropriately quoted the 1977 Convention of the Council of Europe in Strasbourg. I think it is a good pact or at least an excellent start, but it needs first of all to be extended to other Western democratic states, like the United States, Canada, Japan and perhaps, if they should show any interest, Australia, New Zealand and a few others. Anti-terrorist international legislation should not remain the privilege or the burden of European countries only.

The Role of the United Nations

The United Nations, I feel, should not be forgotten in this process. I am sympathetic to the argument of those who do not want to hurt or to diminish in any way this venerable and often ineffective institution. Hence, I would suggest that the free democracies introduce to the United Nations, with the appropriate safe procedures, any proposal that they submit to their limited and safer group. If the free democracies act promptly on their own agreement, we could resign ourselves, without too much sorrow, to seeing our project modified, distorted, deprived of all practical meaning or strength, or simply put aside and lost in the impressive offices of the United Nations.

I do not intend to continue my list. I already announced my last point. It will take too much of your valuable time. Others may elaborate, and our conference should perhaps pass a resolution in order to promote such or other measures. But quite aside from a list of measures, I could not end my statement without touching upon a most delicate and controversial subject which was widely discussed by us in these few days.

Should we denounce in a resolution those states or known groups within other states which we think responsible for assisting, abetting, advising, arming, protecting, giving sanctuary and encouragement to terrorism, national or international — I mean should we do this specifically, nominatively? I have my doubts about the wisdom of such an action. First of all, it may raise discord among ourselves. We have already heard some clear expression of that here. Second, it would mean the raising of a private conference to the level and the responsibility of a group of governments, which we are not. We might embarrass our own governments by doing so and stir some criticism in our own responsible circles at home. Or we might raise in the minds of the criticized governments some misunderstanding about the nature of the governmental connections, the ultimate purpose of this meeting of ours.

I submit as a consequence that we condemn the sins as clearly and forcefully as we can afford, but not name the sinner. Of course I have here in mind only the abettors and the accessories, not the active terrorists themselves and their groups. The treatment for them could and should be different, and I am quite open-minded about any deliberation of ours concerning them.

ERIC BLUMENFELD has been the Hamburg Deputy of the German Bundestag
(CDU) since 1961. He has been a leader in
the successful fight for the abolition of the
Statutes of Limitation of Nazi war criminals.
Mr. Blumenfeld has been an active member
of the Council of Europe, the Western
European Union and the NATO Parliamentary Conference, and is currently a
member of the European Parliament.

"NO" TO TERRORISM IN ANY GUISE

*Mr. Chairman, Ladies and Gentlemen,*I owe you an apology for
not having attended the previous sessions of this great conference. I was still speaking in the German Parliament on Tuesday
night and caught a flight out of Frankfurt yesterday in order
to arrive here to speak to you this afternoon. I haven't therefore been able to prepare a speech. I have made a few notes
and remarks, because I have been very busy indeed during the
past two weeks. I am proud and happy to say that I was
among the majority of 255 legislators in the German Bundestag who voted in favor of the lifting of the statute of limitations for National Socialist murders and for terrorist murders
in the future. Once and for all they will be brought to their
judges and they will be punished.

A great many of my distinguished colleagues and speakers
have during the past two days analyzed the old and yet new
phenomenon of terrorism which is again on the rise. I have
been reading up on their speeches and I find myself in almost
complete agreement with what they have said. I will therefore
try to deal exclusively with the theme of this afternoon, the
countermeasures which our parliamentary democracies will
have to adopt, put into effect, or improve. Let me say at the
outset, ladies and gentlemen, that this is a very cumbersome
task. I am speaking from the same background as did my
colleague Mr. Rees and others before me, as a parliamentarian

or political animal who has been around for the past 25 years in those circles, and who knows how difficult it is to implement effective legislation. I find when listening to our colleagues in the Knesset that they are almost the front runners in this task too.

There is no easy way out. We have to recognize that in order to be effective we must use not only political arguments but also persuasion and political willpower. The latter is lacking sadly, at any rate in the European political forum. As a member of the newly elected European Parliament with a good deal of experience in the previous European Parliament, and as a member also of the venerable body of the Council of Europe to which my other colleague Mr. Van den Bergh has referred with a great deal of truth and knowledge, I want to stress once more: It is up to the politicians and the governments to set the stage because the other responsible body, the media, cannot report on something which has not happened, which has not been legislated, and which has not been put into effect.

Furthermore, it is for the governments and the politicians and the parliaments to assist the intelligence services, the police and all those who are out in the field risking their lives daily by combating terrorism. It is no good for us to sit back and watch them.

In his remarkable speech, Paul Johnson mentioned seven deadly sins of terrorism, and I couldn't agree more with him [applause]. This speech is very much the guideline of this conference. I have also, among others, admired what Hugh Fraser and Lord Chalfont said. I've read Robert Moss' very forthright, very sharp analysis and admire his spirit of attacking things properly; I'm glad that he is one of the European journalists, along with Gerhard Löwenthal, who has the courage to say things out loud [applause] and to print them or to say them on television. I really want to congratulate our two colleagues here on the panel for what they are doing back home. We need more of them, and this has nothing to do with political sympathies — this has to do with the courage of the individual. I wish that some of my political and parliamentary colleagues in the European Parliament and in the German Bundestag would have a little more courage. This goes for some of the leaders in government in my country too.

Where the Blame Lies

But let me take one look at the line of thought which says that our societies or our political system, our ideologies, are to be blamed for the rise of terrorism. I don't think that I can let Mr. Van den Bergh's one remark pass without commenting on it. He said, "Don't blame everything on Soviet Russia. We are also responsible." Yes, we are of course responsible for our own societies, but there is no lack of freedom in our societies, there is no lack of political and other means to improve our social fabric. In some cases there are too many social reforms, and sometimes we severely limit our own freedom and the ability of our economies and industries to work profitably. But is terrorism a product of our societies? Are we to be blamed for this because we supposedly have too few freedoms? On the contrary, it is precisely the great freedoms of liberal democracy that the terrorists are using to an extent which was unknown 10 or 15 years ago. I also believe that the other speakers are quite correct when they say that Soviet Russia and some of their client regimes, including East Germany, are very much responsible for what happens in international terrorism [applause].

It is quite clear from factual evidence which has been gathered that the PLO works closely with other terrorist groups in Europe, Africa and Latin America, but I submit that if there is a difference of motives among these groups, there is none in the criminal acts they perform. When you look at the terrorist gangs operating in the various countries of Europe and the Arab terrorists operating inside or outside of Israel, you see them always attacking, killing or torturing innocent children, women and men.

None of these terrorist assaults is political. They are crimes against humanity and we the politicians, the governments and the parliamentary bodies, and the media, will have to point this out to the public time and time again, advance through political arguments, appropriate legislation and law enforcement, and strengthen our political willpower to defend our liberty. It is *our* liberty we are defending, both our individual liberties and that of our democratic societies as a whole. The younger generation — what we in Germany have termed the schoolbook generation (and this includes women and men up to the age of 45 by now) — has not had the terrible experience of terrorism of the twenties and the early thirties initiated by the radical left, the Communists, and the radical right, the Hitlerites. Hitlerite terrorism at least in part led also to Hitler's rise because people got intimidated, and very few were prepared to stand up and fight back. Today many in Europe, including officials (and this is a sad truth, but it is a truth), become complacent if terrorist attacks cease to occur for say 6 or 8 weeks. Let's face it, very few get very concerned if terrorism shows its ugly head elsewhere, far away, in the Americas or in Israel.

The Soviet Union, East Germany and other authoritarian regimes bear a heavy responsibility for the continued increase of terrorism, not only by supplying arms and money, training facilities and sanctuaries, but equally so by supporting terrorist movements politically and through their propaganda. They call terrorism "liberation" or terrorists "patriotic freedom fighters" as long as they do not operate on their own Communist territory.

The Responsibilities of Government and Media

I believe the two responsible bodies which have to come into the forefront of the fight on terrorism are the political bodies and the media. Political bodies, including parliaments and other organs of government, will have to take legislative action.

The responsibility of the media is also a very heavy one. Mr. Löwenthal and others have drawn our attention to this in their speeches earlier today. I agree with what Mr. Rees has said this morning, drawing on his ministerial experience, and I don't believe that any parliamentarian would think otherwise or speak otherwise. We do not wish to interfere with our free press and all that goes with it. But for instance, why can't we try to choose the senior people for public television with the responsibility and sensitivity to the treatment of terrorism and all that it entails? Why leave it to the ideologists who believe that they can reform our society by calling a terrorist a "freedom fighter" and by giving them extraordinary publicity with enormous TV coverage? This coverage comes into every home and impresses the ordinary citizen as an authoritative statement, something that is almost an announcement by a government.

I believe that a politician should have to undergo not only the scrutiny of the voter but also of the media. He has to stand up and account for what he says, and he has to be voted on for his deeds. Some of our journalists and some of our people in the media should also have a few more thoughts about their responsibilities, specifically when it comes to terrorism. As someone has said during the conference, TV and our print media would not dream of giving an ordinary criminal such front-page coverage unless something truly extraordinary had happened. But as far as terrorism is concerned, the press gives terrorists all the coverage they want and depicts them as misguided young people, or as people who can be reformed if we only went about it decently and democratically. I believe that we need a new kind of education with regard to the young generation of journalists. And lastly, we cannot expect the individual journalist to be brave if governments behave in a cowardly fashion.

Countermeasures

In conclusion, I would like to mention some of the measures that I believe will have to be taken. Some have already been suggested today on this panel.

First, enforce international conventions against terrorism. Starting with the European countries, have the European Convention on Terrorism finally ratified by those countries which have not done so.

Second, urge ratification of an agreement in which the democracies of Europe might be joined by the United States and Canada, which would require concerted economic, diplomatic, and political sanctions against governments or states which support terrorists and grant them refuge.

Third, for Europeans only, institute a Joint European Anti-Terrorist Brigade. We have had in some countries very successful and effective terrorist forces. But Europe is a very difficult continent in which to have concerted action, far different from what can be done in the United States. It has nine Common Market countries, three neutral countries and other states which must agree on action — all with very different legal procedures and social and political fabrics, even though they are all parliamentary democracies. If we could therefore get a European anti-terrorist brigade this would constitute an effective instrument for combating terrorism both nationally and internationally.

Fourth, adopt national legislation for the implementation of the conventions dealing with air piracy and other crimes, which Mr. Ben-Ari has just mentioned.

Fifth, deny political status for terrorist criminals and agree on the procedure for extradition of such criminals, and the application of appropriate penalties in each country.

Sixth, intensify the exchange of intelligence and evidence on terrorism, and agree to adopt proper and legal measures against terrorist activities.

Finally, urge both national and European parliaments to press for all these actions and to control their enforcement.

We have to alert our people that we will not tolerate terrorism in whatever guise any longer. This is what this Conference is about. We have fought Fascism and National Socialism. Millions of Jewish people from all over Europe have been massacred by Hitler and his criminal aides in the period of the Holocaust. Many millions more of soldiers and civilians all over the world were killed in action during World War II, or perished amidst the ruins of their homes. We must not, ladies and gentlemen, permit our societies to sit back complacently and watch another apocalyptic catastrophe shape up because we let ourselves be blackmailed, cajoled and threatened without taking the necessary preemptive measures and actions. Let's stand up and be counted.

Closing Session
Subject:
THE CHALLENGE TO FREE MEN
Evening, July 5, 1979
Chairman: Lord Chalfont

PREFACE

The Closing Session summarized the major issues that had been pondered during the Jerusalem Conference. Further important information was presented about the vital material and political support offered by Soviet bloc and Arab states. The need to create an anti-terror alliance among the democratic nations was stressed once again.

Maj.-Gen. Gazit, Israel's Chief of Intelligence, unmasked the true nature of the PLO and highlighted the role which Moscow played in the training of its members. Russia's designs in its use of terror were analyzed by Maj.-Gen. Keegan, while George Bush discussed the implications of the Soviet tactics for the West.

In the last address, Russian dissident Vladimir Bukovsky made an eloquent plea to all free men to reject all forms of complicity with terrorism and gather their courage to rise vigorously against the spreading evil.

At the close, Senator Jackson read a statement that expressed the views of the majority of the participants, setting forth the minimum measures that should be undertaken by democratic societies to combat and to ultimately conquer the terrorist plague.

LORD CHALFONT'S OPENING REMARKS

Ladies and gentlemen, I have the very great honor to preside over this closing session of the Jerusalem Conference and to present to you a very distinguished panel of speakers.

This Conference has increased my knowledge and my understanding of the problem of terrorism which we have been addressing. Bayard Rustin, in his extremely elegant address to this conference, used the word "clarity," and somewhat to my surprise, that is I think what has come out of this Conference — a certain degree of clarity. A remarkable consensus has emerged. There have of course been differences of approach and differences of opinion. That was not only inevitable in a Conference of this kind, but, in my view, desirable. But there has been general agreement on a number of important concepts. We have been able to agree, without too much contention, upon the nature of terrorism. Without going into legal definitions I think we have all agreed that terrorism — the indiscriminate violence against innocent people — is a crime against humanity. I don't think any of us disagree about that.

I think too there is general consensus about the gravity of the threat. There is a feeling that there is a grave conflict between international terrorism and the liberal democracies. Many people have expressed the opinion that we are at war. Although this is a sentiment with which I agree, I think we should also take note of the cautionary words earlier today of

Signore Brosio, whose experience and wisdom in world affairs command our respect.

We have also agreed that there is an international dimension to terrorism. The links between the various terrorist organizations have been fully documented.

It seems to me that the one area in which there has been some difference is the extent of Soviet involvement in this international terrorist threat. I think that we may all agree that the involvement of the Soviet Union, and the common cause between the Soviets and some of the terrorist organizations, have been established as a matter of incontrovertible fact. In the course of the conference there were a few people who either dissented from that view or who had some different nuances and differences of approach. I must disagree with the view which was put forward by one participant in this conference, that the question of international terrorism and the relations between the Soviet Union and the West are irrelevant. From that proposition I wholly dissent. I believe that there is a general spectrum of menace to the West, a continuous spectrum of threat which stretches from nuclear weapons at the top to the individual terrorist with the grenade in his flight bag at the bottom. Because this conference has very rightly concentrated on one band in that spectrum, we should not believe that it can be separated and isolated from the whole. The free world is everywhere under threat and we must meet it at every level. For this reason I believe we have all agreed that international cooperation is needed at various levels to meet an international threat.

I think it would be wrong to pass over this subject without mentioning the fallacy of what I call the intelligence bogey — the thought that there is something intrinsically evil in the very concept of intelligence. Intelligence is, after all, only the obtaining, collation, and dissemination of information. It seems to me that the emasculation of some of the intelligence services of the West, as a result of a systematic campaign of denigration, has done nothing but reduce and undermine not only the resolve but the capacity of the West to meet the various threats which it faces. This brings me to the delicate subject of the role of the press and the other media.

After all the argument and all the passion have been expended, there has emerged the clear expression of a serious concern about some of the attitudes and standards of the press and the communications media in the Western world. George Will, in the course of what was one of the most elegant and penetrating presentations made at this Conference, advanced the view that the press in the West had adopted a kind of adversary posture towards the establishement, towards the government and the state and the *status quo*. I think this was most vividly demonstrated to me when in the course of the various small gatherings that take place on the margin of conferences like this, someone expressed to me the view that we should not say anything here that would upset the press, because if we did, that would turn out to be the "story," and the real discussions and the real conclusions and considerations of this conference would be ignored.

Whether that is true or not, it reflected the concern of a sophisticated and intelligent member of this conference. It does seem to me to indicate that, whatever the rights and wrongs and the facts and the realities of the situation, there is a serious concern among intelligent people about the way the Western press has handled this problem.

I was depressed to hear a journalist who contributed to the discussion today talking once again about the virtues of "objectivity" in this context. I think this is a search after false sophistication, a desire to get away from what people regard as "oversimplification", a term that has incidentally been used again and again in the proceedings of this Conference. "Don't oversimplify." There is a constant search for what seems to me to be a fictitious sophistication, and I would advance the view that sophistication is not necessarily the enemy of moral choice. You can be sophisticated but you can make clear moral choices at the same time.

The ability to distinguish clearly between good and evil is not a symptom of a feeble mind. Winston Churchill, whom I think no one could accuse of feeblemindedness, once said in the House of Commons, "I do not accept that there is an objective intellectual position as between good and evil." To that I heartily assent.

I think that about one thing we are all clear and we are all agreed. Terrorism, as we have defined it, is evil. It is a menace to the free society within which the free press works and without which a free press will cease to exist. For that reason it seems to me that a free press cannot be neutral in this struggle. It cannot be, whatever is meant by that word, "objective." It must either be an integral part of the defenses of the free world, within which a free press exists, or it aids in the destruction of all free institutions including the institution of a free press.

Finally, ladies and gentlemen, may I just refer to what can be called the ideological fallacy. I detected at a certain stage in this meeting the beginnings of a false clash, conflict, or dichotomy between social democracy on the one hand and what is loosely called the "right wing" of the political spectrum on the other. Like Merlyn Rees, I believe that terrorism, cruelty, oppression, brutality are offensive to the civilized conscience, whether derived from the ideologies of the extreme left or the extreme right. It is the terrorism that matters. It is the brutality and the cruelty that matter. Condemnation and horror of terrorism in all its forms are not the prerogatives of any one wing of the political spectrum. Thank you.

JOSEPH LANE KIRKLAND is President of
the AFL-CIO, America's largest labor
federation. From 1969 to 1979 he served as
Secretary-Treasurer of the organization. Mr.
Kirkland is a member of various Presidential
commissions, as well as of the board of
directors of the Rockefeller Foundation,
the Council on Foreign Relations, the
Carnegie Endowment for International
Peace, and other institutions.

TERRORISM AND THE GULAG

Message to the Conference
Read at the Closing Session, July 5, 1979.

I regret that urgent business prevents my participation in
your Conference on International Terrorism, which could have
no more appropriate sponsor than The Jonathan Institute, itself
a symbol and instrument of the courage required to overcome
this threat to free societies.

If the democracies are to defend themselves against the
rising tide of terrorism, our publics must be brought to a clearer
understanding of what we are up against — all the more because
modern terrorism's target is precisely the public itself, not
merely selected individuals. By victimizing innocents, the terrorist seeks to seize attention, to disorient and intimidate the
public, shattering its sense of security, and thereby destabiliz-
ing democratic governments and institutions.

Your Conference can greatly help educate and arouse the
people of the West by emphasizing that terrorism today represents far more than the sporadic manifestations of frustration on the part of diverse political malcontents. It is the work
of states. It is armed and financed by totalitarian governments
and their clients as a matter of foreign policy. Indeed, modern
terrorism is the projection by totalitarian states into the international arena of the system by which they rule at home.

What, after all, is the Gulag? What is the knock on the door in the middle of the night? The use of psychiatric hospitals as a tool of political repression? What is relentless surveillance? What is the KGB, the Gestapo? What is the whole array of scientific satanism employed by the totally coercive state — what but a highly developed form of terrorism, directed against its own citizens?

The class genocide now underway in Indochina, to which hundreds of thousands of refugees are testament, is but the most blatant expression of a doctrine firmly embedded in the totalitarian state, no matter how conservative or duly bureaucratic it is alleged to have become.

Democratic governments must develop specific and precisely targeted weapons to counter terrorism, while preserving the libertarian features of our societies that make them worth defending. This can only be done on a broad base of public support, in turn based on an understanding that, whatever particular cause it professes to advance in this place or that, terrorism is in fact but one more of the weapons unleashed against democracy itself by the expanding forces of totalitarianism. If those forces are being accommodated or appeased — or affectionately embraced — on all fronts, we cannot expect to triumph over the Carloses, the Arafats, or the Red Brigades. Those in the West who deplore the terrorist's act while defending its source — who, for example, deplore the Red Brigades while condoning Soviet foreign policy objectives — are assets, rather than adversaries of terrorism.

I can assure you that the AFL-CIO will do all that it can to educate the American people as to the nature of the threat, to encourage our governments to take effective steps against it, and to support measures by the democracies to meet the totalitarian challenge all across the board.

GEORGE BUSH is an American diplomat
and a leading figure in the Republican
Party. He served as CIA director in 1976
and 1977. His diplomatic posts include
Chief U.S. Liaison Officer to Peking
(1974-1975) and U.S. Ambassador to
the United Nations (1971-1972). Earlier
he was a member of the 90 and 91st
Congresses, and later served as Chairman
of the Republican National Committee.

THE U.S. AND THE FIGHT AGAINST
INTERNATIONAL TERRORISM

We had a little briefing for all the people you see up here and
there, and I said to Lord Chalfont, "What will I talk about?"
He said, "Talk about eight or ten minutes, because we're
going to speed this up tonight," so I will try to be brief. I
would be remiss if I didn't pay my respects to Prof. Netanyahu
whom I had the pleasure of visiting with privately yesterday.
I had the great honor of being a little fly at the wall at that
lovely memorial service yesterday, and I guess it brought home
to me as much as anything the importance of this conference.

I am privileged to have been a participant in this important and sobering conference. I am pleased to have renewed old
acquaintances, made new ones, and learned more of the most
advanced thinking about this cancer of civilization that we call
international terrorism.

The perpetrators of terrorist acts carry or proclaim
various ideological and political labels — there are major and
minor categories of terrorism which we have discussed here
at the sessions of this conference — methods and scale of terrorist activity differ from incident to incident — but all terrorism retains as a common denominator its totalitarian and anti-
human character. It seeks to destroy the fabric of society, to
disrupt the equilibrium of peaceful commerce. It strikes down

the innocent bystander. It denies the individual. It has murderous contempt for the very basis of human freedom.

Since the roots and motivations of terrorism appear to be so diverse and often irrational, we are far from hoping for any success in its prevention. I know that some argue persuasively that the demonstrated futility of political terrorism ultimately militates against the success and even survival of terrorism as an instrument of international political pressure. I am naturally anxious to see this view vindicated. Certainly there is evidence that terrorism is essentially ineffective in bending political wills to what are, most frequently, poorly articulated political objectives. But that does not give us hope that terrorism will cease to be an instrument for international mischief and destabilization. In the absence of any known cure or prevention, I must urge drastic surgery as the only reasonable course — and by that I mean determined action, firmness under the duress of blackmail, and swift and effective retribution.

You are familiar with the statistics of terrorism. By nationality, North America and Western Europe accounted for three-fourths of the total number of victims of international terrorist attacks in the decade of 1968—78. During the same period, nearly half of all international terrorist incidents took place in that part of the world. The Middle East and Latin America are, of course, in close second or third place.

You are also well familiar with the scant amount of progress achieved so far in the United Nations Organization on the question of terrorism. To put it bluntly — which, as a former chief representative of the United States at the UN, I may be forgiven for doing — that organization has shown neither the ability nor yet the willingness to come close to an acceptable definition of international terrorism to consider its causes and sources; or to give shape to more than minimal cooperative measures designed to prevent or combat this brutal activity. This was brought home most clearly to me in 1972 after the murder of the Munich athletes. The UN wanted to censure Israel's retaliatory raid into Lebanon but would permit no

mention of the terrorism that caused the retaliation. I vetoed
that one-sided resolution.

Official State Terror

Some objective characteristics and definitions *have* been worked out, and, it would seem, *could* be accepted by the international community as the basis for a common front against a
common evil. That this has not been the case points to the
continued existence of a greater evil — and that is, official
state terror. Russian Bolsheviks saw clearly that state terror
was the most efficient form of terror. Its leading practitioner
Stalin is suitably remembered by his pithy comment that one
death is tragedy but millions of deaths are only statistics. The
totalitarian states of today produce terror on a staggering
scale; and, naturally, we tend to fear the isolated act of the
terrorist more than the chronic horror of totalitarianism. At
the same time, our callous indifference to, or ignorance of,
state terror tends to blur our perceptions: who is the freedom
fighter, and who, the international hooligan? What plays an
important role in public perceptions is the often ignored fact
that contemporary state terror does not need to rely on
physical torture and killing. Czechoslovakia in 1968—69 was
the most extensive and explicit recent demonstration of the
workings of modern, sophisticated state terror, which in
that case was certainly infinitely less bloody than its classic
Lubyanka variation. But, make no mistake about it, the sub-
stitution of personal humiliation, individual economic pressure,
debarment from suitable and gainful employment, vindict-
iveness against children and relatives, extinction of national
pride and hope — an entire gamut of fiendishly practiced non-
physical torture — maintained and enhanced the efficacy of
terror.

Soviet Support of Terrorism

By contrast, in future, the so-called "private" terrorist, with
even less well-defined political objectives and decreasing bar-
gaining power, may well reach for highly sophisticated lo-
gistical and weapons technology. Many terrorist organizations

(subsidized by patron states) are affluent and easily armed with advanced weapons. It is likely that soon the traditional view of terrorism as the recourse of the desperate and the weak may need to be re-formulated: desperation and weakness may be supplanted, more precisely, by frustration and destructiveness. Thus, it is time that nations who school and train terrorists be compelled to face the onus of world opinion. Evidence presented at this conference of Soviet involvement must be widely disseminated. If the Soviets want relaxation of tensions, one way to start would be for them to renounce any terrorist training. .

The Possibility of Nuclear Blackmail

As nations continue to substitute nuclear power for oil and other forms of hydrocarbons, we are faced with the possibility of a new form of terrorism — that of nuclear blackmail. If our security plans are lacking, we may find ourselves one day being blackmailed by terrorists — not holding five, ten, or a hundred hostages, but threatening actions that could result in the death of hundreds of thousands of our citizens. While the nuclear age may offer a realistic hope that world dependence on the use of oil will be significantly diminished, each individual nation must begin now to formulate its own programs along with bilateral plans to prevent the horrifying threat that I have just mentioned.

International and transnational terrorism interact, as it were, in the area of so-called "surrogate warfare." Some experts on terrorism, I have noted, believe surrogate warfare will be war on the evolved form of international terrorism, but will provide the future expression of international conflict. It may well be so: it is, however, more difficult for me to share the proposed conclusion — that could fairly be described as hopeful — that this "surrogate warfare" will incidentally reduce the threat of a widespread military conflict. Terrorism must be combatted — it must be stopped — and the job must be done by the free nations of the world. Those who participate must be caught — those who train terrorists must be exposed.

Democracy's Struggle Against Terrorism

William James, psychologist, philosopher and passionate believer in individual freedom, said that the inner mystery of democracy consists of "two inveterate habits carried into political life — habits more precious, perhaps, than any that the human race has gained. . . One of them is the habit of trained and disciplined good temper towards the opposite party when it fairly wins its innings . . . The other is that of *fierce and merciless resentment toward every man or set of men who break the public peace.*"

When the fundamental values of free society are challenged and trampled, when the processes of orderly representative government are jeopardized and abused by lawlessness and terror reaching across national boundaries, free men must act — decisively, effectively and legitimately.

Recent Progress in Fighting Terrorism

During the past year, progress has been made, especially in Europe, in the development of concrete regional mechanisms for cooperative anti-terrorist countermeasures. I believe that the capability for unified action by free nations is essential to the discouragement, prevention and punishment of terrorist activity. Since I do not anticipate that the creation of a truly international anti-terrorist force is likely, I believe that anti-terrorist paramilitary units, closely coordinated by democratic states, are a viable answer to the threat. I find much to commend also in the proposal for a common judicial zone now under consideration in Europe.

I believe that we must maintain effective cooperation in the field of intelligence and, to be precise, counter-intelligence. I hope and trust that the United States' government will use its resources effectively to this end.

As you all know, the last few years have seen the American intelligence mechanism subjected to a systematic campaign to abridge, expose, weaken, and dismantle it. This is neither the place nor the occasion to go over the agony and controversy of the past, but it has been miserable. In my judgment, the pendulum has begun its reverse swing. The dilemma, mind you, has been a real one, and well articulated by Brian Crozier: "The problem for the open society is now to have, build up and preserve this essential tool of defence — which in the long run is indispensable for the protection of ordinary people — and not so outrage the liberal conscience that the legitimate exercise of state power is frustrated." I believe we have further improved the ways in which intelligence is accountable to the people, and we should strive vigorously to shape and utilize this important capability in the fight against international terrorism. You may be assured that I will do all I can to bring this about.

A Merciless Struggle Against the Disrupters of Public Tranquility

In a world of nation-states, state terror, confined to national boundaries, enjoys the protection of sovereignty and claims immunity from external interference. Lest we blunt our own devotion to individual freedom, we must not close our eyes to the existence of terror in any form anywhere in the world, for such tolerance makes us vulnerable to the cancer of international terrorism by weakening our confidence and our resolve. Specifically, we cannot rely on much aid and comfort from non-democratic states in protecting our institutions and our way of life — the threat of terrorism is to freedom and not to totalitarianism. Progress in regional cooperation has been minimal. Much more remains to be done. Above all, as free men, we must assiduously cultivate the habit of fierce and merciless resentment towards all those who disrupt public tranquility; this habit will make us safe and keep us free.

MAJ. GEN. GEORGE J. KEEGAN, JR.
served as Chief of U.S. Air Force Intelligence
from 1972 to 1977. He has had extensive
experience in combat operations, command
and strategic planning. General Keegan is
recognized as one of America's top military
experts on the Soviet Union and is widely
known as a writer and lecturer. He served as
President of the U.S. Strategic Institute and
as Military Editor of *Strategic Review*, a
journal on strategic affairs.

THE PREFERRED ROUTE

I consider the Jonathan Institute's first Conference on International Terrorism to be the single most important step taken
against international terrorism since World War II. In bringing
a great body of experts together in open deliberations this
Conference has fulfilled the first task of modern intelligence —
to identify and characterize the threat. In the process, it has
managed to clear the air of a vast body of illusion and misconception about the nature of terrorism.

Secondly, the Conference has rendered a great service by
piercing through the fog of causation and making it clear,
possibly for the first time in an open forum, the true nature of
the Soviet Union's perfidious role in the direction and support
of global terror as an instrument of strategic warfare.

By exposing these deliberations to some of the free
world's most responsible journalists it has assured that there
shall be light and truth — casting aside the veil of silence that
for too long has obscured from public view the true nature of
modern terrorism.

Among other areas, it has brought light and knowledge
into an area long deliberately obscured by the U.S., lest disclo-
sure jeopardize pursuit of the illusory politics of seeking peace
through unilateral disarmament and appeasement of the most
aggressive imperialism in modern history.

It is altogether fitting that the counter-assault against international terrorism begin here in Israel — where the world finds the only liberal democracy not yet so immobilized by illusion that it cannot still deal effectively with the reality of survival. Obviously, such people are not destined to be popular, but this should not trouble them, for it is survival that is the first obligation of government to its people.

It is fitting also because the Israeli uniformed professionals and a few of their distinguished political leaders are among the few groups in the Free World who have held correctly that the Soviet Union means ultimately to subjugate or dominate all who are free, that their weapons of conflict encompass the entire spectrum of direct and indirect means of human capacity for deceit, treachery and violence, and that terrorism — in its strategic form — is in the main a product of the Soviet Union's leadership, direction and support.

The global context wherein international terror thrives is but *one* facet of the most expansive strategic imperialism in history which emanates from the Kremlin.

War Preparations

It is fact that the Soviet Union is in the midst of the greatest war preparations in peacetime history, that it has long since surpassed the U.S. and the free world in strategic nuclear power and in conventional naval and para-military capability, and has thus decisively altered the balance of power in each area.

For instance, were the Soviet Union to mount an attack against the nuclear powers today — an eventuality which for the time being I do not anticipate or consider logical, noting only that the Soviet capability for such an undertaking is virtually complete — at least 160 million fatalities could be inflicted on the U.S., while in retaliation the USSR would have fewer than 10 million fatalities. This is due in the main to the Soviet development of the world's most extensive system of wartime sheltering and Civil Defense preparations for the protection of their civil and military leaders, factory workers, essential urban population and nuclear weapons.

In the conventional area of land, sea and air capability, I know of no single geographic area where free world forces are not now at a serious operational disadvantage. It is my studied conviction, after twenty years of the most exhaustive personal examination of Warsaw Pact war preparations, that the Soviet Union today, in launching a giant, unreinforced surprise attack, could impose a surrender on Europe in less than 4 days without firing a single nuclear weapon. While all indications are that the Soviet leadership, patient as it has proven to be, anticipates hegemony over Western Europe without such violent action, my question is: Why should they spend so much on military preparations ranging far beyond their defensive needs?

Parenthetically, I would note that we in U.S. military intelligence would not have known of the qualitative capabilities of Soviet weapons were it not for the Soviet arms provided to U.S. military intelligence by Israel's Defence Forces, a debt which I am trying to repay by my public defense of Israel's legitimate security needs — needs which, if met, serve our own.

A Systematic Assault

Although the excessive military preparations of the Soviet Union are disquieting to say the least, terrorism is the preferred Soviet route for global domination. Under the growing world perception of Soviet military invincibility and power, terrorism has opened the way to intimidation and revolution through indiscriminate violence against all classes of society. Meanwhile world stability is affected. The possible denial of access to fuel energy and raw material by both the Third World and the industrial world threatens economic disorder on an unprecedented scale.

In this, the Soviets are aided most by the world press' legitimization of violence through language which tends to render heroic that which is utterly depraved. The U.S. probably bears more responsibility for this latter development than any other nation.

Despite repeated warnings provided the U.S. by Israel, Saudi Arabia and France concerning direct and indirect Soviet support for the assault upon Iran, the U.S. was somehow surprised by the events there.

The truth concerning the Marxist connection was obscured by U.S. press and television which struggled to relabel the Communist-allied PLO and KGB Afghan units as "urban terrorists," "urban guerrillas" and "leftist radicals" — this during the single most effective use of mass terror in recent times.

A more sophisticated form of subversive penetration has occurred throughout Western Europe, Japan and above all in Latin America. In the latter the main faculties of the more important universities are under strong Marxist influence. The states so targeted are slowly ripened for revolutionary take-over. And it is here that terrorism is introduced to play a key role.

Since the fall of Vietnam, now viewed by communist leadership as their greatest achievement to date, the unprecedented assault upon the Third World has been accelerated. This can only be understood in the light of Brezhnev's continuing commitment to Lenin's ideological definition of Third World targets (witness Brezhnev's 25th Party Congress speech).

Soviet actions in the Middle East are part of this process. To date three wars against Israel have been made possible solely through Soviet aid. In 1955, the USSR shifted 75% of its foreign economic and military aid to the Middle East with the hope someday of cutting off the flow of oil to NATO and Japan.

Sixteen African countries are now under systematic communist penetration in the Soviet hope that the experience of Angola, Mozambique, Rhodesia, Ethiopia, Somalia, Eritrea and Yemen can be repeated.

A Long-Standing Policy
The evidence accumulated over the years, yet seldom revealed, leaves no doubt that the Soviets view the use of terror on an international basis as the single most cost-effective adjunct to

their global efforts in the military, diplomatic and economic areas as well as in subversive penetration. Party directives, Comintern protocols, and Party Congress directives in 1919, 1927 and 1929 set early guidelines for the covert establishment of revolutionary terrorism. By 1932, more than fifty training camps had been established in the Soviet Union and abroad for the training of terrorists and guerrillas. By 1936, more than a hundred military academies and service schools had established adjunct courses, with operational standards set by a special branch of the General Staff and political guidance emanating from party schools set up by the Lenin School of Revolution in Moscow.

Following the extraordinary success of the paramilitary partisans of World War II, Stalin established the present system of training which now involves thousands of full time KGB, GRU and military personnel and the use of over 100 major facilities within the Soviet Union for training of foreign terrorists and cadre. This gives you an indication of the scale and the scope of the investment in terrorism and subversion. The overseas scope of Soviet supported activities has been fully documented by other speakers, especially Mssrs. Brian Crozier and Robert Moss.

In 60 years the Soviets have gone to great extremes to conceal their role while presumably condemning terrorism. A first step to counter this deception has now been taken through these open deliberations. Meanwhile, a few good men and women will continue to enlarge public awareness. That is the essential first step to perception of the truth and thus ultimately to motivation and political action — in which we regain proper leadership.

MAJ. GEN. SHLOMO GAZIT was head of
Israel's Military Intelligence from 1974 to
1979. Prior to this he held staff positions
with the Army Chief of Staff and the
General Staff, and also served in diplomatic
posts in France. In the Six-Day War he
served as Senior Officer in Army
Intelligence.

THE MYTH AND THE REALITY OF THE PLO

I have to apologize. I am afraid that my paper, at this closing session of the Conference, is an anti-climax. It is a descriptive paper, dealing with facts and not with conclusions or propositions. My paper tries to analyze what makes the Palestinian Arab terrorists different from the other terrorist organizations.

We have been going in depth into the characteristics of international terrorism during the four days of this symposium. And all these characteristics are relevant to the Palestinians. But there is much more that characterizes them in goals and methods.

Let me begin with the goals. The final goal of the P.L.O. and of all Palestinian terrorists is threefold:

1. To take over a country and dismantle it politically.
2. To expel the present Jewish population of that country, the population which today forms a vast majority there.
3. To replace this population with another population, brought in from the outside.

In brief, as Mr. Begin has so justly described it at the opening session, the goal is *politicide* combined with *genocide*!

Further, it is totally wrong to assume that Palestinian goals are limited to the liberation of the territories we occupied in 1967. It is totally wrong to assume that the P.L.O. would be satisfied with the establishment of a Palestinian Arab state in these territories. Let me remind you of some facts just twelve years old:

1. Palestinian terrorists began operating against Israel as early as the 1950's.
2. The P.L.O. and Fatah were established two years *before* the Six Day War, *before* the occupation of these territories.
3. The P.L.O. refuses obstinately to recognize the Security Council's Resolution 242 (which means recognizing Israel's right to exist as an independent state).
4. In spite of hints and promises, the P.L.O. refuses to enter political negotiations towards peace in the Middle East.

Now let us examine the methods, and look for the distinguishing aspects of Palestinian terrorism.

What Makes the PLO different?

The first point of distinction of the P.T.A. (Palestinian Terrorist Activity) is the fact that it is a "De Luxe Terrorism," terrorism on a "Silver Platter." They are not the classic terrorists, always persecuted and hiding. On the contrary — they move in the open, in independent and legal (from the point of view of their Arab host countries) camps, wearing their uniforms, having their own weapons' arsenals, recruiting offices, command posts, administration, legal magazines and radio stations. They enjoy the infrastructure of Arab diplomatic services — as diplomatic couriers immune from search. They receive all the personal documents they need: identity cards and blank and false passports. And, in case of emergency, they always find the open door of an Arab Embassy, enjoying its extraterritorial status.

The second point of distinction of the P.T.A. is their concentration on operations outside Israel, the target country. On June 20, 1967, immediately after the "Six Day War," Al Assifa (at that time the name of the Palestinian Terrorist Organization) published in Beirut a communiqué, in which they declared the transfer of their General Command Post into the territories occupied by Israel. The Communiqué added:

"The organization is determined to continue the struggle against the Zionist Occupation; however, we plan to operate deep inside the enemy's territory, and far away from the bordering Arab countries, so that Israel will have no pretext to retaliate against those countries in revenge following Fedayeen operations."

But there was a wide gap between intention and reality. For some time Yassir Arafat tried to direct operations while hiding in the Nablus and Jerusalem areas. Then when things became too dangerous he left the area in September 1967, crossed back to Jordan, and that was the first and last endeavor to operate from inside Israel. Since then, for the last twelve years, the command post has always been outside our borders.

That noble idea not to endanger the Arab countries by P.T.A. was short-lived. The P.T.A. established itself in Arab territory like a cancer, imposing its presence on Arab hospitality and becoming a permanent threat to its hosts. As we have seen, the command post moved outside Israel, and since then P.T.A. operations against Israel are carried out on five different fronts.

The First Front is P.T.A. Inside Our Borders

This activity is carried out by member terrorists living and operating inside our borders, while receiving all their orders, directives, training and equipment from the outside. Yes, even they hardly use any locally produced weapons or explosives; nor have they ever tried to acquire weapons by attacking Israeli military installations. Almost their entire arsenal is smuggled in. Just recently, we succeeded in uncovering two new channels of smuggling weapons:

1. Use of the drug traffic into Israel.
2. Use of U.N. observers who are immune to search and control.

I am the last person to underestimate the threat of P.T.A. inside our borders, but the success and effectiveness of our security services and measures and the very low standard of the Palestinian terrorist's professional achievements make the overall impact of this activity on Israel rather limited. Just to give you an idea — during the last fifteen months, beginning on April, 1978 we had twenty-eight Israelis killed (civilian and military) by that kind of P.T.A. This should be compared to about seven hundred persons killed in road accidents during the same period.

The Second Front is Border P.T.A.
I mean here operations originating from installations and bases inside the protected areas of the Arab host country (now mainly from the Lebanon). We identify three modes of operation from across the border: *The easiest and safest act* is firing at Israeli targets with various weapons, including heavy artillery (e.g. 130 mm with a range of 27 km) and heavy Katyushas (with a range of almost 21 km). *Somewhat less secure* is the short penetration, just a few hundred yards, to lay a mine or to ambush Israeli vehicles close to the border. The infamous attack on a busload of Avivim school children was an operation of this kind. And *the third and much more dangerous* mode of operation is the deep penetration by land or sea. The terrorists' main problem in a case like that is the almost zero chance of escape once they are encountered. Their difficult choice is between death in battle or surrender. A great many of them prefer an Israeli prison to an heroic death.

The Third, Fourth and Fifth Fronts
The third front is P.T.A. from a neutral country. The idea here is to avoid the strong security measures along the borders and seashore. The plan is quite simple — to mix with the large traffic of passengers and tourists flying into Israel. The two most prominent operations of this kind were the hijacking of a Sabena Aircraft on May 9, 1972, and landing it in Israel, and three weeks later, the murderous attack by three Japanese Red Army terrorists at the Ben Gurion Air Terminal.
    The fourth front is P.T.A. against Israeli installations and institutions abroad. Here, once we took the necessary precautions, the direct attacks by P.L.O. terrorists against

EL AL planes, Israeli embassies, etc., stopped almost completely. What they still try from time to time is to shoot down an EL AL plane with an anti-aircraft missile (Rome, Nairobi), or to attack Israeli citizens in various neutral places, like hotel lobbies, airport terminals, etc.

The last, and fifth front is the attack on completely neutral targets. Such operations are so indirect that one has to ask onself, how do they serve the terrorists' purpose? Furthermore, such acts are very unpopular in international public opinion. This is why Fatah, as the biggest Palestinian Terrorist Organization, never admits its responsibility and tries to hide behind cover names like "Black September " or "Black June."

The P.L.O. is realistic; they do not delude themselves that these operations will bring about Israel's destruction. Their real intention in these acts is to enlist the Arab states in the Holy War against Israel. The terrorists consider themselves the spearhead of the overall Arab struggle against Israel.

The Search for Easy Targets
The terrorists are looking for safe and uncomplicated targets. This is an important principle of operations for them. Most resistance movements are careful to choose targets that will best serve their goals. Thus, they go after governmental installations, military bases, major civilian infrastructures and prominent enemy figures. Not so the Palestinians. They purposely avoid any target that has even minimum protection. They prefer innocent civilian objectives like a marketplace, a bus station, or innocent passengers on a bus. This phenomenon has another aspect. With P.T.A. there is no such thing as determination in achieving their goal. After all, since they don't go after special objectives and are only interested in hurting Israelis, what difference would it make if they planted their bomb on a bus, in a garbage can or under a pile of tomatoes in the market?

Also, the Palestinian terrorist is not the kamikaze type; he does not knowingly join a suicide mission. Of course, the very encounter with Israeli security forces is already very dangerous. Many of the PLO men who penetrated Israel by

ground, sea or air did not come out alive. But their original
plan of operation always included safe withdrawal or surrender
to our forces. This stereotypic line of operation makes the
Japanese Red Army attack at the Ben Gurion Terminal so
flagrantly different. It also explains Palestinian terrorists' behavior in our prisons. They never commit suicide, and they
cooperate freely and completely with their interrogators.

International Support of P.L.O. Terrorism

Palestinian terrorism is a rich man's terrorism. It is a "spoiled"
terrorist's organization. I have already mentioned the "Silver
Platter " of P.T.A. This means they have all the money they
want, without any need to fight for it. They are perhaps the
only terrorist organization that has no need for fund raising
operations.   But while their money comes from the rich Arab
oil-producing countries, most of their military needs are looked after by the Soviet Union. Thus, they receive weapons and
equipment directly from the Soviet Union or from the Eastern Bloc Countries and use training facilities all over the Eastern
Bloc. During a period of 15 months in 1966– 67 Palestinian
terrorists participated in fifty different military schools and
courses, some forty in the Soviet Union itself and the rest in
Red China, North Korea and East Germany. Compared to any
other terrorist organization, the P.L.O. do it the easy way.
They were born with a silver spoon in their mouths.

   Another indication of strong international support for
the P.L.O. is the close relations between the P.L.O. and other
terrorist organizations. The very existence of the P.L.O. and
its rich infrastructure within the Arab world makes them a
great attraction to all terrorist and resistance movements all
over the world. The P.L.O.'s assistance with facilities and
shelter has very much changed the *modus operandi* of International Terrorism. I won't elaborate, since this aspect has already been discussed at length during the symposium. I would,
however, like to examine the assistance the P.T.A. receives
from the different international terrorist organizations.

   First is the collecting of intelligence on targets in Israel
and on security measures at the different Israeli border sta-

tions. This is carried out by tourists who arrive in Israel posing as totally innocent visitors, attracting no suspicion.

Second is non-Arab terrorists who act as messengers, delivering equipment, weapons and explosives through and from neutral countries.

And third is non-Arabs participating actively in a Palestinian terrorist act, together with a Palestinian team or — in very rare cases — even committing the acts by themselves with no Palestinian participation.

Palestinian Terrorism's Bluff

When I sum up and examine all the points that distinguish the P.L.O. from all other terrorist organizations, I cannot but ask myself — what do they have in common with other international organizations? They carry the name of terrorists, but their "De luxe" facilities make them so different.

They do not operate in real underground conditions. They do not operate in poverty, and they don't suffer from want. They are not persecuted and they are not on the run. Thus, the biggest bluff of the Palestinians is their success in selling the underdog image.

It is the duty of this symposium to uncover this bluff. I hope very much that world-wide publicity of the proceedings of the conference held here in Jerusalem may serve this purpose.

VLADIMIR BUKOVSKY is a Russian
dissident and author. Prior to his expulsion
from Russia in 1976 he was arrested several
times in the USSR and placed in a "psychiatric ward." In 1972 he was sentenced to a
term of 12 years on a charge of "anti-Soviet
activities." His "crimes" were campaigning
for human rights in the USSR and exposing
the Soviet use of psychiatry against political
dissenters. Mr. Bukovsky is the author of
To Build a Castle, an autobiographical work
which dissects the reality of Soviet life.

THE CURSE OF COMPLICITY

Mr. Chairman, dear friends, I am not a scholar, I am not a journalist, I am not a legal expert. But one of the major subjects
we are discussing at this Conference is complicity in evil —
terrorism and its support, especially by such countries as the
Soviet Union. I think I can say something about these two
subjects — complicity in evil and the Soviet Union.

Every day we learn about new acts of terror all over the
world. Every day we receive a fresh portion of horrifying
stories about murdered children, hostages taken, or a crowd of
people blown up, and we begin to accept it as normal. Moreover, we are almost used to the idea that at any moment any
one of us or our friends could be killed by some "freedom
fighter." Terror has entered our lives to such an extent that we
no longer remember its sources.

I happened to be in Italy when Aldo Moro was kidnapped.
The fictitious trial "in the name of the people" without any
legal defense or legal indictment, without any jury or freely-
elected judges, but with the inevitable death sentence guaranteed even before the trial started, and with the defendant
repenting in an attempt to save his life — all of this did not fail
to remind me of the Moscow show trials of the 1930's. It was
the language of the leaflets distributed by the terrorists that
impressed me most of all, as if something revoltingly familiar
from childhood haunted my mind — the picture of a Bolshevik

kommissar, draped with bands of bullets. It was all the same: the same jargon, same faces, same ideology, same actions, same results.

The only difference is that all these countless "red brigades," "red armies" or "liberation movements" have not managed so far to take power, that is, to concentrate in their hands economic, administrative, political and spiritual power, uncontrolled and unlimited.

Their spiritual fathers in 1917 were more successful. The result of 62 years of their rule is 46 million killed and 260 million frightened people. And even more than that, if we remember the East European countries, China, Cuba, Vietnam, Cambodia, Angola. A very long list of countries. All these "red brigades" and "red armies" are just the sparks, the embers of the huge fire set in the world 62 years ago.

Many people at this Conference have mentioned the Soviet role in international terrorism. Some other people here have said they do not believe this, that it must be exaggerated, people are just imagining things, and so on. Perhaps it really is still a question for someone here as to whether these terrorists are actively supported and exploited by the Kremlin. For those of us who lived in the Soviet Union — not as tourists or diplomats — there never has been the slightest doubt about it. And it is not such a secret conspiracy that only a KGB man would know about it. What do you think happens when Habash and Arafat go to Moscow several times a year? Or to Cuba?

This policy of supporting terrorism has become official Kremlin policy, openly proclaimed at the 25th Party Congress. The presence of the famous Katyushas not far from here, and the Russian maps of training camps found on PLO people in Lebanon, are sufficient proof of this. And, of course, East Germany and Cuba are simply used as agents of the Soviets in this respect.

The Psychology of Compromise

I would like to talk about complicity, about stupidity, about people living in freedom, with all the information and the truth available to them, who refuse to see things as they are.

How do people in the West develop, and even seem to be proud of, the mental disease of our age? That mental disease is shown as well in their refusal to recognize, to condemn and to fight absolutely against such evils as terrorism and its brother, totalitarianism.

I must say the democratic societies have proved themselves almost unable to cope with this problem. Some of the suggestions made here seem to me impractical. An attempt to restrict our liberties might recruit more sympathizers of terrorism and would be exploited by certain political groups. Censorship of the press might increase panicky rumors and the circulation of underground leaflets. The introduction of the death penalty may make terrorists more desperate and ruthless.

Some people suggested that we create an intelligence international. Notwithstanding the political impracticability of implementing such an idea, I doubt the effectiveness of this proposed brotherhood. It was, of course, incredibly stupid to attack and weaken our intelligence organizations. But while this damage can't be remedied at once, other things can be done more quickly.

Mr. Moss rightly proposed the economic boycott of those countries supporting and exporting terrorism. But who is going to do that? You know better than I that from the very beginning of the Soviet-state the western countries readily assisted in building, strengthening and enriching its monstrous system of oppression. Don't we know that western businessmen would sell the rope they will be hanged with? Actually, it is very often business interests that collaborate in a certain way with the Soviets and prevent attacks on terrorism around the world, because of oil or Pepsi Cola or some other liquid or solid.

The psychology of compromise which is quite useful in solving internal problems of democratic societies has proved fatal in dealing with terrorism and totalitarianism. We are told that international terrorism increased ten-fold between 1968 and 1978. This corresponds with the growth of Soviet aggressive power. In both cases, western countries tried to follow the policy of so-called "détente." They readily negotiated with bandits as if they were equal partners. The aircraft, millions in ransom money, and applause, were provided with amazing speed. Are we really surprised that the criminals are now called by the glamorous names of "Freedom Fighters", "Liberation Army", or "Guerrillas", and that they demand the exchange of "Prisoners of War"?

The American Congress calculated that in forty years the Soviet Union violated twenty-five treaties, and yet America now considers signing another one. Is it not clear that it is irrelevant how many new and promising treaties one signs, if one has not the guts to insist on the fulfillment of the previous accords?

Violence derives equally from the behavior of the victim and his tormentor.

I was born and brought up in the country where terror, state terror, has been state policy for more than sixty-two years. I was in the criminal camps together with murderers and gangsters where terror was regarded as a means of survival. Now, when I hear the politicians and policymakers in the West argue seriously whether the fed communist is better than the hungry one, or whether unilateral disarmament can prevent war, I begin to feel I was safer in my prison.

Opening the Doors

The problems of democratic societies trying to fight terrorism and the problems of the free world confronted with the threat of totalitarianism are similar. Such difficulties remind me of our struggle for human rights in the Soviet terroristic state. We, too, could not compete with the Communist rulers in cruelty and meanness without giving up our human values. At the same time we did not pretend to cultivate peaceful co-existence when they confined us to psychiatric hospitals. To participate fully in their political reality would mean for us to become KGB agents. But at least we knew our enemy. We understood that the power of the Soviets — like that of terrorists — derives mainly from the people's readiness to submit, to yield, to give up because they are tired or afraid. Terror and totalitarianism cannot exist in a vacuum. They need accomplices, and they create them by tying everybody up in a bloody circle, *krovavaya porooka*, as Dostoevsky said.

Only when Stalin died and his crimes were exposed did we realize that everybody had been guilty. Not only those directly involved in the crimes, but also those who kept silent. It is known that at the 20th Party Congress, after Khrushchev had made his speech, somebody from the audience sent him a note saying:

"Where were you, when all these crimes were committed?"

Khrushchev read the question over the microphone and asked:

"Would whoever wrote this please get up."

Naturally, nobody got up.

"Well" — said Khrushchev — *"I was in exactly the same place where you are now."*

The source of our movement is based on this idea — that we must stand up, ourselves, and also make others, too, ashamed to collaborate. This is exactly what our rulers were afraid of.

In one of the camps I met an old man who had been imprisoned for murdering Jews during the Second World War.

"I never killed anybody," explained the man. *"My work was just to open the door to the gas-chamber. To close it was another man's job."*

Ladies and Gentlemen! We are here to condemn terrorism — the cold-blooded murder of innocent people in order to achieve political goals. We are here to condemn those whom I cannot even describe as animals since animals are much more human. These people are potential Stalins and Hitlers, if we permit them to exist. But what about all of those who just *opened the door*, like the man I met in that camp — opened the doors of our society to this disgusting crime?

I am referring to those who are silent and obedient, irresponsible and unscrupulous, such as highly intellectual professors in France or Italy, Germany or America, who love to hold forth about what Communism or the Soviet Union is really like, or about the happy life in the Socialist countries, or about the wonderful new society in Cuba, or about the "righteous struggle" of those murderers who receive applause at the U.N.

and who proudly take credit for bashing in the heads of four-year-old girls. For these people, sitting safely in the West with their houses and cars, and writing exactly what people would like them to write — that is, the slogans and clichés that fill their brains instead of thoughts — this is a matter of fashion, of saying what others say, and forgetting that no matter what people say, there is still good and still evil and we should be able to tell the difference between them.

I am referring to philosophers and writers, sociologists and journalists, who help to spread — maybe out of stupidity more than out of malice — disinformation and slander, help create the atmosphere of hatred and murder in our world. They have poisoned the minds of countless young people all over the world — in Italy and Germany and in the United States, in Africa, and elsewhere. They have supplied the ideological justification for the terrorists, the way many of them supplied, after 1917, reasons to justify the Soviet State.

Why was it so long, so very long, before anyone could hear the moans and cries from the Soviet *Kantslagery*? Why did we have to wait until the last decades for all people, including the people who follow intellectual fashion, who have all the so-called "right" views — that is "tolerant", "progressive" and so on — to see Soviet reality as it is? And now they want to paint a nice picture, with lots of rosy colors, of the terrorists? Evil always has a way of collaborating with evil. We should not be surprised that the Soviets support and use the PLO, the German terrorists or others. We should not be surprised that the ideology that was fed to the killers of Aldo Moro was the same sort of ideology that elevated Mr. Brezhnev, Mr. Mao, Mr. Arafat, and even, sometimes, Mr. Idi Amin. It would be much more surprising if the opposite were the case.

Real Villains, Real Heroes
These people in the West create the image of the valiant "Freedom Fighter", who needs publicity for his "Just Cause". But if one wants to have publicity, does one have to machine-gun a room full of little school girls to get it? Why not just

jump off the Eiffel Tower to get it rather than buy it with the blood of children?

In the East, where there is real oppression, and where we are not just seasick but drowning, the real Freedom Fighter, the young Czech student Jan Palach, burnt himself in protest against the Soviet Invasion of 1968.

There is a mysterious law that where there is real injustice and real oppression, then there are real martyrdom and real heroes. But when the cause is a false one, based on the thrill of violence, boredom with one's graduate work in sociology, or even the racist hatred that inspires certain terrorists to kill any Jewish person because it is felt that a tiny piece of land must belong to some gigantic "Sacred Arab Nation," then there are never any martyrs or heroes. I do not know of any terrorist group that has ever shown real courage or real heroism, not in Italy, or Germany, or Spain, or in the Middle East or anywhere. I would like to know of a single brave deed any of them has ever accomplished. Of course there are none. Actually, where there are real tyrants, and the worst oppression, we do not see such violence. We would be more justified than anybody to kill our rulers, but we have never even thought of this, let alone indiscriminate murder. Never was real freedom based on the blood of innocents, but totalitarianism — that of Hitler, Stalin and all their friends and imitators — always is.

Ladies and Gentlemen, we cannot all be expected to go out everyday in uniform and fight the terrorist criminals. I do not ask you to do this, just as I do not expect people in the West to spend every waking moment fighting against Soviet totalitarianism. But is it so very much to ask that you not be accomplices to the crimes? That you do not justify them, explain them away, sympathize with them, use the kind of language that is simply neutral and supposedly "objective"? If television had existed in the 1930's it is not hard to imagine long interviews with Adolph Hitler or Josef Stalin. Such a man would be questioned respectfully by several interviewers, as Arafat was on the American program "Face the Nation" or the West German terrorist on German Television, perhaps even pausing or nodding thoughtfully before giving his answer.

Some people would find this television performer reasonable, justified, perhaps even sympathetic if he had a nice smile. And, of course, aren't we supposed to let everyone express his "point of view"?

Ladies and Gentlemen, personally most of us can do very little to fight terrorism. We can only admire Jonathan who gave a remarkable example to the free world. But we can, and we must, fight against *complicity*. Do not be collaborators! There is no need to curtail our freedoms or to distort our democratic institutions if we believe they are worth defending. Western civilization, Western democracy, is not a myth, not a fantasy, not a lie, not something we should simply give up because of occasional wrongs, or because we are fed up with the consumer society or with the stupidity of this or that particular set of leaders. Let us use these institutions and everything won with such difficulty through hundreds, even thousands of years of history, but use them better than we have.

I want to employ some terms from the biological laboratory. I think we see a kind of nutritious culture provided for the bacteria of evil, in which they grow and flourish. Let us stop feeding this evil and throw out these intellectual petri dishes in which it thrives. Let us not reward terrorism by giving terrorist organizations what they demand. If crime pays for one group, all of them will be encouraged in their bloody work. Let us not bring into being terrorist states that would simply be Soviet agents, which all of our history tells us encourage the destruction of Western positions, everywhere in the area.

Do Not Forget

The great Russian poet Nekrasov wrote about a hundred years ago, *Bredit Amerikoy Rus*, which means "Russia thinks, dreams, is obsessed by, America." Actually, we could say this is even more true today — that everyone in the Soviet empire is obsessed not just with America, but with the West, with the great world of freedom outside that empire. Despite the very large dimensions of our concentration camp — some 6,000 miles in one direction, some 3,000 miles in another — sooner or later, everything you do here in the West becomes known to us

there, in that empire. Every time you yield, every time you
seem to abandon your own principles, whether in Africa, the
Middle East or Europe, you give us a great blow, a great
wound, you make it more difficult for us — *Tam*, over there —
to breathe, to continue our fight. I am trying to speak not
only for myself but for, I believe, many others still in that
empire and in those camps. Please do not collaborate with evil,
not for the promise of selling Pepsi Cola at the olympic games,
or selling tractors, not for the promise of another million barrels of oil from a feudal state, not for any smiles or promises.
The Soviet Union and all its satellites live only by lies: every
day, in small ways, we have to lie in that country. But why
should anyone do it here, where it is possible to breathe? This
has been, from the viewpoint of humans, a very bad century,
and I will not recite the long list of crimes. Probably many
people in this audience have suffered from more than one of
these historic crimes. But please — and here I ask all the democracies, and above all the United States — do not forget
what you have always stood for, and do not make still longer
the catalogue of those crimes.

LORD CHALFONT'S CLOSING REMARKS

Ladies and gentlemen, I think it would be a very hard heart that wasn't moved by that appeal from Vladimir Bukovsky. Of all the appalling images that he evoked there were many that will live in my mind, but perhaps the one that stands out most was the sentence about the West's mental disease and its inability to recognize and fight against the evils which threaten it. If we were to remember nothing else of his talk tonight then we should at least remember that sentence.

Before I close the Conference I would like to say that for me and for a great number of people, this Conference has demonstrated three things which I will list briefly. The first is the importance of an intellectual inquiry into the problems of terrorism. In dealing with this problem, we must move in the world of ideas so that we can combat and resist the nihilistic and brutalizing philosophies of violence.

The second point which has emerged with enormous clarity throughout this Conference has been that one of the chief aids to such moral subversion and confusion is the degradation of language. We take with us the imperative of using language with precision and care. Language is after all not merely a method of simple communication. Monkeys and dogs can do that. What we have is a precise and precious instrument, and unless we use it with exactitude, we shall neither understand the problems nor even begin to solve them.

The third message concerns something that Vladimir Bukovsky underlined so powerfully and so movingly in the speech which brought this Conference to an end: The will of the West to fight against those things that threaten it. Do we have that will or do we not?

I would like, if I may, to read you one quotation on that subject: "Free men, if they are willing to fight, if they are ready to apply their courage and wisdom, and channel all of their resources into a concerted action, can overcome ruthless evil, however dreadful and threatening." That was said by Benjamin Netanyahu in a tribute to his brother Yoni after the Operation at Entebbe. I believe it is that kind of philosophy with which we should go forward from this Conference. May I express the hope that this Conference will mark a new phase in the struggle of democratic societies against the forces of darkness which threaten them. Indeed, I believe that this Conference, when we look back on it many years ahead, will have proved to be a historic milestone in the struggle against terrorism.

There is a quotation from an English philosopher and parliamentarian with which I should like to leave you. It is one which I have carried in my mind through most of my adult life: "All that is necessary for the triumph of evil is that good men do nothing." When all the arguments are over, we must go from here and do something. The Jonathan Institute, The Jerusalem Conference, and Israel have shown us the way. Thank you.

CONFERENCE SUMMARY STATEMENT
Read by Senator Henry Jackson
at the Closing Session, July 5, 1979

The Jerusalem Conference on International Terrorism defines terrorism as "the deliberate, systematic murder, maiming and menacing of the innocent to inspire fear in order to gain political ends."

The majority view of the Conference is that terrorism is a serious and growing threat to the people of all states which live under the rule of law; that it is no longer a national problem, but a global one; that it cannot be contained, let alone eliminated, except by concerted international action; and that the case for such action should not jeopardize fundamental civil liberties.

There was profound concern at the accumulating volume of evidence that terrorists now have access to ample funds, modern weapons, regular training programs, ever-available sanctuaries and other support services provided by sovereign states belonging to the Soviet and Arab blocs.

The evidence is now sufficient to justify use of the phrase "Terrorist International" to describe the many and growing links between separate terrorist organizations, their use of communal services and their systematic exchange of information, resources and techniques.

While there is still debate over the extent to which the Soviet government, either directly or through its allies and satellites, exercises central control over certain terrorist organizations, the view of the majority is that Soviet bloc weapons, training, finance, protective services and diplomatic assistance now constitute an important element in the scale and success of terrorism. Whatever the ideological or nationalist aspirations of individual terrorist groups, they have a common interest, which they share with the Soviet Union, in destroying the fabric of democratic, lawful societies all over the world.

Many believe that the response of the democracies to the threat posed by international terrorism has been hesitant and inadequate.

The civilized world is learning — but it is learning too slowly. Many participants believe the time has come for the leading democratic nations to convene a conference of all states which respect the principles of democracy and the rule of law, with a view to formulating concerted measures against the terrorist forces and their backers. It is suggested such action should include the following:

(1) A unanimous condemnation of terrorism without qualification or reserve.

(2) Enforcement of an international convention against terrorism, for which the European Convention on Terrorism would serve as a working model, and which would cover the definition of terrorism as an international crime, the denial of political status for criminals so defined, common procedures for extradition, appropriate penalties, and the exchange of evidence.

(3) A complementary agreement to take concerted measures, including diplomatic, economic and other sanctions, against states which aid terrorists by supplying them with money and arms, according them facilities for training and propaganda, and granting them refuge.

(4) An undertaking to adopt legislation for the effective enforcement of The Hague, Tokyo and Montreal Conventions dealing with air piracy and related crimes.

(5) Agreement to take all necessary, proper and legal measures for the effective exchange of information on terrorist activities.

(6) An energetic and continuing effort to alert public opinion to the dangers of terrorism to civil liberties and to the rights of individuals in a free society and the need for effective measures to combat it.

The majority view of the participants in the Jerusalem Conference on International Terrorism is that the above measures represent the minimum necessary to defend the democratic and lawful states from the threat which faces them, and it calls on governments and peoples throughout the civilized world to unite behind this program.

INDEX

INDEX